Disappointing the Dragon

DISAPPOINTING THE DRAGON

How Australia should stand up to the Communist Party of China

Bob Breen

DEDICATION

This book is dedicated to those who have lost their lives or been physically and mentally injured protecting Australia's national interests.

It is written to minimise the loss of life and wellbeing of those the nation will call again.

Bob Breen
March 3, 2022

ACKNOWLEDGEMENTS

Emeritus Professor David Horner has been and continues to be my inspiration and benchmark for scholarly standards. Much of this book originated in a collaboration with Brigadier Ian Langford DSC and Bars while I supervised his PhD candidature. Colleagues and friends, including Dr Ross Babbage AM, Dr Alan Dupont AO, Mark Hoare, Professor Clive Hamilton AM, Air Commodore Peter McDermott AM CSC, Major General Roger Noble AO, DSC, CSC, Senator Jim Molan AO, DSC, and Jeff Wilkinson AM gave early ideas 'a kick and a punch'. The book is better argued and its conclusions and recommendations more pragmatic because of their constructive criticism.

Thank you to Marcus Fielding, a true patriot, for having the courage to publish this book knowing the risks of retribution.

Finally, my wife, Rhonda, deserves equal acknowledgement for her encouragement, love and emotional support.

First Published in 2022 by Echo Books

Echo Books is an imprint of Superscript Publishing Pty Ltd,
ABN 76 644 812 395
Registered Office: Suite 401, 140 Bourke St, Melbourne, VIC, 3000
www.echobooks.com.au

ISBN: 978-1-922603-07-4 (paperback)

CONTENTS

Executive Summary

The book's seven chapters propose a de-escalation strategy and the establishment of a Response Force and Strike Force to counter a Communist Party of China (CPC) grey zone campaign by answering seven questions.

Chapter Question	Answers	Evidence/Arguments
Part 1 – The Threat 1. Should Australia be afraid?	Yes. The CPC has begun a grey zone campaign to coerce Australia to trade on China's terms as a tribute state after Australia makes political concessions and dissociates from the US-led Western alliance.	Warnings from Australian Security and Intelligence Organisation, think tanks, experts and the media.
2. What should be feared?	A CPC grey zone campaign borrows from Russia whereby political, economic and informational coercion accompanied by cyberattacks escalate without warning to hybrid warfare.	There is expert literature on political, information, hybrid, and cyberwarfare in the grey zone and two credible scenarios.
Part 2 – Responding to the threat 3. What is being done about it?	Reflexive legislation and inter-agency taskforces are not hard enough to counter a grey zone campaign. Australian strategic policies are incomplete. More money for conventional military deterrence is not enough. The ADF is still a 'one punch force'. There is no strategy, plan or institutional machinery for countering an escalating CPC grey zone campaign nationally, regionally or internationally.	Analysis of reflexive responses to CPC grey zone escalations. Analysis of contemporary Australian strategic guidance, concluding that conventional military forces and their deterrent effects are mainly irrelevant to countering an escalating grey zone campaign. There is the 2020 Strategic Update but no strategic plan.

Part 3 – Dealing with the threat 4. What is a De-escalation Strategy and Response Power?	A de-escalation strategy is a fair and firm assertion of Australia's sovereignty and values to counter grey zone campaigns. Its pillars are detection, deterrence, information actions and de-escalation. It paces Phase 1, 2 and 3 escalations of grey zone campaigns while always seeking negotiation and rapprochement. The frontline for this strategy is 'anywhere' combined with a readiness level of 'anytime'. The aim is to engage grey zone threats 'upstream' overseas rather than risk surprise 'downstream' in Australia. It involves: Detect and 'stare' to comprehend threats and warn to deter, dissuade and reconcile. Detain and prosecute grey zone combatants in the courts where possible. De-escalate to force attention and demand negotiation. Regional de-escalation strategy is based on partnership, leverage engagement and constraint. Response Power underpins the de-escalation strategy by providing the ways and means for acquiring intelligence, enabling precise targeting and de-escalating anywhere and anytime. Response Power gives Australia sovereign options to shape, understand and influence operating environments across the competition, conflict and warfare spectrum overseas where threats are in different stages of development.	Australia must anticipate and counter escalations of a grey zone campaign progressing towards a military threshold. Deterrence to stop grey zone escalation cannot be achieved without credible and forceful consequences for continuing coercion. It is better to: • detect, 'stare' discreetly, develop options and pace escalation thresholds in phases than respond reflexively or retaliate with conventional force; • remain engaged and constrain rather than disengage and try to contain; and • de-escalate and reconcile rather than retaliate and risk further escalation. This strategy complements collaboration with allies. It enables Australia to join partners in operations below the threshold of limited war in the grey zone. Response Power is required because the grey zone is an 'anywhere' at 'anytime' battlespace, and grey zone activities are covert, clandestine, deniable and population-centric. Response Power accords with the 2020 Strategic Update's emphasis on shaping and enhancing deterrent capabilities and responding with credible force further from Australia's homeland.

Part 4 – New instruments for national security in the grey zone 5. The ways and means for a de-escalation strategy	Grey zone legislation is required to harden Australia's defences in the grey zone. A new AFP Response Force should be responsible for countering escalating Phase 1 and 2 grey zone campaigns in the homeland and near region, including counter-terrorism. A new ASIS Strike Force should be an ultimate deterrent and sanction, but only for countering Phase 3 escalation to hybrid warfare while attempting to deter and de-escalate in Phases 1 and 2. Response Force paces and responds to escalation at home and in the near region in Phase 1. Strike Force stares at and reacts to Phase 1 escalations internationally. Response Force collaborates with 'called out' Special Forces in Phase 2. Response Force, Strike Force and Special Forces respond to Phase 3 escalation.	Australia must simplify the law enforcement and strike capabilities for the grey zone. **Argument 1** – Separate Federal and State/ Territory jurisdictions impede anywhere/anytime responses to homeland Phase 1 and 2 grey zone escalations. **Argument 2** – There is merit in extending Australia's counter-terrorism legislation and arrangements for countering grey zone campaigns. **Argument 3** – Law enforcement options are better for Phase 1 and 2 deterrence and de-escalation because there is no military threat yet.

6. Strike Force Attributes?	Australia had an unfulfilled 'Fourth Fighting Force' in 1942–45. Australia should take a sovereign approach to threats in the grey zone by developing a new Strike Force founded on best operational and ethical practices with multi-domain capabilities and political and cultural sophistication for operating in the grey zone. The Australian Secret Intelligence Service (ASIS) has the technology, lawful ethos, collaborative culture and international cross-cultural sophistication to select, train and manage Strike Force	Australia can draw on the traditions and ethos of Special Operations Australia in the Pacific War for Strike Force, leaving Special Forces to support ADF operations. Strike Force operations can build on ASIS intelligence-gathering capabilities and develop strike capabilities inspired by Special Operations Australia in the Pacific War. Covert and clandestine strike and enabling operations accompanied by electromagnetic operations optimise Australia's deterrence in the grey zone. Enabling operations optimise the capabilities of Australia's regional allies to create deterrence in the grey zone.
Part 5 – The way ahead 7. What are the steps to implementing a de-escalation strategy, creating Response Power and establishing a Response Force and a Strike Force?	Appoint a National Grey Zone Security Advisor and assemble an Inter-Departmental Task Force to develop and communicate plans, draft legislation, and propose the appropriate authority, responsibility, accountability arrangements and resource allocations. Recruit, train, equip a diverse military, law enforcement and civilian full time and part-time Response Power workforce and develop and conduct contingency operations.	No single department or agency can develop and implement a de-escalation strategy. The collaboration of all departments and agencies charged with Australia's national security, including the corporate sector, is required. Australia needs a diverse, capable grey zone workforce comprised of law enforcement, corporate, intelligence and military personnel.

Preface

I am prophesying the Communist Party of China's [CPC] intentions for Australia. The CPC does not want war. It aspires to achieve its strategic objectives in the grey zone where coercive actions are not acts of war – where war is not war. I offer evidence of Russian and Chinese grey zone campaigns. Hopefully, most readers will appreciate my analysis and welcome a de-escalation strategy. If some adjudge it useless, I look forward to someone offering a better plan.

The CPC is bullying Australia. The metaphorical Australian Pub Test applies – if bullies have no adverse consequences, they will not stop. Originating in arrogance and condescension, they grow to enjoy what they do unless they are opposed firmly. Appeasement is not an option, even to buy time. Hoping the United States will meet Australia's CPC grey zone threat is insulting our nationhood. We have sovereign responsibilities.

Australia's conventional military capabilities and the US–Australian alliance will not deter more bullying. Grey zone campaigns by-pass navies, armies, air forces, alliances and coalitions. Ask the Ukrainians how a grey zone campaign feels. These three-Phase campaigns initially undermine societal confidence by applying economic, political and informational pressure, including cyberattacks. Recruitment and inducement of political, corporate and civil society leaders to argue that Australia must find a way to make concessions and restore trading relations accompany Phase 1. If this pressure is not successful, light-grey, non-violent tactics may escalate to darker grey Phase 2 disruption, economic intimidation and sporadic violence. This escalation involves the employment of proxies to infiltrate political parties, manipulate grievance groups and concoct civil protests. While denying any involvement, the aim is to frighten the Australian population into applying pressure on political leaders and their parties to change policies towards China.

The Australian Government's 2020 Strategic Update acknowledges the threat from the grey zone. Still, there is no strategy or action plan, just reflexive responses, such as stricter legislation and inter-departmental counter-cyber, counter-espionage and counter-foreign interference task forces. For trade troubles with China, Australia looks to allies to protest and the World Trade Organisation to adjudicate. These instinctive legislative and institutional responses are not pacing escalating phases effectively. Reflexive responses leave the CPC with the initiative to make the next move and keep Australia on the back foot until submission.

I warn about escalation to hybrid warfare, Phase 3 of a grey zone campaign. This escalation is a remote possibility for some readers because hybrid warfare is Russia's so-called '5D Next Generation Warfare', not China's. The Russians have set the benchmarks and achieved success in their neighbourhood thousands of kilometres away from Australia. However, China's history of emulating Russian strategies for opposing the West and Russia's military technology transfer to China suggests that a Chinese variant of Russian hybrid warfare is likely.

The CPC already has a grey zone doctrine. Twenty years ago, two Chinese colonels articulated China's variant of hybrid warfare as 'unrestricted warfare'. In 2019 the Chinese armed services outlined the 'informationalised local warfare' doctrine with the 'look and feel' of hybrid warfare. The CPC's oppressive revolutionary history points to its capacity to cow populations into compliance. The CPC's repression in Hong Kong is a contemporary example. Incorporating Tibet as a tribute state is a past example. Its escalating grey zone campaigns in the South China Sea and Taiwan are instructive and have ominous implications for Australia.

The government relies on conventional military deterrence. More money for longer-range missiles, nuclear-powered submarines, fighter aircraft and counter cyber warfare capabilities accords with public understanding and sentiment. It is also comfortable to support the Home Affairs portfolio with stricter legislation, new task forces and capabilities to harden homeland defence. If more hardening is required, it is traditional to rely on the ADF to adapt to meet new challenges on the home front. Inconveniently, the ADF's capabilities are not suited to countering a grey zone campaign that escalates suddenly.

It is politically hard to persuade Australian departments and security agencies to redirect resources and effort to create new national security capabilities and instruments. However, creating the Home Affairs portfolio suggests that new capabilities and arrangements are possible if the threat is real, escalation is imminent, and an urgent response is required. My de-escalation strategy and call for establishing a Response Force and a secret Strike Force anticipate and deter the CPC from escalating its grey zone campaign. It is a sovereign, lawful and carefully nuanced strategy that complements but neither replaces nor depends on the Australia US–UK (AUKUS) alliance or the QUAD. It does not rely on more submarines, armoured vehicles, longer-range missiles and strike fighters. It depends on Australian ingenuity and lessons from Special Operations Australia in the Pacific War.

When releasing the 2020 Strategic Update, Prime Minister Scott Morrison alluded to the 1930s. He called for Australia to shape its strategic environment and deter and respond to threats. He was 'spot on'. But I believe that the Australian people's understanding of the threat and the timing and nature of government responses need enhancement. Australia's submarines, ships, and missiles investments are at least ten years away from delivery. It is like being ready for the Japanese southern thrust by 1948. Or more colloquially, trying to create deterrence by warning about the guard dog Australia plans to have in ten years rather than having a dog ready bite now. My de-escalation strategy can start now and be optimised affordably in two years.

Prophets often have a hard time in their homeland, and I also may incur 'Cassandra's curse'. However, silence is not an option when there are so many warning signs. I cannot sit back and hope for the best. I am joining the national conversation on Australia's security. I hope this book is published in time to make a difference.

Bob Breen
Canberra
2022

Primer

The Threat

Over 20 years ago, two Chinese colonels published *Unrestricted Warfare,* a so-called master plan for China to dominate the United States and its liberal democratic allies. The strategy is to coerce others to serve the interests of the Communist Party of China [CPC] by prosecuting a new way of warfare when no war is declared. Since its publication in 1999, China has risen economically and militarily and refined its doctrine for 'informationalised local wars'. Under President for life, Xi Jinping, China implements so-called Wolf Warrior statecraft and has established military bases in the South China Sea without incurring severe opposition. China can now project military power throughout Southeast Asia. Books and commentary have appeared on China's 'hundred-year marathon', 'silent invasion' and 'hidden hand'. There is an intense debate in the United States and among its allies about China's ambitions and the inevitability of a new Cold War or escalation to the nightmare of a Third World War.

In 2020, Australian intelligence agencies, think tanks, academics and media warned that an early non-violent but disruptive Phase of *Unrestricted Warfare* had come to Australia and its regional neighbourhood. The CPC has begun an intimidatory economic and political campaign that includes arbitrary and punitive trade sanctions and espionage and interference and information operations in a battlespace between peace and war called the grey zone. Suppose peace is the colour 'white' and war is figuratively 'black'. In this case, this new way of pursuing national interests and achieving dominance is a range of coercive, warlike activities in 'the grey zone' that escalate through shades of grey between white and black. It is warlike statecraft that ultimately seeks dominance. If non-violent intimidation fails, more violent, disruptive and destructive tactics follow.

The Russians have set the benchmarks for hybrid warfare in Estonia (2007), Georgia (2008) and then in Crimea 2014 and Ukraine (ongoing). There is an alarming increase in the scale and frequency of cyber-attacks. Hackers at a distance and proxies on the ground escalated political warfare to dark-grey violent and coercive tactics, including cyberattacks, concocted civil disorder and sabotage. Evidence is mounting that the CPC could borrow from the Russian hybrid warfare playbook akin to tactics espoused in *Unrestricted Warfare* and more recent Chinese military doctrine related to 'informationalised warfare'. The intention would be to cause sufficient disruption, violence and intimidation to persuade Australia to act in China's interests – the ultimate objective of unrestricted warfare. I call for urgent action so that Australia does not succumb in the grey zone or, when distracted and floundering there, 'sleepwalk' to war with a major Asian trading partner again – under-prepared and dependent on powerful allies to protect the Australian homeland.

Responding to the threat

Australia responds to the escalating grey zone threat with stricter legislation and hardened institutional machinery – but I ask whether the tempo and type of response are sufficient? Does Australia 'get it'? Is the Australian Government anticipating the next move or responding reflexively to each escalating Phase of a grey zone campaign? In the context of employing reflexive tactics without strategy, are these responses echoing Sun Tzu's 'Noise before defeat'?

Australia's traditional strategic posture is incomplete if those prosecuting a grey zone campaign disrupt the economy; launch cyberattacks to closedown essential services, online commerce and utilities; subvert the political system, and intimidate people into compliance through proxies located on Australian soil. Unless there is a whole-of-government deterrence and de-escalation strategy, law enforcement and intelligence agencies become the hunted rather than the hunters. The ADF is left to 'stare' at the air-sea gap around the continent while a grey zone campaign triumphs behind them.

In a Defence Department 2020 Strategic Update, the Australian Government acknowledged the grey zone for the first time, promising to deter and respond to those pursuing 'grey zone activities' in Australia and its near region 'in the future' with $270 billion of additional expenditure on defence. The future is now. I am trying to move Australia's response from a commendable and firm 'Update' and a promised response to a precise strategy and a definitive action plan. Prime Minister Morrison evoked the pre-war 1930s when releasing the 2020 Strategic Update, stating there is no longer ten years of strategic warning time. I agree. The CPC might suddenly escalate its grey zone campaign, especially after success in Taiwan.

Dealing with the threat

My proposed de-escalation strategy is a fair, firm and lawful assertion of Australia's sovereignty. Colloquially, it is a 'nip in the bud' strategy. It paces and prevents rather than provokes. It de-escalates rather than retaliates. It is about developing a new national power instrument called 'Response Power' that complements conventional maritime, land and air power. If Australia's existing defence strategy is a chair, the grey zone exposes it as having only three legs – maritime, land and air power. All are mostly conventional, and all need a declaration of war or civil emergency to mobilise. None directly impacts the grey zone because grey zone campaigns bypass conventional military deterrence and ignore whatever referred deterrence comes from alliances. Figuratively speaking, the ADF's first strategic priority is to fight 'in front' of the Australian people to defend them against inbound enemy forces. The Department of Home Affairs, the National Intelligence Community [NIC] and law enforcement agencies are left to protect the Australian population and maintain law and order in the homeland with the assistance of ADF Reserves. These security instruments do not have sufficient deterrence or lethal responsiveness to defend the homeland from an escalating grey zone campaign. Response Power gives Response Force and Strike Force options.

The fourth leg of Australia's defence strategy chair should be Response Power underpinned by a Home Affairs Response Force and a Foreign Affairs Strike Force. These capabilities integrate and bolster counter-cyber warfare, counter-foreign interference, counter-information warfare capabilities with deterrent clandestine and electromagnetic spectrum and carefully-calibrated surgical response operations anywhere and at any time. The paradox of deterrence is that credible and potent ultimate sanctions that 'hurt' must exist.

Response Power paces the three phases of an escalating grey zone campaign. For Phase 1 it involves extending counter-terrorism and counter-espionage legislation with empowering 'grey zone' legislation and establishing a Response Force. The government should categorise those preparing, planning and conducting 'dark grey' hybrid warfare in the same way as terrorists. They are politically motivated and possess and employ methods and means for disruption, destruction and violence. Counter-terrorism legislation already authorises law enforcement agencies and the NIC to detect and deter plots, detain plotters, bring them to justice, and de-escalate terrorist acts. Grey zone legislation would categorise grey zone combatants in the same category as terrorists for targeting by Response Force.

It is better to disappoint than provoke and remain engaged and constrain rather than focus on isolating and containing. Aggregating regional de-escalation complements aggregating conventional regional military power. There is still sufficient time to de-escalate in a way that complements and strengthens Australia's longer-term traditional hard power deterrent strategy. It is an 'and/and' rather than 'either/or' approach, or, for that matter, a third way. Figuratively speaking, it is 'the guard dog' to be beware of now rather than the 'pack of dogs' Australia will have in ten to 15 years. One analogy would be that a person who persists with hostile actions and is unwilling to communicate or negotiate can choose to ignore a person who has a dog on a lead. That person would most likely pay attention, complain and negotiate after the dog has bitten them once. Another analogy would be that a jab to the nose or a sting to the ear would force the same hostile person to pay attention and negotiate in fear of further discomfort.

New national security instruments for the grey zone

Grey zone legislation would categorise those preparing, planning and perpetrating disruptive and destructive cyberattacks and recruiting and controlling others for violent action as grey zone combatants. Legislation should authorise their lawful detection and detention in the first instance. If deterrence and negotiations for rapprochement with their sponsors fail, police and Response Force teams will de-escalate them in proportion to their threat to life and property. If there is a likelihood of an escalation to Phase 2 that approaches the Phase 3 military threshold, the government can call out the ADF's Special Forces. The new Response Power capability is a Strike Force that lives and works overseas. This is an additional ASIS capability designed to detect and de-escalate threats overseas – 'upstream' – rather than 'downstream' in Australia.

Response Power changes Australia's responses from reflexive to proactive. An AFP Response Force will be a hardened, coordinated and integrated organisation with legislation and institutional machinery to pace and de-escalate escalating espionage, foreign interference and cyberattacks in the Australian homeland and its near region. It is about the NIC, the AFP, in conjunction with their State and Territory counterparts, and Response Force capabilities detecting and 'staring' at grey zone threats, deterring threats from becoming dangerous, and if deterrence fails, striking with carefully-calibrated force to de-escalate them. The AFP and the NIC are the most appropriate partners for assisting Australia's neighbours in the near region to implement de-escalation strategies.

The Home Affairs portfolio should lead the whole-of-government de-escalation strategy as part of a national security strategy. Response Force must stand with Border Force to defend the Australian homeland with collaborative multi-agency taskforces. Task forces anticipate light-grey political coercion escalating to a 'dark-grey' hybrid war by pacing escalation rather than provoking retaliation. They are anticipatory, preparatory, and potent. They warn first and physically respond as a last resort if sponsors ignore warnings. In the future, rather than the Australian Government and its intelligence agencies only expressing concern about cyberattacks, espionage and foreign interference, as well as intimidation of Australian citizens through CPC proxies in their own country, the Prime Minister can warn of consequences for not respecting Australia's sovereignty and the rights of its citizens.

If pressure escalates through the shades of grey, Australia's Response Force transitions from deterrence to de-escalatory forceful responses or 'stings' intended to prevent further escalation.

There is an advantage of establishing a new law enforcement entity rather than enhancing Special Forces' counter-terrorism military capabilities for countering a Phase 1 grey zone campaign. Military instruments suggest a warlike response when there is no overt or covert military threat. It is provocative and 'too much too soon'. This type of response is not sufficiently nuanced or agile for the Information Age or an international security environment of oscillating cooperation, competition and conflict. It looks like warlike retaliation rather than a well-calibrated hardening of law enforcement responses to a Phase 1 grey zone campaign, its light grey non-violent but illegal and criminal phase.

There is also an operational disadvantage for building on military foundations for homeland defence. A Special Forces approach to countering acts of violence in the grey zone institutionalises a two-step emergency response process. Every armed military response has to cross immutable Federal, State and Territory legislative and institutional divides. Defence legislation is different from legislation for national law enforcement. The ADF is a separate organisation to the AFP and Australia's federation of law enforcement agencies and the NIC. It is better to have one organisation enabled by its customised legislation countering a Phase 1 grey zone campaign at home and in the near region.

Intense political and diplomatic communication always accompanies Response Force operations. The approach is to express disappointment rather than antagonise, but it does give the CPC sponsorship of illegal coercive behaviour in Australia and the near region consequences. It aims to get along with and firmly and lawfully stand up to the CPC. For regional de-escalation, Australia would partner with neighbours who are also uncomfortable with CPC grey zone coercion. Australia's Response Force would collaborate with regional law enforcement agencies to apply de-escalation strategies customised to their strategic circumstances, capabilities and sovereign preferences.

The Foreign Affairs portfolio needs to harden up for the grey zone. Its secret intelligence service, ASIS, has the political, diplomatic and cross-cultural sophistication to detect threats in the grey zone but cannot create deterrence by having a forceful option if grey zone combatants and their sponsors do not wish to negotiate or desist from planning or conducting violence after detection and warning. I am proposing a new Strike Force for ASIS founded on the attributes of Response Power, but with greater capacities and capabilities to 'hurt' for deterrence and de-escalation.

Why create a Strike Force? Arguably, Special Forces are a honed and capable force to respond to Phase 3 escalations of a grey zone campaign as it transitions to hybrid warfare and approaches a conventional military threshold with acts of war. An ASIS Strike Force is an appropriate de-escalation instrument because it will be nested in Australia's Foreign Affairs portfolio, where diplomacy and negotiation are also instruments. In effect, the Response Force is Australia's homeland frontline force in the grey zone. Strike Force is Australia's international frontline force. The ADF and Special Forces are Australia's enduring instruments when war is imminent.

The way ahead

Leadership for implementing a de-escalation strategy and raising Response Force and Strike Force will have to come from the top. This top-down requirement was the case for the development of Special Operations Australia in 1942 for the Pacific War against opposition from the ministers for the Navy, Army and Air Force and all armed Services. Currently, the Prime Minister's Cabinet colleagues are unlikely to support redirecting allocated funds and departmental effort to implement a Home Affairs-led whole-of-government answer to countering a grey zone campaign that could escalate to hybrid warfare in Australia. There will also be opposition to creating an international Strike force that will be likened to Israel's Mossad, America's CIA and Canada's Security Intelligence Service, the British Secret Intelligence Service, formerly MI6. All of these intelligence services have strike capabilities.

The Prime Minister should appoint a National Grey Zone Security

Adviser to direct an Inter-Departmental Task Force to produce unclassified and classified versions of Australia's de-escalation strategy, Response Power requirements and propose Response Force and Strike Force roles and structures. After Cabinet's approval, the government should communicate this new strategy through legislation and a public information campaign.

How will Response Force and Strike Force be established? The Prime Minister's Inter-Departmental Taskforce will establish them by developing a plan and conducting a selective mobilisation. Australia will need to astutely and confidentially marshal its most innovative and capable people to become members. This process will require a sophisticated selection and education and training system integrated with departmental and agency structures.

How will Response Force be commanded? For Response Force, the Minister for Home Affairs will command. This portfolio has already been drawn into operations in the grey zone and is under pressure. The NIC gives the portfolio detection instruments. Law enforcement agencies provide detention and judicial response options that create some deterrence. Response Force offers a deterrence and de-escalation capability alongside Border Force. The command and control arrangements for Border Force would include Response Force.

How will Strike Force be commanded? The Foreign Minister would command Strike Force. Department of Foreign Affairs and Trade (DFAT) would raise a De-escalation Operations Branch (DOB) within ASIS. DOB would be responsible for raising, training and sustaining Strike Force. The Director-General of ASIS would conduct Strike Force operations on behalf of the Minister for Foreign Affairs.

What will Response Force do? Its mission is to counter an escalating grey zone campaign at home and in the near region, including counter-terrorism. Response Force multi-agency operations will detect, deter and de-escalate organisations, groups and individuals and their operations sponsoring politically motivated violence in the grey zone, both at home and in the near region. Response Force will be a law enforcement organisation capable of operating at sea, on land and in the air, and the cyber, electronic, informational and space domains. Defence would transfer its counter-terrorism responsibilities to

Home Affairs in a transition process that maintains capability while building enhanced law enforcement counter-terrorism capabilities and capacities concurrently. Response Force will work collaboratively with Defence, Prime Minister and Cabinet and DFAT, Home Affairs law enforcement and other agencies charged with keeping Australia safe. It would also partner with regional neighbours to implement their sovereign de-escalation strategies.

What will Strike Force do? It is a deterrent force to counter a grey zone campaign that originates overseas and is escalating beyond the law enforcement threshold. Ultimately, it is a negotiating tool that firmly seeks reconciliation and a return to cooperation. Strike Force will be a civilian-led organisation capable of operating at sea, on land and in the air, and the cyber, electronic, informational and space domains. If deterrence fails, it can strike an adversary in their homeland and elsewhere to hurt their national interests. It is a force that can strike anywhere and anytime with strategic effect and optimised informational impact.

How will these forces be governed? Response Force and Strike Force must maintain the confidence and trust of the Australian government, the Australian people and national and international partners. Governance arrangements must guarantee the lawful application of force, nationally, regionally and internationally. Parliamentary scrutiny is mandatory. The Australian Commission for Law Enforcement Integrity and, for operations, the *modus operandi* and principles guiding the AFP Professional Standards Operations Monitoring Centre should inform Response Force and Strike Force governance.

How will these forces be selected and trained? Hopefully, the call to defend Australia by participating in a de-escalation strategy will resonate with educated and exceptional Australians from all ethnic backgrounds who prefer to prevent war now rather than mobilise and train for one later. Home Affairs will select and train Response Force in conjunction with Defence, DFAT and Prime Minister and Cabinet portfolios. Response Force will comprise law enforcement and civilian full-time and part-time workforce until it can grow a fully-integrated workforce from entry-level to senior leadership level. Selection, training, and contingency exercises combined with

Response Forces' mission importance will bind, bond, and build a homogenous, ethical and lawful culture and specialist capabilities in the interim.

ASIS will select and train Strike Force in conjunction with Home Affairs, DFAT, Defence and Prime Minister and Cabinet portfolios. Strike Force will have to draw on the military, law enforcement and civilian full-time and part-time workforces until it can grow a fully integrated workforce from entry-level to senior leadership level. The difference between Response Force and Strike Force selection, training and employment is between law enforcement and para-military forces for national security. However, both forces will have clear rules of engagement for applying lethal force. The other difference is that Response Force de-escalates armed operatives, malicious insiders and unarmed operatives such as hackers in the homeland. Strike Force de-escalates the same grey zone combatants overseas.

Special Forces mobilise and intervene when a military threshold is likely to be exceeded with the employment of foreign Special Forces and proxy groups with violent and destructive capabilities, as well as crewed or uncrewed vessels and aircraft.

What are the messages for friends and foes?

- Australia is defending its sovereignty and national interests preventatively rather than provocatively;
- Australia prefers to deter, de-escalate and negotiate rather than retaliate.
- Response Power sharpens the diplomatic, informational, military and economic instruments of Australian national power;
- Australia has a Response Force to counter Phase 1 and Phase 2 escalations of a grey zone campaign that detects threats and will de-escalate them before they harm – precautionary, lawful and ethical, but ultimately potent.
- Australia has a Strike Force that will hurt an adversary's national interests anywhere and at any time overseas if their grey zone campaign escalates;
- Australian Special Forces remain Australia's ultimate deterrent sanction against the escalation of a grey zone campaign to the military threshold of acts of war; and

- Australia stands ready with conventional military power, supplemented with new grey zone capabilities, to defend its sovereignty and national interests, preferably in the company of allies.

The following Parts 1, 2, 3, 4 and 5 elaborate on the primer and make my case.

Part 1 – The Threat

CHAPTER 1

Should Australia be afraid?

Introduction

Over 20 years ago, two Chinese colonels, Qiao Liang and Wang Xiangsui, published *Unrestricted Warfare,* a so-called master plan to destroy America. In their Preface, they opined:

> ... war will be reborn in another form and in another arena, becoming an instrument of enormous power in the hands of all those who harbor intentions of controlling other countries or regions. ... The new principles of war are no longer 'using armed force to compel the enemy to submit to one's will,' but rather a 'using all means, including armed force or non-armed force, military or non-military, and lethal and non-lethal means to compel the enemy to accept one's interests.[1]

They assessed that the 1991 Gulf War, where the US-led Western alliance ejected Iraqi forces from Kuwait in 42 days, was the last time traditional warfare would achieve a decisive victory. Though the United States would lead another coalition to occupy Iraq in 2003 after another display of conventional military might, these Chinese predictions appear to have been vindicated. Naval vessels, tens of thousands of troops and air power have not achieved enduring victory for the West in Iraq and Afghanistan after almost 20 years of campaigning. Sub-national groups such as the Taliban, Islamic State in Syria [ISIS] and a plethora of hostile jihadist movements remain active and potent in the Middle East and worldwide.

The essence of how these two colonels broadened the definition of war is embodied in this extract:

---

1 Liang, Q & Xiangsui, W, 1999, Preface

> In unrestricted warfare, there is no longer any distinction between what is or is not the battlefield. Spaces in nature including the ground, the seas, the air, and outer space are battlefields, but social spaces such as the military, politics, economics, culture, and the psyche are also battlefields. And the technological space linking these two great spaces is even more so the battlefield over which all antagonists spare no effort in contesting. *National Power can be military, or it can be quasi-military, or it can be non-military. It can use violence, or it can be nonviolent. It can be a confrontation between professional soldiers, or one between newly emerging forces consisting primarily of ordinary people or experts* [author's emphasis]. These characteristics of *Unrestricted Warfare* mark the watershed between it and traditional warfare, as well as the starting line for new types of warfare.[2]

China, Russia and Iran have learned from the 1991 and 2003 Gulf Wars. During the second decade of the 21st Century, they began pursuing their totalitarian objectives using 'grey zone' strategies to avoid provoking a US-led conventional military response. Russia's unopposed annexation of the Crimea in 2014 and China's uncontested militarisation of the South China Sea are measures of their early success.[3] If war is figuratively 'black' and peace is the colour 'white', this new way of pursuing national interests and achieving dominance is a range of coercive, warlike activities in 'the grey zone', between black and white – and there are different shades of grey. Borrowing David Kilcullen's book title, this is 'How the rest learned to fight the West.'[4]

William Birnes, the American publisher of the 2017 edition of *Unrestricted Warfare,* captures the essence of why the 20-year-old writings of two Chinese colonels should concern Australia:

---

2 Ibid., p. 2

3 Norberg, J, 2016, 'The use of Russia's military in the Crimea crisis', Norberg, J, Westerlund, F & Franke, U, 2014, 'The Crimea operation. Implications for future Russian military interventions' and Kofman, M & Rojansky, M, 2015, 'A closer look at Russia's 'Hybrid War'

4 Kilcullen, D, 2020, *The Dragons and the Snakes*

> *Unrestricted Warfare* is the People's Liberation Army [PLA] manual for asymmetric warfare ... not too dissimilar from Sun Tzu's Art of War [that] is about impeding the enemy's ability to wage war and to defend itself against *a barrage of attacks against its economy, its civil institutions, its governmental structures, and its actual belief system* [author's emphasis].
>
> This is not a manual for achieving an overnight victory. Rather, it is a recipe for a slow but inexorable assault on an enemy's institutions, often without the enemy's knowledge that it is even being attacked. As Sun Tzu once wrote, 'If one party is at war with another, and the other party does not realize it is at war, the party who knows it is at war almost always has the advantage and usually wins.' And this is the strategy set forth in *Unrestricted Warfare*: waging a war on an adversary with methods so covert at first and seemingly so benign that the party being attacked does not realize it's being attacked.
>
> ... Readers, therefore, should take this little manual as a dire warning. Complacency cripples. Hubris kills. ... Thus, although this book was written almost twenty years ago, it should be regarded as the playbook for the destruction of not only the United States but of Western democracies in general. Be afraid. Be very afraid.[5]

Should Australia be afraid? What is there to fear? What is being done about it? What should be done about it? I argue for developing unique Australian Response Power to implement a detection, deterrence and de-escalation strategy. Response Power is an autonomous capability that does not depend on allies or massive investments in conventional military deterrence. It complements working with partners and enhances traditional military deterrence.

Chinese and Russian strategic ambitions

Let's begin with the big picture. There is a plethora of scholarly literature and official British and American government warnings about China and Russia's strategic intentions to dominate in their self-designated

---

5 Birnes, WJ, 2017, Foreword, in Liang, Q & Xiangsui, W, 1999

spheres of influence to suit their interests.[6] The post-Cold War era is over. A new era of intense competition, possibly a new version of the Cold War, is being fought in the grey zone. Though they are rivals, Emeritus Professor Paul Dibb, a doyen of Australian military strategy, warns that China and Russia may combine in mutual self-interest to achieve their strategic objectives coercively.[7] In 2019 and 2020, there has been increasing military cooperation and technological transfer between Russia and China.[8]

There are some realities for Australia. Australia has a significant trading relationship with China. There are substantial revenues from exporting raw materials and agricultural products, 'full-fee' Chinese students studying in Australia's university sector and Chinese tourism. Australia has supply chains from China that create a relationship between the well-being of Australia's economy and China's willingness to supply manufactured goods. The vast majority of transactions with the Chinese people are optimistic, warm and mutually beneficial. There is an immense reservoir of goodwill, and Australia should make every effort to continue to foster good relations, especially in the face of self-serving provocations from Communist Party of China [CPC] hard-line nationalists. This book does not confuse the majority of the Chinese people and their corporate and civil society sectors with their rulers. Its recommended de-escalation strategy encourages the CPC to have second thoughts on escalating its grey zone campaign. It enables moderate CPC and corporate leaders to make a case to return to

---

6 Friedburg, AL, 2011, *A Contest for Supremacy:*, Pillsbury, M, 2015, *The Hundred-Year Marathon*, Ikenberry GJ, 2015, *America, China, and the Struggle for World Order*, Allison, G, 2017, *Destined for war*, Bachmann, S, Oliver, V, Dowse, A & Gunneriusson, H, 2019, 'Competition Short of War, US Department of Defense 2017, *Russia Military Power*, and US Department of Defense 2019, *China Military Power*

7 Dibb, P, 2019, 'How the geopolitical partnership between China and Russia threatens the West'

8 Bendett, S and Kania, E, 2019, 'A New Sino–Russian High Tech Partnership', Bendett, S and Kania, E, 2020, 'The Resilience of Sino–Russian High-Tech Cooperation'; Kendall-Taylor, A, Shullman, D and MacCormick, D, 2020, *Navigating Sino–Russian Defense Cooperation*; Kofman, M, 2020, *The Emperor's League: Understanding Sino–Russian Defense Cooperation*; Segal, A, 2020, Peering into the Future of Sino–Russian Cyber Security Cooperation

mutually agreeable trade relations and respectful acknowledgement of political and cultural differences.

This book focuses on what a reasonable person would agree is threatening, sometimes described in commentary as 'bullying' behaviour and the assertive agenda of CPC nationalistic hardliners in Australia and its near region. If the CPC reversed the situation, it would not tolerate the Australian Government prosecuting unrestricted warfare in China or against Chinese national interests elsewhere. Though it may be naïve to evoke this 'Golden Rule' in the context of this serious discussion about international relations and 'pseudo-war', this book's message is, 'Do to others what you would want others to do to you.' It recommends a firm, lawful and fair response to intimidation that accords with the sentiments and values of the vast majority of Australian and Chinese citizens and their societal decision-making elites. Still, it increases consequences for the CPC's subversive and threatening behaviour.

Australia is a member of a Western alliance of nations that seeks to preserve the rules-based global order, uphold the United Nations Charter and support liberal democracy and human rights. This membership and a continuing closeness to the United States obligates Australia to comprehend China and Russia's nationalistic aspirations. Aside from 'freedom of navigation' exercises in the South China Sea and outrage after the downing of Malaysian Airlines MH17 in Ukraine in 2014, Australia has not had to confront China or Russia, respectively. It is worth noting that after Prime Minister Tony Abbott's threat to 'shirtfront' Russian President Vladimir Putin over the MH17 incident at a G20 meeting in Australia, several Russian warships appeared brazenly off Australia's northern coast.[9] Only theatre, but an example of the contemporary Russian mindset and the potential for hostile acts against Australian interests.

Since 9/11, Australia has made modest military contributions to US-led Western alliance military operations in the Middle East and Afghanistan as a participant in a US-declared' War on Terror' and

9 Pearlman, J, Parfitt S & Parfitt, T, 2014, 'Russia has sent a convoy of warships to Australia northern maritime border'

continues to do so.[10] Arguably, while the United States and those allies in Europe who are closer to the jihadist terrorist threat and disruptive State-sponsored behaviour 'hold the line' and bear the burden of military action, Australia should not be afraid.

But is there something closer to home to fear? In recent years there have been several severe warnings about the growing influence of the CPC in Australia and its near region. They come from the Australian Security and Intelligence Organisation [ASIO], from think tanks and academics in the United States, Australia and New Zealand, and journalists and commentators in the media. China's 2019 Defence White Paper outlines an emerging strategy of conducting 'informationalised local wars' to further China's strategic interests.[11]

The CPC will not publish its strategic game plan. Typically, the CPC narrative for its use of armed force is defensive, accompanied by hubris about assured devasting retaliation. Looking behind the nationalistic rhetoric, the 2019 Defence White Paper reveals broader intentions for remote operations 'in the far seas'. The United Work Front, discussed below, is the CPC's non-violent instrument for prosecuting Professor Clive Hamilton's 'Silent Invasion'. Xi Jinping has created a Strategic Strike Force [SSF] within the Chinese armed forces to prosecute localised information warfare that brings together space, cyberspace and the electromagnetic spectrum domains.[12] Well before the appearance of an invasion fleet in the Indonesian-Melanesia archipelago, the SSF has capabilities to conduct an 'Electronic Invasion' that disables Australia's computer-dependent economy, financial system, and essential services including food, water and energy supply. At the same time, Australia's satellite and electromagnetic spectrum dependent communications system would collapse.

The Morrison Government issued a strategic update on 1 July

---

10 Department of Defence, 'Global Operations', Brangwin, N, 2020, *Australia's military involvement in Afghanistan since 2001: a chronology*

11 Burke, EJ, Gunness, K, Cooper CA III, Mark Cozad MI, 2020, *People's Liberation Army Operational Concepts*, Bekjr Ilhan, *China's Evolving Military Doctrine after the Cold War* and Kania, E, 2020, Innovation in the New Era of Chinese Military Power

12 Costello, J and McReynolds, J, 2020, 'China's Strategic Support Force', p. 446

2020, warning of a more uncertain world and the collapse of strategic warning time and introducing the notion of an ominous 'grey zone'.[13] Australia's strategic warning lights were blinking. Let's quickly run through the warnings of unrestricted warfare in Australia before the discussion turns to what it is and could be, as well as what is being done about it.

Warnings from intelligence agencies

For the fifth year in a row, ASIO has warned in 2020 of unprecedented levels of foreign interference, cyber disruption and espionage in Australia. The current Director-General, Mike Burgess, cautioned that,

> The level of threat we face from foreign espionage and interference activities is currently unprecedented. *It is higher now than it was at the height of the Cold War.* [author's emphasis]... There are more foreign intelligence officers and their proxies operating in Australia now than at the height of the Cold War, and many of them have the requisite level of capability; the intent and the persistence to cause significant harm to our national security. But the character and focus of that espionage activity will continue to evolve.
>
> ... ASIO has uncovered cases where foreign spies have travelled to Australia with the intention of setting up sophisticated hacking infrastructure targeting computers containing sensitive and classified information. ... And perhaps most disturbingly, *hostile intelligence services have directly threatened and intimidated Australians* [author's emphasis] in this country.
>
> Those threats across the terrorism, espionage and foreign interference domains are formidable and continually evolving. They will require us to deploy a range of imaginative and sophisticated effects to *harden our environment* [author's emphasis] to make sure we continue to detect threats and *raise the cost of entry* [author's emphasis] for our adversaries.[14]

---

13 Department of Defence, 2020, *2020 Defence Strategic Update*, Canberra, 1 July 2020, para 1.5

14 Burgess, M, 2020, 'Director-General's Annual Threat Assessment 2020'

On retirement, Burgess's two predecessors, Duncan Lewis and David Irvine, had nothing to lose by naming the CPC; Burgess was constrained because he was a government official.[15] Let's be clear: the only organisation conducting unprecedented levels of espionage, cyber disruption, foreign interference, influence operations and intimidation of citizens in Australia is the CPC. Jihadist sub-national groups plotting terrorist acts and Far-Right extremists, possibly inspired by the Christchurch massacre in 2019, still threatened, but they did not constitute a strategic threat. The Russian Communist Party does not have any strategic, ideological or political affinities with Australia, but the Russians are not the 'Reds under the bed' this time.

Extremism with global reach has not gone away. The Federal Government's 2017 Independent Intelligence Review [IIR] assessed that:

> extremism with global reach will continue and diversify over the coming decade. Fundamentalist advocacy of violence in the name of religion will continue to inspire attacks, especially from Islamist terrorist organisations.[16] ... These will include the activities and networks of Australian 'foreign fighters' involved in international extremist and terrorist causes ... The time taken between radicalisation and a terrorist attack is shortening, further challenging intelligence agencies' *detection and response capabilities* [author's emphasis].[17]

Adding to his warnings about foreign interference and espionage, Mike Burgess publicly and plainly stated:

> So let me be clear: the threat of terrorism at home is PROBABLE [Burgess's emphasis] and will remain unacceptably high for the foreseeable future. The unfortunate reality is that, right now, terrorists are still plotting to harm Australians. ... The number of terrorism leads

---

15 Irvine, D, 2013, 'Director-General Speech: Address to the Security in Government Conference', Grattan M, 2014, 'In conversation with ASIO chief David Irvine' and Lewis, D, 2019, 'Address to the Lowy Institute'

16 Australian Government, 2017, *2017 Independent Intelligence Review*, para 1.14

17 Ibid., para 1.15

> we are investigating right now *has doubled since this time last year.* [author's emphasis] The character of terrorism will continue to evolve, and we believe that it will take on a more dispersed and diversified face.[18]

The IIR added a dimension to public warnings about 'rogue state and non-state actors' by emphasising 'the security and societal consequences of accelerating technological change'.[19]

> Technology is changing the way in which economies work, and societies evolve, making the intersection of economics, politics, and security more difficult to manage. ... One of the most worrying aspects of technological change is the way it is helping to place enormously destructive capabilities within easier reach of rogue states and non-state actors. This trend is not reversible, and it will lead to an even more threatening international environment than now exists.[20]
>
> ... More generally, the cyber domain will likely feature even more prominently than it currently does in attempts to undermine economies, societies and national governments. It offers a relatively inexpensive but potentially effective way of achieving a wide range of effects – from influencing political processes to disrupting financial systems and key aspects of national infrastructure.[21]

The IIR was right to warn of an environment of change, increased complexity and technological enablement. Australia's safety will depend critically on how well its governments understand this complex threat environment as it evolves – to keep pace with and, ideally, one step ahead of the threat. However, the IIR fell short of Ganor's compelling connection of modern jihadist terrorism to a new type of armed conflict that he describes as 'multidimensional warfare', another name for unrestricted warfare.[22] Hostile sub-national groups,

---

18 Burgess, M, 2020, 'Director-General's Annual Threat Assessment 2020'

19 Australian Government, 2017, *2017 Independent Intelligence Review*, para 3.1

20 Ibid., para 1.18

21 Ibid., para 1.22

22 Ganor, B, 2015, *Global Alert*

inspired by ISIS, have the role model organisation, imagination and technology to prosecute a jihadi version of unrestricted warfare that incorporates terrorism. The question is whether CPC operatives could manipulate aspirational terrorist groups or 'lone wolves' in Australia for disruptive purposes to support a grey zone campaign?

Far-Right extremists are another group that could be manipulated for participation in unrestricted warfare. Burgess issued a clear warning in 2020:

> In Australia, the extreme right-wing threat is real, and it is growing. In suburbs around Australia, small cells regularly meet to salute Nazi flags, inspect weapons, train in combat and share their hateful ideology. ... We continue to see some Australian extremists seeking to connect with like-minded individuals in other parts of the world, sometimes in person. They are not merely seeking to share ideology and tactics. ... We expect such groups will remain an enduring threat, making more use of online propaganda to spread their messages of hate.
>
> While we would expect any right-wing, extremist inspired attack in Australia to be low capability, i.e. a knife, gun or vehicle attack, more sophisticated attacks are possible. And we also *need to be mindful of state-sponsored terrorism as states seek to use terrorism to further their goals* [author's emphasis].[23]

Paradoxically, the Far Right's racist and xenophobic response to CPC political warfare allows the CPC to manipulate them to destabilise Australia's political order and mobilise Australians of Chinese and Asian heritage to support CPC interests. Consider CPC agents provoking or co-opting Far-Right extremists to attack persons of Asian ancestry while at the same time disseminating a narrative that the Australian Government cannot protect citizens of Asian heritage, as well as Asian students and tourists. In June 2020, the CPC advised Chinese parents not to send their children to study in Australia and cautioned Chinese citizens from travelling to Australia because of the risks of racist attacks. Escalating this narrative after several Far-Right

23 Burgess, M, 2020, 'Director-General's Annual Threat Assessment 2020'

extremist attacks and violent demonstrations would be simple. There is potential for Far-Right groups, possibly in conjunction with criminal networks, to be infiltrated and co-opted for a grey zone campaign. Russia set an example in Crimea in 2014, and the Indonesian armed forces set a precedent for Australia's near region in East Timor in 1998–99 to thwart an UN-endorsed referendum on independence.[24]

In summary, those recruiting for unrestricted warfare have a range of grievance groups and individuals available in Australia for small group and lone-wolf terrorist acts. The spike of media condemnation of the activities of groups of young men of African heritage in Melbourne in 2018–19 alienated members of those groups. There are still groups of alienated men of Middle Eastern and Asian sub-continental heritage who might be susceptible to narratives calling for action against authorities and institutions. Members of Far-Right extremist groups may listen to calls for radical political change and act violently against political, ethnic, religious, and racial groups in the name of Australian patriotism. Recruiters may also adopt coercive techniques prevalent in the Middle East, such as threatening family members to compel cooperation for illegal and violent acts. Concocting this dystopian nightmare of ideological, political, racial and ethnic violence in a targeted country is the stuff of unrestricted warfare explained in terms of hybrid warfare described in Chapter 2.

Warnings from think tanks and academics

What about think tanks and academics? Similar warnings? Ross Babbage, an eminent Australian strategist and Senior Fellow at the US think tank, Center for Strategic and Budgetary Assessments [CSBA], has published with his CSBA colleagues ominous assessments of unrestricted Chinese warfare.[25] They include case studies of CPC

---

24 McDonald, H, Ball, D, Dunn, J, van Kinken, G, Bourchier, D, Kammen, D & Tanter R, 2002, *Masters of Terror, Indonesia's military and violence in East Timor in 1999*

25 Babbage, R, 2016, *Countering Chinese Adventurism in the South-China Sea,* and Babbage, R, Mahnken, T and Toshihara, T, 2018, *Countering Comprehensive Coercion-Competitive strategies against authoritarian political warfare*

political operations in Australia, New Zealand and the Pacific Islands.[26] More generally, they warn:

> The political warfare undertaken by the regimes in Russia and China is, at its core, driven by the obsessions of Vladimir Putin and Xi Jinping to protect their personal rule. These leaders feel deeply threatened by the liberties and practices prized by liberal democracies. Hence, in order to defend themselves, rally domestic support, keep their enemies off-balance, and weaken and potentially overthrow democratic states, *they have refined powerful versions of political warfare as a means of progressing their interests at relatively low cost and risk* [author's emphasis]. They appreciate that by operating aggressively and in a nimble fashion in the gray zone between the Western conceptions of peace and war, they are exploiting a substantial advantage over the United States and its allies, who are more traditionally minded, conventionally structured, and bureaucratically sluggish.
>
> ... Moscow and Beijing employ a much wider range of instruments, many of which involve highly intrusive intelligence operations and deeply subversive espionage, cyber, military, and other active measures to disorientate, distract, confuse, coerce, undermine, and potentially cause the collapse of targeted societies.[27]

Clive Hamilton, Professor of Public Ethics at the Centre for Applied Philosophy and Public Ethics, at Charles Sturt University, observed in his book, *Silent Invasion: China's influence in Australia*:

> Today, few understand the dangers [of Chinese influence in Australia] sufficiently to feel we [Australia] need to begin taking steps to regain our independence and keep at it despite the inevitable retaliation [from those consciously or unwittingly supporting the CPC agenda]. Our naivety and our complacency are Beijing's strongest assets. *Boy Scouts up against Don Corleone* [author's emphasis]. Once Australians

---

26 Babbage, R, 2019, *Stealing a March*; Babbage, R, 2019, *Winning Without Fighting: Chinese and Russian Political Warfare Campaigns*

27 Babbage, R, Mahnken, T and Toshihara, T, 2018, *Countering Comprehensive Coercion*

> of all ethnic backgrounds understand the danger, we can begin to protect our freedoms from the new totalitarianism.[28]

Anne-Marie Brady, Professor of Political Science at the University of Canterbury in New Zealand and an eminent Sinologist published a paper in 2017 describing Chinese President Xi Jinping's 'Magic Weapons' of political warfare to influence targeted Western countries. It highlighted CPC influence in New Zealand.[29] Reportedly, CPC agents, working directly or through proxies, have harassed Professor Brady and her family through a burglary of their home, office break-ins, tampering with their family car and threatening letters, phone calls and e-mails. Chinese Ministry of State officials have visited and intimidated her academic colleagues in China. She opines, 'Here is an actual challenge to our sovereignty – and a New Zealand family who have had their safety threatened – and our government is not defending them.'[30] As this book shows below, the CPC targets families and individuals in Australia. There is little evidence of the government backing off perpetrators whose covert intimidation cunningly avoids law enforcement and legal prosecution.

For several years, Alan Dupont, well-respected CEO, Cognoscenti Group, has been sounding warnings about China's political warfare in Australia. He also warns of a new way of war at Australia's doorstep.[31] In 2016, prompted by disclosures of impropriety between Australian Labor Party [ALP] Senator, Sam Dastyari and Chinese businessman, Huang Xiangmo, Dr Peter Jennings, Head of the Australian Strategic Policy Institute [ASPI], identified widening and deepening CPC influence through political donations in Australia and 'debt trap' aid in the Pacific Islands and Timor Leste.[32] His assessments have sharpened

---

28 Hamilton, C, 2018, *Silent Invasion: China's influence in Australia*, p. 281

29 Brady AM, 2017, 'Magic Weapons: China's political influence activities under Xi Jinping'

30 Ainge Roy, E, 2019, 'I'm being watched': Anne-Marie Brady, the China critic living in fear of Beijing'

31 Dupont, A, 2019, 'A New Type of War at Our Door', and Dupont, A, 2020, 'Australia must stand strong against Beijing's political warfare'

32 Jennings, P, 2016, 'Peter Jennings on China, Australia and soft power'

over time. In 2020 he called for Australia to harden its position on Chinese bullying and applauded the Morrison Government's tightening of restrictions on foreign investment in security-sensitive industries and infrastructure.[33] On 9 June 2020, ASPI released Alex Joske's policy paper, *The Party Speaks for You*, containing compelling evidence that the CPC is stepping up its political warfare in Australia.[34] He describes the 'united front system', a grouping of agencies, social organisations, businesses, universities, research institutes and individuals carrying out united front work to persuade the Australian political system, the corporate sector and civil society to favour CPC interests. In February 2022, ASPI released a comprehensive description of the levels of influence China has achieved in Australia's States and territories – exemplars of Phase 1 political, economical and information operations escalating to foreign interference.[35]

John Blaxland, Professor of International Security and Intelligence Studies at the Australian National University [ANU], has identified eleven threats to Australia's security.[36] The first was CPC foreign interference, the second was cyber warfare and religious and politically motivated violence as the next major threat. He is right to mention CPC interference enabled by cyber warfare' upfront' in the order of threats to Australia's national interests.

Warnings from the media

There continues to be a lively, sometimes sensationalised, national discussion in the Australian media about CPC surveillance, infiltration and influence in Australia.[37] The Dastyari affair dominated the discourse in 2016 and 2017.[38] Late in 2019, there was a flurry

---

33 Jennings, P, 2020, 'Party's over for the bullies of Beijing', 'The many ways China is pushing us around ... without resistance' and 'China will be surprised how long it took us to act'

34 Joske, A, 2020, 'The Party Speaks for You'

35 Fitzgerald, J, (ed) 2022, 'Taking the Low Road: China's Influence in Australia's States and Territories'

36 Blaxland, J, 2019, 'A Geostrategic SWOT Analysis for Australia'

37 Hamilton, C, 2018, 'Why do we keep turning a blind eye to Chinese political interference?'

38 Sweeny, L et al. 2017, 'Sam Dastyari resignation: How we got there'

of interest in a Chinese defector seeking asylum in Australia. His interviews on the Channel 9 60 minutes TV program confirmed CPC interest in increasing its influence in Australia.[39] But there are doubts about the defector's authenticity.[40] Another spike of interest occurred in 2019 over an alleged 'Manchurian candidate', the late Nick Zhao Bao, for the Federal Electorate of Chisolm in Victoria.[41] Since the election of Hong Kong-born Gladys Liu as the Member for Chisolm, there has been speculation in the media about her ties to the CPC. There are photos of her meeting Nick Zhao Bao and her involvement with Chinese businessman Brian Chen Chunsheng, photographed in a Chinese military uniform.[42]

The Murdoch press has questioned the Victorian Premier, Daniel Andrews, and his government for signing agreements related to the Chinese Belt and Road Initiative. Articles point to CPC agents of influence and imply that former politicians promote CPC interests in Australia.[43] Greg Sheridan, *The Australian* newspaper's foreign editor and prominent media commentator, has numerous articles warning of CPC influence in Australia and the near region.[44] Late in June 2020, ASIO officials and AFP officers raided the home and NSW

---

39 McKenzie, N, 2019, 'China's Spy Secrets', and McKenzie, N, 2019, 'World Exclusive: Chinese spy spills secrets to expose Communist espionage'

40 Grenfell, O, 2019, 'Australian media's 'Chinese spy defection story' unravels'

41 Australian Associated Press 2019, 'ASIO investigating Chinese plot to plant spy in Australia's parliament after Liberal party member found dead'

42 Hartcher, P, 2019, 'Red Flag: Waking up to China's challenge', p. 62. Hamilton, C, 2019, 'Why Gladys Liu must answer to parliament about alleged links to the Chinese government', Harris, R, 2019, Gladys Liu's Beijing confession deepens dispute over loyalty, Burke, K, 2019, 'Chinese spy scandal puts spotlight back on Liberals' Gladys Liu, and Sakkal, P & Mackenzie, N, 2019, 'How Nick Zhao made enemies, faced charges, and was allegedly asked to spy for China' and McKenzie, N, Sakkal, P & Tobin, G, 2019, 'China tried to plant its candidate in Federal Parliament'

43 Packham, B, 2020, 'Influencer cosied up to Chinese leaders', *The Australian*, The Nation, 1 June, p. 3, Varga, R, 2020, 'Key BRI advisor linked to Communist Party', *The Australian*, The Nation, 1 June, p. 3, Baxendale, R, 2020, China-linked staffer's corona conspiracy, *The Australian*, The Nation, 2 June, p. 5 and Baxendale, R, 2020, 'Andrews staffer did Chinese propaganda course', *The Australian*, 29 June, p. 2

44 Sheridan, G, 2020, 'Scott Morrison right to say times as dangerous as 1930s'

parliamentary office of ALP MP, Shaoquett Moselmane, and the home and office of John Zhang, one of Moselmane's staff, on suspicion of their complicity in CPC influence operations.[45] Significantly, these raids were the first conducted under provisions of new legislation aimed at quelling foreign interference.[46] Clive Hamilton commented that these raids were further evidence of CPC infiltration of the NSW ALP. *The Australian* newspaper headlined that ASIO was investigating the CPC infiltration of the NSW Parliament.[47] This contested evidence suggests a lively interest in the media of any signs of CPC influence. Still, evidence of an unrestricted warfare campaign is elusive, but there is sufficient revelation that the CPC asserts its influence covertly in Australia.[48]

For me, ASIO, journalists Peter Hartcher and Greg Sheridan, and academics John Fitzgerald, Clive Hamilton and Alex Joske provide sufficient evidence that Australia should be afraid of and do something about the CPC's growing influence in Australia. The CPC has 'form'. The party's infiltration and surveillance operations, followed by the detention of minorities and dissident groups in China, such as Uighurs, Falun Gong and 'under-ground' Christians, confirm a *modus operandi* of suppression that is akin to unrestricted warfare.[49] The eruption of civil protests in Hong Kong in 2019 and arrest and detention of 15 pro-democracy dissidents in April 2020, and more arrests of over 300 democracy activists in July after the passage of more restrictive security legislation has brought the discussion about CPC strategies

---

45 Kelly, J & Benson, S, 2020, 'Raided Labor MP in fundraising boast'and Norington, B, 2020, 'MP China-link raids underline ASIO's anxiety'

46 Kelly, J & Packham, B, 2020, 'Sweeps first test of laws on foreign interference', p. 4

47 Hamilton, C, 2020, 'Sheets pulled back in search for reds in bed with ALP', p. 4 and Bashen, 2020, 'ASIO chases agents in the House', p. 1

48 Kelly, P, 2020, 'Shift on Beijing was Turnbull's gift to Morrison', p. 14

49 US Embassies and Consulates in China, 2019, '2018 Report on International Religious Freedom'

for infiltrating and controlling populations into sharper focus.[50] Suppression in Hong Kong is likely to continue until submission as a tribute state. The arrest of more than 50 political activists on 7 January 2021 confirms this inevitable trend.[51] The West will probably not know how to respond effectively. The CPC will extinguish democracy there while maintaining that Hong Konger patriots loyal to China have overcome dissident and disruptive pro-democracy separatists.[52] Are there signs of this type of suppression and 'fake news' beginning in Australia?

Peter Hartcher, the Political and International Editor of the *Sydney Morning Herald* and Fellow at the Lowy Institute, in his paper, *Red Flag, Waking up to China's Challenges*, warns of China's 'insatiable appetite' for influence in Australia.[53] He identifies 'Document No 9' as Xi Jinping's aspiration for ridding the world of liberal democratic ideas.[54] Hartcher illustrates how the CPC operates in Australia through six anecdotes of Chinese millionaires and officials behaving in ways that fictional Mafia boss, Don Corleone, would admire. These actions involve former Federal Treasurer Joe Hockey, former Labor Senators Stephen Conroy and Sam Dastyari, and current Labor politicians, Penny Wong, Bill Shorten and Richard Marles, Australian journalist John Garnaut, and former Chief Secretary of Hong Kong, Anson Chan.[55] He also points to eleven case studies of CPC international economic intimidation and 'calls out' four of the CPC's 'useful idiots' in Australian public life.[56] Hartcher warns that Australia must become self-reliant in the future:

> Australia needs to concentrate on strengthening itself, *making itself*

---

50 Reuters/ABC News 2020, 'US, UK condemns arrests of 15 Hong Kong democracy activists in raids', Agence France-Presse, 'Beijing passes feared Hong Kong security laws', p. 8 and Agence France-Presse, 'HK erupts over China law 180 held', p. 9

51 Korporaal, G, 2021, 'Hong Kong activists arrested in China show of force'

52 Callick, R, 2021, 'Farewell to China's Most Sparkling Gem', 20–21 January, Inquirer, *The Weekend Australian*, pp. 13–14

53 Hartcher, P, 2019, *Red Flag: Waking up to China's challenge*, p. 9

54 Ibid., pp. 4–5, Buckley, C, 2013, 'China takes aim at Western ideas'

55 Hartcher, P, 2019, *Red Flag: Waking up to China's challenge*, pp. 11–28

56 Ibid., pp. 44–52

> *armour-plated against foreign subversion* [author's emphasis] so that it can engage confidently with China and the world because it cannot count on anyone else.[57]

Hartcher highlights examples of CPC agents harassing prominent citizens and their families that echo the intimidation of Anne-Marie Brady and her family in New Zealand. He reports on CPC harassment of journalist John Garnaut and his wife after Garnaut authored a classified report on CPC interference in Australia for the Turnbull Government in 2015. It illustrates that the CPC likes to 'get up close and personal'.[58] Garnaut's report prompted the Morrison Government to introduce legislation countering CPC covert intrusions in 2018.[59] Another example is the continuing campaign against Australian Olympic swimmer Mack Horton and his family exposed in the media in 2020. Horton 'called out' Chinese swimmer, Sun Yang, a three-time Olympic Gold medallist and 11-time world champion at the 2016 Olympics, for being a drug cheat and refused to stand on the dais with him at the 2019 World Swimming Championships. Interestingly, Brazilian authorities were sufficiently concerned about the safety of Horton and his parents in Rio de Janeiro in 2016 to assign armed Special Forces commandos to keep them safe. The Horton family reportedly received regular briefings from ASIO officials for their safety in 2020, even after Sun Yang's suspension from international swimming competitions for eight years for drug testing offences.[60]

Another example of CPC intimidation in 2020 was the physical attack on and continuing harassment of University of Queensland activist student Drew Pavlou for his support for the pro-democracy movement in Hong Kong.[61] Pavlou has since called out the University of Queensland for hosting a CPC-funded Confucius Institute and

---

57 Ibid., p. 89

58 Ibid., pp. 60–61

59 Australian Parliament 2018, National Security Legislation Amendment (Espionage and Foreign Interference) Act 2018, No. 67

60 Slattery, L, 2020, 'Hitting Home'

61 Zhou, N & Smee B, 2020, 'We cannot be seen: the fallout from the University of Queensland's Hong Kong protests'

permitting CPC agents to mobilise Chinese students to shut down peaceful pro-Hong Kong democracy protests on campus violently.[62] The University of Queensland has suspended Pavlou for two years. He has appealed this decision. His fate in the courts will be worth watching.

John Garnaut, Mack Horton and Drew Pavlou are publicised examples of the CPC intimidating Australians in their own country. It is worth pondering how many citizens CPC agents threaten directly or through criminal and radicalised Chinese student proxies and if numbers are growing? More particularly, how might Australia detect, deter and de-escalate these illegal activities that must be dreadfully distressing for victims and their families? So far, no perpetrators appear to have been brought to justice or even named and shamed. The proposed de-escalation strategy in this book would draw a line on this type of intimidation and create uncomfortable consequences for perpetrators.

Silent invasion?

Clive Hamilton has put together even more convincing evidence of the beginnings of CPC unrestricted warfare in Australia and has published another book exposing the CPC's international campaign.[63] This second book, *Hidden Hand*, begins:

> The Chinese Communist Party is determined to transform the international order, to shape the world in its own image, *without a shot being fired.* [author's emphasis] Rather than challenging from the outside, it has been eroding resistance to it from within, by winning supporters, silencing critics and subverting institutions. ... and while many in the West remain reluctant to acknowledge this, democracies *urgently need to become more resilient if they are to survive.* [author's emphasis] ... As Beijing is emboldened by the feebleness of resistance, its tactics of coercion and intimidation are being used against an increasingly broad spectrum of people.[64]

62 Condon, M, 2020, 'The boy who kicked the hornet's nest'

63 Hamilton, C & Onlbereg, M, 2020, *Hidden Hand*

64 Ibid., Preface and p. 1

Hamilton is explicit and specific about the CPC threat in Australia in *Silent Invasion*. His comprehensive exposition covers the expected battlespaces of unrestricted warfare – the political system, the economy, trade, corporations, the education system, the media, entertainment and cultural organisations and civil society more generally. In sum, for this book, *Silent Invasion* and Alex Joske's ASPI policy paper provide compelling proof that something sinister is going on and, in the author's opinion, will escalate unless there is detection, deterrence and de-escalation.[65]

I could not find a think tank, academic, journalist, commentator, expert or publication that satisfactorily counters Hamilton or Joske's evidence or arguments comprehensively. Some commentary opposing their views call for pragmatism, realism, and a more subtle, nuanced and sophisticated relationship with China, even suggesting a 'new China' is emerging that will overtake the CPC's authoritarian rule.[66] Former Australian Ambassador to China, Geoff Raby, articulates this desire to accommodate China in his 2020 book, *China's Grand Strategy and Australia's Future in the New Global Order* that echoes Martin Jacques's 2014 edition of *When China Rules the World*.[67] Former Prime Minister Paul Keating opines that Australia should accept the reality that, 'Big states are rude and nasty – but that does not mean we can afford not to deal with them – whether it be the United States or China.'[68] He dismisses ASIO warnings about the CPC and asserts cuttingly that 'nutters' are in charge of Australia's domestic intelligence and that security agencies have 'gone Berko' about China.[69]

Hugh White, probably Australia's most high-profile publicised strategist, rightly points out that Australia has to address uncomfortable questions about China and derive a better way of engaging

---

65 Joske, A, 2020, 'The Party Speaks for You'

66 Hayward-Jones, J, 2013, 'Big Enough for All of Us: Geo-strategic Competition in the Pacific Islands', and Croucher, G & Powell D, 2019, 'Our ties to China must be subtle and nuanced'

67 Raby, G, 2020, *China's Grand Strategy and Australia's Future in the New Global Order*, and Martin Jacques, 2014, *When China Rules the World, When China Rules The World*

68 Keating, P, 2019, 'Paul Keating's speech on Australia's China policy'

69 Keating, P, 2019, Video: 'China is a great state'

the CPC. Still, he avoids directly challenging Hamilton or Joske on CPC activities and disquieting events in Australia.[70] Professor of History at the ANU Frank Bongiorno's thoughtful but qualified review of *Silent Invasion* criticises instances of exaggeration but not its substance.[71] Rory Medcalf, Professor and Head of the National Security College at the ANU, calls out critics of *Silent Invasion* for confecting racism with reasonable concern about the CPC. He is right. Hamilton does not question the behaviour of the Chinese people, in general, or Australians of Chinese heritage in particular, many of whom contributed to *Silent Invasion* and attended its launch.[72] Kevin Carrico, a Senior Lecturer in Chinese Studies at Monash University, correctly assesses most criticisms of *Silent Invasion* as 'rants' and possibly economically self-interested or ideological rather than reasoned, evidence-based critiques.[73] Borrowing from Paul Keating, the question is, 'What should be done about the CPC's 'rude and nasty' behaviour in Australia, especially towards Australians of Chinese heritage?' How does Australia get on with China and stand up to China?

Pressure on Australians of Chinese heritage

Hamilton, Joske, Hartcher and John Fitzgerald, Emeritus Professor in the Centre for Social Impact at the Swinburne University of Technology, describe increasing CPC pressure on Australians of Chinese heritage.[74] They join New Zealanders, Anne-Marie Brady and her protégé, James Jian Hua To, warning of the CPC's '*qiaowu*' strategy.[75] This strategy

70 White, H, 2017, 'China's Power and the Future of Australia' and White, H, 2017, 'We need to talk about China'

71 Bongiorno, F, 2017, 'Up to a point, Professor Hamilton'

72 Medcalf, R, 2018, 'Silent Invasion: the question of race'

73 Carrico, K, 2019, 'In defence of Silent Invasion'

74 Hamilton, C, 2018, *Silent Invasion*, pp. 25–52, Hartcher, P, 2019, 'Red Flag, pp. 19–22, p. 63, pp. 80–82, Joske, A, 2020, 'The Party Speaks for You' and Fitzgerald, J, 2016, 'Beijing's quoqing versus Australia's way of life'

75 Brady, AM, 2003, *Making the foreign serve China: managing foreigners in the People's Republic*, Brady, AM ed. 2010, 'Looking North, Looking South: China, Taiwan, and the South Pacific'; Brady, AM ed., 2012, *China's Thought Management*, Jian Hua To, J, 2014, *Qiaowu: Extra-Territorial Policies for the Overseas Chinese*, Brady AM, 2017, 'Magic Weapons: China's political influence activities under Xi Jinping'

aims to use the Chinese diaspora worldwide to subvert democratic political systems, civil society and economies to accept, or at least be ambivalent to the CPC's strategic interests – the main objective of unrestricted warfare.[76]

Why might Australians of Chinese heritage be a significant battlespace for unrestricted warfare in Australia? According to Hamilton and Joske, the CPC's United Front Work Department and its allied agencies are infiltrating this community and marshalling the Chinese diaspora living and studying in Australia. Their tactics involve silencing CPC critics and independent Chinese–Australian media and encouraging allegiance to a unified patriotic notion of China.[77] They recruit 'influencers' and cultivate former political leaders, facilitate Chinese investment in critical infrastructure, especially telecommunications, and prosecute information warfare, including sponsored cultural events, to manipulate narratives in favour of the CPC's broader agenda.[78] Hartcher describes deep divisions within the Chinese–Australian community, with most wavering between anti-CPC and pro-CPC factions who work assiduously to sway the vast majority who just want to get on with their lives.[79] The pro-CPC camp can call on the resources of the United Front Work Department. The anti-CPC grouping can only look to the Australian Government and its security agencies to recognise and respond to intimidation and manipulation.

This book is not questioning and warmly affirms the loyalty, values and law-abiding nature of the 1.2 million-strong community of Australians of Chinese heritage. Australia has been and should continue to be grateful for its contribution to national life. But this community may be the first battlespace for countering unrestricted warfare in the grey zone. The Australian Government should comprehend the

---

76 Hamilton, C, 2018, *Silent invasion*, Chapters 3, 7 and 12

77 Ibid., Joske, A, 2020, 'The Party Speaks for You' and Sun, W, 2019, 'What do we learn about the experience of Mandarin-speaking migrants from Chinese-language media in Australia?'

78 Fitzgerald, J, 2018, 'Australia on its own when managing foreign influence on Australian soil'

79 Hartcher, P, 2019, *Red Flag: Waking up to China's challenge*, pp. 20–23, pp. 80–81

protection of this community from an escalation in CPC coercion. This community is most under threat and a potential vector for unrestricted warfare if the Australian Government takes no action. It is the most effective community to support Australian security agency efforts to detect, deter and de-escalate the CPC's threatening behaviour and stop a transition to more assertive coercive and violent tactics associated with hybrid warfare.

The anxiousness of the Australian people

The Australian people are anxious about their security. According to the annual Lowy Institute Opinion poll, 'Australians are feeling extremely anxious in 2020, with only 50 per cent of the country saying they feel safe, a sizeable 28-point drop from 2018.'[80] Only 23 per cent of respondents say they trust China to 'act responsibly in the world', in a 30-point fall since 2018, and 78 per cent do not trust Xi Jinping 'to do the right thing', the lowest level of trust in a Chinese leader ever recorded in Lowy Institute polling.[81] An average of 42 per cent of respondents assess that foreign interference in Australian affairs, international terrorism, and dissemination of 'fake news' are critical threats to Australia's vital interests.[82] In 2020, an average of 62 per cent of respondents nominated cyberattacks, presumably from China, and a Chinese base in a Pacific Island nation as critical threats to Australia. Furthermore, 44 per cent said 'protecting Australians from foreign state intrusion' should be the government's priority when considering which foreign companies should be allowed to supply new technology for essential services.[83]

The indicative messages from the 2020 Lowy Institute Poll are that the Australian people 'feel far more distrustful, pessimistic and less secure than at any point in the 16-year Lowy Poll's history'.[84] Respondents have recognised CPC strategic ambitions and are beginning to detect those ambitions in Australia and its near region.

---

80 Lowy Institute 2020, '2020 Lowy Institute Opinion Poll'
81 Ibid.
82 Ibid.
83 Munro, K, 2019, 'Australian attitudes to China shift: 2019 Lowy Poll'
84 Oliver, A & Kassam, N, 2020, 'Happy to hop away from these bounders', p. 10

Still, the Lowy Institute and respondents to its poll in 2020 have not given names to what is going on or developed a way of thinking about it, let alone looking at response options if it gets worse. This book does.

Conclusion

In answer to the question 'What is going on?', there is sufficient *prima facie* evidence that the battle lines of CPC political warfare are now drawn: Australia's political parties, corporate boardrooms, think tanks, media, civil society, as well as among Australians of Chinese heritage and on university campuses. While there is no evidence yet of systematic political violence, the physical attacks on Chinese students supporting the Hong Kong protests on university campuses in 2019 and previous 'rumbling' of pro-Tibet and Falun Gong demonstrations testify to CPC methods and penchant for violence through proxies.[85] The intimidation of Mack Horton and his family and John Garnaut and his wife and student activist Drew Pavlou point to the potential for more brazen efforts to intimidate Australian citizens and others. Think of Hong Kong. The question is whether Australia is anticipating this sort of development and responding to ASIO's call for hardening its opposition to these repressive activities and increasing the CPC's 'price of entry'?

The CPC is coercing Australia to agree to political concessions, including distancing the US–Australian alliance and persuading Australia to act in China's interests as a tribute state. In exchange, the CPC would assure Australia of reasonable trading arrangements and respect for Australia's sovereignty and values – a 'Hong Kong promise'. Across the Tasman Sea, New Zealand appears to have already accepted the CPC's 'Hong Kong promise'. In late January 2021, the New Zealand Trade Minister, Damien O'Connor, after signing an upgraded Free Trade Agreement [FTA] with China, cautioned Australia 'to follow us and show respect … to China'.[86] Under the title 'Building on a Success

---

85 Needham, K, 2019, 'Beijing supports 'patriotic' protests against Hong Kong students in Australia'

86 Dziedzic, S, 2021, 'New Zealand Trade Minister advises Australia to show China more 'respect'

Story', the New Zealand Ministry of Foreign Affairs and Trade website boasted:

> The New Zealand-China Free Trade Agreement, first signed in 2008, is a success story for both countries. It has opened up significant trade and economic opportunities and has been a catalyst for closer cooperation across a number of areas. China is now New Zealand's largest trading partner. Two-way trade (exports and imports of goods and services) has quadrupled from $8 billion to over $32 billion since the free trade agreement was signed. ... Trade is a key driver of New Zealand's prosperity ... Upgrading our free trade agreement with China delivers on one of the pillars of New Zealand's Trade Recovery Strategy [post-COVID pandemic].[87]

New Zealand appears to be on its way to a 'partnership for peace and prosperity.' An example of its separation from Western allies was its absence from a joint statement issued on 10 January 2021 from the so-called 'Five-Eyes' intelligence community [US, Canada, UK, Australia and NZ] condemning the detention of 55 pro-democracy advocates in Hong Kong.[88] China's 'Wolf Warrior' response to the joint statement was a threat to 'poke out the eyes' of the Five Eyes intelligence collaboration.[89] The absence of New Zealand from the joint statement suggests that one 'Eye' has closed without the need to pluck it out. It is unlikely that the New Zealand Government will harden its capabilities to counter a CPC grey zone campaign that it is accommodating. Australia should not be so naïve.

---

87 New Zealand Ministry of Foreign Affairs and Trade, 'Building on a Success Story'

88 Payne, M, 2021, 'Joint statement on arrests in Hong Kong'

89 Walden, M, 2021, 'China again blames Australia for diplomatic spat, issues warning to Five Eyes intelligence partners'

CHAPTER 2

What should be feared?

Political and hybrid warfare in the grey zone

So far, I conclude that something is going on in Australia and the near region that looks like the early phases of unrestricted warfare. Before discussing a de-escalation strategy, defining and discussing what should be feared is essential. What are totalitarian nations such as China and Russia doing? Concepts such as the grey zone and hybrid warfare are not prominent in Australia's national security and defence conversation. The 2016 Defence White Paper is silent. The 2020 Strategic Update mentions 'grey zone activities' for the first time in strategic guidance. Public discourse is still sparse. This chapter maps out what should be feared.

The Australian Government is alert to the threat described in Chapter 1. Its 2020 Defence Strategic Update defines the grey zone briefly and mentions 'grey zone activities' in the Indo-Pacific region.[90] It does not elaborate or identify who is responsible. However, there is a $274 billion investment in longer-range missiles and counter-cyber capabilities between 2020 and 2030.[91] The Update does not go far enough. It does not offer a strategy related to the grey zone, specific new capability development initiatives, adjustments to institutional machinery or any particular counter-measures.[92] While acknowledging the cyber and space domains, it is rooted in conventional military deterrence – ships, submarines, tanks, strike aircraft and longer-range missile systems, an extension of the 2016 Defence White Paper.

This chapter warns about the CPC's political warfare in Australia

---

90 Australian Government, 2020, *2020 Defence Strategic Update*, para 2.23

91 Morrison, S, 2020, 'Address – Launch of the 2020 Defence Strategic Update'

92 Australian Government, *2020 Defence Strategic Update*, Foreword

escalating to something more sinister and violent – from light grey to dark grey. Accordingly, readers need to understand the nature and significance of what might happen if what is going on now is not countered urgently. Preparations need to be made to deter and de-escalate what might happen next. Let's quickly elaborate on concepts of the grey zone, political, information and hybrid warfare, including cyberattacks, to underpin the argument that a de-escalation strategy is required because things could worsen suddenly.

The grey zone

Though aggressive statecraft short of war is centuries old, the origins of contemporary grey zone campaigns go back to the end of the Cold War. Professor Hew Strachan, Chichele Professor of the History of War at Oxford University, observed astutely in 2013 what most commentators would agree is warfare in the grey zone without coining the term:

> ... the clear distinction between war and peace, which prevailed in the era of so-called 'total war' has been eroded. Since 1990 America's and Britain's forces have been engaged in various forms of conflict, virtually without pause. Yet neither has been a state formally at war in the sense that both were in the two world wars. Most citizens have conducted their lives as though their countries have been at peace. They have been affected by these conflicts indirectly through the media but in most cases not directly – since the burdens of war have been borne by professional armed forces drawn from a small sector of society, and in some cases by Special Forces.[93]

Inadvertently, Strachan describes a 'forever war' since the end of the Cold War – a dichotomy of 'when war is not war'. Had he waited three more years before publishing *The Directions of War* in 2013, he would have identified Chinese and Russian manifestations of political, information and hybrid war in the grey zone. While the United States and its allies focussed on destroying terrorist networks and battling insurgencies in the Middle East and Afghanistan after 9/11, China and

---

93 Strachan, H, 2018, *The Direction of War*, p. 82

Russia took to the grey zone. Neither country wants conventional war with the West, but both seek strategic advantage by other ways and means. David Kilcullen describes this phenomenon in some detail in his book, *The Dragons and the Snakes: How the Rest Learned to Fight the West* and references *Unrestricted Warfare* to illustrate how the CPC operates in the world.[94] Clive Hamilton and Mareike Ohlberg clarified the CPC's worldwide grey zone campaign in *Hidden Hand*, and Ross Babbage and colleagues have sharpened Western alliance perceptions of China's strategic trajectory in *Which Way the Dragon?*.[95]

In its recent *2020 Strategic Update*, Australia's Department of Defence offers a definition:

> Grey zone is one of a range of terms used to describe activities designed to coerce countries in ways that seek to avoid military conflict. Examples include using para-military forces, militarisation of disputed features, exploiting influence, interference operations and the coercive use of trade and economic levers. These tactics are not new. But they are now being used in our immediate region against shared interests in security and stability. They are facilitated by technological developments, including cyber warfare.[96]

Grey zone campaigns involve non-violent and violent actions by a nation, like China, or a sub-national group, like a terrorist organisation, that are harmful while remaining below the threshold of what is usually considered acts of war. China and Russia's prosecution of political, information and hybrid warfare is figuratively in a 'grey', shadow-like zone. There is no transparency or truthful public declarations of strategic intentions and actions, just contrived narratives and public denials. Mazarr describes a grey zone campaign as 'gradualist and coercive in nature, and it is unconventional in the tools it employs.'[97]

---

94 Kilcullen, D, 2020, *The Dragons and the Snakes*, Chapter 4 and 5

95 Babbage, R, 2020, *Which Way the Dragon: sharpening allied perceptions of China's strategic trajectory*

96 Australian Government, 2020, *2020 Defence Strategic Update*, para 1.5

97 Mazarr, MJ, 2015, *Mastering the gray zone: understanding a changing era of conflict*, p. 4

Nationalistic and religious narratives of entitlement and destiny legitimise and disguise real intentions and strategies.

The Australian Government's 2017 Foreign Policy White Paper provides a practical 'big picture' description of the grey zone:

> The international order is also being contested in other ways. Some states have increased their use of 'measures short of war' to pursue political and security objectives. Such measures include the use of non-state actors and other proxies, covert and paramilitary operations, economic coercion, cyberattacks, misinformation and media manipulation. ... International rules designed to help maintain peace and minimise the use of coercion are also being challenged.
>
> Australia's security is maintained primarily through our own strength, our alliance with the United States and our partnerships with other countries. Australia's security and prosperity would nonetheless suffer in a world governed by power alone. It is strongly in Australia's interests to seek to prevent the erosion of hard-won international rules and agreed norms of behaviour that promote global security. ...
>
> Like all great powers, China will seek to influence the region to suit its own interests. As it does, a number of factors suggest we will face an increasingly complex and contested Indo-Pacific.[98]

The United States Army does not use the term 'grey zone' in its doctrine but defines competition below the threshold of conflict that epitomises the grey zone. Competition precedes conflict and escalates from non-violent actions to warlike violent, disruptive and destructive actions. The US Army acknowledges grey zone competition:

> Although the idea of competition is not new, the current and future operating environments require a holistic approach to campaigning that links activities short of armed conflict with the execution of armed conflict.
>
> Peer adversaries compete to separate alliances and defeat

98 Australian Government, 2017, 2017 Foreign Policy White Paper, Canberra, p. 24 and p. 26

> partners below the threshold of armed conflict and challenge the traditional metrics of deterrence by conducting operations that *make unclear the distinctions between peace and war* [author's emphasis].[99]

Geography does not matter in the grey zone battlespace. Grey zone campaigns hold back on traditional battles and physical invasion until their non-attributable and deniable operations have undermined an opponent. The phases of a grey zone campaign gradually and deniably damage and disrupt political institutions and democratic processes, economic activity, social systems and essential services with the aim of unsettling governments and populations sufficiently before final subjugation. The ultimate objective is a *fait accompli* achieved 'without firing a shot'.[100] The invasion of Ukraine in 2022 came after years of grey zone intimidation.

Figuratively, the grey zone is an area of operations inhabited by organised criminal networks such as drug cartels, pirates, and people traffickers. Cohabitating are terrorist groups, 'semi-legitimate' organisations cooperating and enabling these groups, counterintelligence organisations, private military companies, mercenaries and other violent groups sponsored by nation-states or sub-national groups. An analogy might be the notion of the 'Dark Web' that operates within the recesses of the Internet. Those prosecuting political, information and hybrid warfare have carved out their grey zone battlespace expertly. It sits astride Australia's traditional understanding of war and conflict. More particularly, in an Australian context, it is figuratively located in an institutional blind spot between Australia's Defence, Foreign Affairs and Trade [DFAT] and Home Affairs departments. This positioning frustrates the use of conventional military power and diffuses and complicates how Australia employs its national law enforcement powers and police and judicial instruments to the best deterrent effect.

A grey zone campaign makes it difficult for a targeted nation to

---

99 US Army 2017, *Multi-Domain Battle: Evolution of Combined Arms for the 21st Century 2025–2040*, p. 2

100 Ibid.

maintain situational awareness because of the number, randomness, secrecy, surprise and simultaneity of hostile actions. In the absence of a defined or enforceable demarcation, peace and war in the 21st Century act as a 'fog' with one another, its blended thickness or shades of grey from political, cyber, informational and economic to hybrid warfare determining the degree of violence. As the fog lifts, so too do the real intentions of antagonists and the scale of violence they apply to achieve their ends.[101] Western Europe and Ukraine remained conflicted, confused and duped before the fog lifted on Russia's annexation of Crimea in 2014.[102]

Another metaphor to illustrate the complexity of a grey zone campaign and its gradualist and increasingly coercive nature is that there are several shades of grey. A fictional example could be that perpetrators assessed that intimidation of Mack Horton's family mentioned above did not send a strong enough message about the consequences of embarrassing a national hero and, by implication, China and the China Swimming Association. Throwing smashed glass into the family swimming pool was 'nasty', but the CPC might have deemed this action not to be 'rude' enough. The escalation moves from a lighter to a darker shade of grey in the form of a bomb going off at the headquarters of Swimming Australia in York Street, South Melbourne, causing damage but no loss of life. The CPC denies any involvement in response to Australian and international media outrage and accusation. Chinese media accuse those attributing the bomb to Chinese revenge as racists and caution that public humiliation of China may arouse intense Chinese patriotism among Chinese diaspora that is reprehensible if violent, but understandable – a CPC grey zone message has been sent.

The Australian public response to a bombing of Swimming Australia's headquarters would far exceed the reaction to the Hilton Hotel Bombing in 1978 for several reasons. Culturally, professional

---

101 Byman, D & Merritt, I, 2018, 'The New American Way of War: Special Operations Forces in the War on Terrorism', Cronin, PM ed. 2008, *The Impenetrable Fog of War: Reflections on Modern Warfare and Strategic Surprise,* and Sechser, TS, 2011, 'Militarized Compellent Threats, 1918–2001'

102 Barber, N, 2017, 'A warning from the Crimea', pp. 46–58

and community-level sport is deeply integrated into Australian national sentiment, recreation, pride and identity. Morally, Australians would view a violent attack on a nationally prominent not-for-profit organisation as cowardly and immoral. Emotionally, the Australian people, who are already unsettled by Chinese connections to the COVID19 pandemic and have increasing distrust of the CPC according to the Lowy Poll, would have their fears of the CPC deepen and demand decisive government action. Arguably, the potential bonuses for the CPC might be a series of disruptive anti-Chinese demonstrations by Far-Right extremists in Melbourne, Sydney and Perth and unprovoked attacks on several Australian citizens of Chinese heritage.

The point to be made from this fictional, and for some readers improbable, Swimming Australia example is that grey zone activities can escalate quickly and can achieve significant impact for a modest investment. Terrorists and revolutionaries have known this for centuries. It is no surprise that those who are developing grey zone strategies in the Information Age draw on this knowledge when deciding on escalation phases from political to hybrid warfare. The challenge for liberal democracies is to detect changes in the shades of grey and have lawful proportional responses that befit their values and ethical codes.

The Morrison Government has acknowledged that grey zone activities have expanded in the Indo-Pacific region:

> These activities involve military and non-military forms of assertiveness and coercion aimed at achieving strategic goals without provoking conflict. In the Indo-Pacific, these activities have ranged from militarisation of the South China Sea to active interference, disinformation campaigns and economic coercion. Defence must be better prepared to respond to these activities, including by working more closely with other elements of Australia's national power.[103]

This promise of integration of Australia's instruments of national power to respond to grey zone activities is stepping in the right

103 Department of Defence, *2020 Defence Strategic Update*, Foreword

direction. This book proposes further steps that would have given the Australian Government more options for responding to a fictional Swimming Australia office bombing and may have even stopped it from occurring.

Information warfare

Information warfare is not a new phenomenon, but it has become more potent and ubiquitous in the 21st Century. The Internet facilitates instantaneous global informational reach with minimal entry costs for nations and sub-national groups. The Information Environment is the aggregate of individuals, organisations or systems that collect, process or disseminate information, and Information Warfare is the contest played out in the Information Environment.[104] Reilly argues that information warfare seeks to influence, compel or coerce.[105] Campbell asserts that it aims to subvert, undermine, influence, subdue, and disrupt a targeted nation or sub-national group.[106] Information warfare is a feature of grey zone campaigns from their non-violent beginnings throughout their escalation phases. The Information Age has weaponised social media and amplified the impact of messaging between adversaries in warfare and between adversaries and populations in the grey zone and *vice versa.*

In the grey zone, information warfare includes traditional psychological warfare and encompasses cyber, electronic and information actions. Cyber and electronic actions have different intensity levels regarding persistence, coverage, and impact. Information and psychological actions have different intensity levels in terms of dissemination and inundation and aggressive and provocative content: cyber actions attack Information Technology and Communications [ICT] systems. Electronic actions deny adversaries access to the Electro-Magnetic Spectrum [EMS], colloquially described as 'jamming'. Information actions manipulate and disseminate narratives, traditionally called propaganda, to influence people's attitudes and actions.

104 Australian Defence Force, 2020, *Information Warfare*, pp. 8–9
105 Reilly, J, 2018, 'The Multi-Domain Operations Strategist'
106 Campbell, A, 2019, 'Political Warfare'

The convergence and increase in cyber, electronic and information actions escalate a grey zone campaign. Cyberattacks are primarily enhancements of information warfare rather than a variant of conflict. Information actions, particularly in the cyber domain, ignore borders and provide a nation and sub-national group the means to realise political goals through precisely targeted propaganda.[107] Unlike conventional warfare that targets an adversary's military forces, information warfare targets populations. Regarding cyberattacks, populations and their public and private sectors lose online access to a range of essential services for economic activity and everyday life. For electronic attacks, they lose the means for communication. They are instantly exposed to pernicious narratives because they live in a 'hyper-transparent, hyper-connected world' that is more exposed and discoverable.[108]

In the 21st Century, nations and sub-national groups have weaponised social media for Information warfare.[109] In *LikeWar*, Singer and Brooking provide a compelling case regarding the weaponisation of information through social media and its near-instantaneous access to nations and sub-national groups to distribute narratives and shape public opinion.[110] Arguably, the CPC has the means to target the Australian population and grievance groups within it with increasingly personal messages that relate to their circumstances, preferences and fears. I agree with Singer and Brooking that 'attacking an adversary's most important centre of gravity – the spirit of its people – no longer requires massive bombing runs or reams of propaganda; all it takes is a smartphone and a few idle seconds.' They state 'five key elements to [weaponised] social media: narrative, emotion, authenticity, community and inundation'. All combine to intimidate populations, mobilise hostile groups and concoct civil unrest.[111]

---

107 Chansoria, M, 2012, 'Defying Borders in Future Conflict in East Asia', pp. 105–06

108 Seidman, D, 2011, *How: Why HOW We Do Anything Means Everything*

109 Singer, PW and Brooking, ET, 2018, *LikeWar*, Schake, K, 2019 'Social Media as War?', Sanger, DE, 2018, *The Perfect Weapon*, and Chansoria, M, 2012, 'Defying Borders in Future Conflict in East Asia'

110 Singer, PW and Brooking, ET, 2018, *LikeWar*

111 Ibid., p. 18

An example of weaponised social media was the radicalisation of Australians to join the Islamic State in Syria [ISIS] in the Middle East in the second decade of the 21st Century. Other hostile sub-national groups, such as Far-Right Extremists and many jihadist terrorist networks, disseminate their narratives and enhance their influence over citizens in targeted nations via social media. The Islamic State Propaganda Handbook claims that 'media weapons [can] be more potent than atomic bombs' highlights that governments and their armed forces no longer monopolise information warfare. There are now three threat vectors: governments, organisations, and individuals.[112]

Cyberattacks intensify Information Warfare to escalate grey zone campaigns. The US Army observes that:

> With increasing frequency, adversaries conduct cyber-attacks on civil targets to affect a targeted nation's decision making. Also, the adversary seeks to undermine security cooperation activities and forces. Adversaries sometimes generate a flood of messages without regard for the truth to confuse, disrupt, and divert debate about their actions.[113]

Modern information warfare integrates cyber, electronic and informational actions. This integration can increase in intensity. An intensifying information campaign, accompanied by cyber and electronic actions, is central to escalating a grey zone campaign. The most significant point is that the escalation is electronic, not physical. Arguably, a grey zone campaign involves three 'invasion' escalations to force political and economic concessions: Phase 1 Political subversion and economic pressure; Phase 2 Political subversion, economic pressure and cyber/electronic attack; and Phase 3 Political subversion, economic pressure, cyber/electronic attack and hybrid war.

---

112 Ibid., p. 148

113 US Army 2017, *Multi-Domain Battle: Evolution of Combined Arms for the 21st Century 2025–2040*, p. 6

Political Warfare

During the Cold War, George Kenna, a former US Secretary of State, defined political warfare as 'the employment of all the means at a nation's command, short of war, to achieve its national objectives,' essentially a grand strategy.[114] Plato's Law 626a states, 'every State is, by a law of nature, engaged perpetually in an informal war with every other State', and 'peace' is nothing but a name.[115] If Plato is correct, then CPC political warfare is an Information Age variant of statecraft that is understandable and constitutes an enduring traditional 'law of nature' in international affairs. But that does not make it either acceptable, tolerable or trivial. It must be opposed because the CPC's competitive intentions coerce Australia to favour China's national interests. This so-called Wolf Warrior political statecraft is reminiscent of the Cold War.[116]

The means for prosecuting political warfare are espionage, subversion, propaganda, foreign interference and, when escalated to hybrid war, combined with unmarked military forces and armed spies and provocateurs.[117] Political warfare involves 'diverse operations to influence, persuade, and coerce nation-states, organisations and individuals to operate according to one's strategic interests without employing kinetic force'.[118] It echoes the prescriptions of *Unrestricted Warfare.* The US Center for Strategic and Budgetary Assessments [CSBA] opines that:

> The regimes in Moscow and Beijing believe that they are already engaged in an intense form of warfare, but it is a political conflict and not kinetic [conventional] warfare. Their primary operational focus at present is on employing a range of non-military instruments in non-

---

114 Kennan, GF, 1948, 'The Inauguration of Organized Political Warfare [redacted version]'

115 Bury, RG, 1967, *Plato in Twelve Volumes*

116 Australian Security and Intelligence Organisation, 2020, Counter Espionage and Foreign Interference

117 Paterson, T, 2019, 'The Grey Zone: Political Warfare is Back'

118 Babbage, R, 2019, *Stealing a March,* p. 1

> traditional ways below the threshold of large-scale military operations to win strategic gains.[119]

The CPC's political war with the world is relevant to Australia. Firstly, it would be strategic folly to misread or underestimate China's political encroachments in Australia's near region and its 'Silent Invasion' of the homeland. The penetrative political operations against democracy in Hong Kong and Taiwan are instructive for Australia.[120] Secondly, Australia should not depend on allies to moderate Chinese influence in its homeland, Pacific Islands, and Timor Leste, Australia's regional backyard. Thirdly, it is Australia's national responsibility to deter political warfare while at the same time maintaining trade relations – a firm but fair and ethical de-escalation strategy. Before discussing Australia's de-escalation options for responding to CPC political warfare, it is essential to come to terms with the possible next Phase – cyber and electronic warfare-enabled hybrid war. A grey zone campaign begins with a non-violent subversive political and informational contest to persuade another nation to act in one's interests. It can escalate to violent hybrid war if the aim is not achieved non-violently.

Hybrid warfare

Since 2006, the term 'hybrid' has become prominent in contemporary and future warfare's expert and academic discourse. The label 'hybrid' encompasses centuries-old modalities of conventional and unconventional warfare, and there is a lively, esoteric semantic contest befitting Western intellectual discourse.[121] Evolving technology, including cyber and electronic warfare and autonomous systems, combines with the Internet and social media to enhance the multi-domain 21st Century modality. No matter the label or the semantics, it's new; it's dangerous, and it's here now.

---

119 Ibid., p. 49

120 Hai-Chi Loo, J, Shiu Hing Lo, S and Chung-Fun Hung, S, 2019, *China's New United Front Work in Hong Kong,* and Yu-shek Cheng, J, 2020, *Political Development in Hong Kong*

121 Stoker, D & Whiteside, C, 2020, 'Blurred Lines: Gray-Zone Conflict and Hybrid'

Academics, strategists and policymakers, and military leaders assert that a 'hybrid' conceptual framework is a basis for contemporary and future military strategies.[122] The US CSBA opines: 'Competitors of the United States and its close allies will likely favour hybrid warfare over other forms of warfare.'[123] The grey zone in which hybrid threats emerge is not a distraction from great power competition but a central environment where the race to shape the international system will take place.[124]

The US Army, mindful of Russian success with hybrid warfare in the Crimea in 2014, offered this definition in 2017:

> Hybrid war is the combination of operations by a state against one or more other states through non-attributable proxies and methods to destabilise the target state and achieve the aggressor state's strategic objectives short of war.
>
> Its techniques leverage conventional and attributable capabilities in threatening ways that reinforce the non-attributable efforts. It intends to achieve military and political objectives rapidly and present a *fait accompli* – a thing accomplished and presumably irreversible – before a conventional military response can prevent it.[125]

A British Government-sponsored multi-national report concluded in 2017 that hybrid warfare is a 'whole-of-government' activity involving military and civilian institutional machinery and capabilities:

> Hybrid warfare involves the synchronized use of military and non-military means against specific vulnerabilities to create effects against its opponent. Its instruments can be ratcheted up and down

---

122 Hoffman, F, 2007, *Conflict in the 21st Century: The Rise of Hybrid War*, Hoffman, F, 2007, *Thoughts on 21st century warfare*, and Glenn, RW, 2009, 'Thoughts on 'Hybrid Conflict'

123 Kouretsos, P, 2019, 'A Literature Review' in Annex A: Contextualising Chinese Hybrid Warfare

124 Mazarr, MJ, 2015, *Mastering the gray zone*: p. 4

125 US Army 2017, *Multi-Domain Battle: Evolution of Combined Arms for the 21st Century* p. 2

simultaneously, using different tools against different targets, across the whole of society.

In this respect, hybrid warfare expands the battlefield. It also creatively exploits our cognitive predisposition to emphasise the military instrument of power, allowing opponents to leverage non-military ... means against a wider set of unconventional targets. This, in turn, allows hybrid warfare actors, at least initially, to operate ambiguously below the target's thresholds of detection and response.

In practice, this can make identifying the starting point of hybrid warfare very difficult. *Moreover, it increases the possibility of a hybrid warfare actor inflicting significant damage on its opponent before that opponent can respond to, or possibly even detect, a hybrid warfare attack.* [author's emphasis]

This strong and fluid element of ambiguity within hybrid warfare adds a new dimension to how coercion, aggression, conflict and war are to be understood. In this respect, new geostrategic contexts, new applications of technologies, and new organizational forms suggest the likelihood that this form of warfare will persist and continue to evolve into the future.[126]

Hybrid warfare involves the use of military, para-military and civilian agencies equipped and authorised to use violence to coerce nation-states, organisations and individuals to operate in accord with one's strategic interests. The definition's first layer is straightforward. The Devil is in the detail. More specificity reveals a level of complexity that defies easy explanation and has stimulated differing interpretations in a proliferation of literature since 2014 when Russia annexed Crimea unexpectedly.[127] One Australian expert questions whether there is anything 'new' in hybrid warfare but argues that the Australian Government needs to grasp its meaning

---

126 UK Government, 2017 *Understanding Hybrid Warfare*, p. 26 and UK Government, 2019, *Countering Hybrid Warfare, Countering Hybrid Warfare*

127 UK Government, 2017, p. 3 and Babbage, R, Mahnken, T & Yoshihara T, 2018, *Countering Comprehensive Coercion-Competitive strategies against authoritarian political warfare*, pp. 6–8

for strategic policy.[128] For this chapter, a helpful definition of hybrid warfare is when an adversary escalates through some combination of (1) political, military, economic, social, and informational means and (2) conventional, irregular, catastrophic, terrorism, and disruptive/criminal warfare methods. It may include a combination of state and non-state actors'.[129] This continuum corresponds to the three escalation phases mentioned earlier: Phase 1 Political subversion and economic pressure; Phase 2 Political subversion, economic pressure and cyber/electronic attack; and Phase 3 Political subversion, economic pressure, cyber/electronic attack and hybrid war.

Hybrid warfare creates 'friction', a fundamental feature of war. Friction means the impact of a combination of random and unpredictable hostile, destructive and disruptive events, including terrorism, that inherently complicate the simplest of organisational tasks, especially responses.[130] This friction or convergence of violent and disruptive actions can collapse economic activity and essential services and disrupt civil society. The Russians applied 'friction' through multiple acts of violence, concocted public protests, cyberattacks and disruption of services in Crimea in 2014.[131] Cyberattacks both enable and magnify the friction caused by nations and sub-national groups employing terrorist and other disruptive and destructive tactics associated with hybrid warfare.[132] More on cyberattacks later.

Over the past eight years, Russia has taken hybrid war to a new level by violently furthering its national interests in the Baltic States, Crimea and Ukraine, and other European and Arctic border areas.[133] In effect, a member of the United Nations Security Council has and continues to

---

128 Buchanan, E, 2019, 'Hybrid warfare: Australia's (not so) new normal'

129 Glenn, RW, 2009, 'Thoughts on 'Hybrid Conflict', p. 2

130 Clausewitz, C, 1984, Howard, M & Paret, P eds., *On War*, pp. 119–21

131 Norberg, J, Westerlund, F, and Franke, U, 2014, 'The Crimea operation. Implications for future Russian military interventions', pp. 41–50 and Chivvis, C, 2017, *Understanding Russian Hybrid Warfare*

132 Australian Government, 2015, National Cyber Security Strategy

133 Kofman, M & Rojansky, M, 2015, 'A closer look at Russia's 'Hybrid War', Fox, AC, 2017, *Hybrid Warfare: The 21st Century Russian Way of War*, and Chivvis, C, 2017, 'Understanding Russian 'Hybrid Warfare'

employ Special Forces, in conjunction with civilian security agencies, to raise, train, employ and sustain proxy political allies and militias. Russia has vigorously denied any involvement and characterised any discovered actions as responding logically and empathetically to the calls from oppressed patriotic Russians and grievance groups living in Ukraine and the Baltic States.[134]

Hybrid operations, employed for the invasion of the Republic of Georgia in 2008, and then more deftly in 2014 in Crimea and eastern Ukraine, and ongoing in Ukraine, the Baltic States and elsewhere, showcases the effectiveness of Russia's Special Forces.[135] Russian political and military leaders adroitly coordinated special operations, information operations, State-controlled media, economic sanctions, cyber-attacks, terrorism, deterrence and criminal coercion to achieve territorial hegemony over Crimea.[136] No invasion risked the opprobrium of the community of nations, as exemplified in the international response in February 1991 to the Iraqi invasion of Kuwait in August 1990. Strategically surprised, NATO 'sat on its hands' in 2014 because it could not mobilise forces in time and, even if NATO had contemplated mobilisation, no one dependent on the Russians for oil and gas in the middle of winter wanted to pick a fight with them.

Professor Julian Lindley-French, the Senior Fellow of the Institute of Statecraft, London, summarises Russia's grey zone campaign as 'complex strategic coercion':

> Russia's military modernisation must thus be seen first and foremost as the foundation instrument for the application of complex strategic coercion across 5D continuous warfare – disinformation, destabilisation, disruption, deception and implied destruction – in pursuit

---

134 White, J, 2016, 'Dismiss, Distort, Distract, and Dismay'

135 Kilcullen, D, 2020, *The Dragons and the Snakes,* pp. 141–148 and Dew, A, 2008, 'The Erosion of Constraints in Armed-Group Warfare', p. 32

136 Renz, B, 2016, 'Russia and 'hybrid war', pp. 283–300, Renz, B & Smith H, 2016, *Russia and hybrid warfare. Going beyond the label,* Norberg, J, Westerlund, F & Franke, U, 2014, 'The Crimea operation', and Norberg, J, 2016, 'The use of Russia's military in the Crimea crisis'

> of the greatest influence at the least warfighting cost to the Russian Federation.[137]

While this concept of '5D continuous warfare' in the grey zone is a Russian innovation, it accords with the underpinning operational concepts of unrestricted, informationalised Chinese warfare – more on Chinese hybrid warfare below.

The Russians appear to have been the first to develop hybrid war as a 'whole-of-government' activity. A lack of coordination between different agencies constrained and weakened previous Russian military interventions, such as in Afghanistan in the 1980s and counter-insurgency operations in Chechnya in the 1990s.[138] In 2014, after the New Look Reforms, the newly formed Russian National Centre for the Management of Defence improved coordination for disrupting local political and administrative control and acquiring control in Crimea. This organisation developed and implemented a Special Forces-led campaign in the grey zone to project coercive force in support of Russian civilian agencies conducting political warfare in eastern Ukraine. The campaign simultaneously employs 'hybrid' and political and information warfare tactics to trouble the public and keep the initiative away from Ukrainian military and security forces.[139]

David Kilcullen in *The Dragons and the Snakes* offers a new conceptual framework called 'liminal warfare' that elaborates on the complexity and sophistication of hybrid warfare. He writes of a 'detection threshold' ... a movable boundary between clandestine and covert operations, on the one hand, and overt actions on the other'. For this book, his exposition about detection, attribution and response thresholds, as well as 'pre-conflict shaping', are instructive.[140] He is explaining the 'shades of grey'.

Before looking more closely at Chinese hybrid warfare, it is oppor-

---

137 Lindley-French, J, 2019, 'Briefing: Complex Strategic Coercion and Russian Military Modernisation', also The Lindley-French Analysis: 'Speaking Truth Unto Power', blog

138 Norberg, J, Westerlund, F & Franke, U, 2014, 'The Crimea operation', p. 23

139 Norberg, J, 2016, 'The use of Russia's military in the Crimea crisis'

140 Kilcullen, D, 2020, *The Dragons and the Snakes*, pp.150–160

tune to reflect on Russian and Chinese Special Forces. The Russians have assigned their Special Forces roles for prosecuting hybrid warfare. My concern is that the CPC may employ PLA Special Forces similarly amongst the Chinese diaspora and among the community of 1.2 million Australians of Chinese heritage.

For hybrid warfare, China and Russia will employ their Special Forces and armed intelligence services. China's People's Liberation Army (PLA) has elevated its strategic thinking about Special Forces for the prosecution of grey zone campaigns by defining Campaign Special Operations as:

> ... irregular operational activities conducted by specially formed, trained and equipped crack units (and small units) using special warfare to achieve specific campaign and strategic goals. The main purpose of its objectives is to assault vital enemy targets, paralyse enemy operational systems, reduce enemy operational capabilities, and interfere, delay, and disrupt enemy operational activities to create favourable conditions for main force units. ... SOF [Special Operations Force] units concentrate on special reconnaissance, raids, sabotage, and harassment while other non-SOF units conduct most special technical warfare tasks such as computer network attack.[141]

According to Blasko, the PLA seeks to employ their Special Forces outside of mainland China in conflicts that are most likely to be dominated by maritime and airstrike and their strategic rocket forces.[142] This force projection intention warns that Chinese Special Forces may deploy covertly to further Chinese national interests in the foreseeable future, possibly to orchestrate hybrid warfare.[143]

Though the deployment of Russian Special Forces against Australia's national interests is less likely, the PLA is undoubtedly aware of Russian capabilities and employment in hybrid warfare. Russia employs its Special Forces as elite specialised reaction forces

---

141 Blasko, D, 2015, 'Chinese Special Forces: Not like 'Back at Bragg'

142 Ibid.

143 Florcruz, M, 2014, 'Chinese Military Professor', p. 1

characterised by speed, surprise, manoeuvre and lethality. Russian special forces, called *Spetsnaz*, are highly mobile and able to put light mobile teams in the field to conduct combined-arms warfare and a range of covert operations. *Spetsnaz* has played significant roles in virtually every major Soviet or Russian operation since World War II. Senior military leadership direct this so-called 'fire brigade' capability outside the conventional chain of command.[144]

For the past few decades, *Spetsnaz* has been conducting special warfare outside Russia as the instrument for prosecuting a hybrid war.[145] Russian Chief of the General Staff, General Valery Gerasimov, stated that a hybrid approach to non-military means was used four times more often in modern conflicts than traditional conventional military measures.[146] Though there is debate about the so-called Gerasimov Doctrine, it is clear that Russia employs its Special Forces as a national coercive instrument for strategic effect.[147] There is less evidence of China doing so, but it cannot be discounted as a means for China's hybrid warfare.

Chinese hybrid warfare

It is improbable that Russia will prosecute a hybrid war against Australia, but could the CPC emulate Russia and prosecute its version accompanied by deniable cyberattacks? Could the CPC, frustrated by lack of success in the light grey phases of its grey zone campaign, launch a multi-domain political, cyber, economic, trade and information attack? Could the Australian Government be forced to negotiate terms that compromise Australian sovereignty under pressure from an Australian political movement calling for closer relations with China in this dramatic and disrupted environment? Could all this happen while

144 Chivvis, C, 2017, *Understanding Russian Hybrid Warfare*, p. 20

145 Chivvis, C, 2017, 'Understanding Russian 'Hybrid Warfare' and What Can Be Done about it', Testimony

146 Gerasimov, V, 2013, 'The Value of Science is in the Foresight' and Jonsson, O, 2019, *The Russian Understanding of War*, p. 5

147 Thornton, R, 2015, 'The Changing Nature of Modern Warfare', pp. 40–48, Jonsson, O, 2019, *The Russian Understanding of War*, Johnston, R, 2018, 'Hybrid War and Its Countermeasures', pp. 141–163 and Renz, B, 2016, 'Russia and 'hybrid war'', pp. 283–300

Australia's traditional allies protest but do not intervene because, like the Australian Government, they are trying to avoid a Third World War and are confused and unsure about what to do?

Readers should be sceptical of this scenario. No one will ever know the mind of Xi Jinping and his CPC colleagues. There is no public evidence that the CPC intends to escalate political and information warfare identified in warnings described in Chapter 1 to hybrid warfare in Australia. But the CPC has 'form' in the grey zone. The US Center for Strategic and Budgetary Assessments [CSBA] has analysed six CPC hybrid warfare case studies in the Indo-Pacific. It begins with the annexation of Tibet in the 1950s. It culminates with China's coercive posturing in the Senkaku's islands in a territorial competition with Japan and its maritime grey zone campaign that has successfully established military bases in the territorially-contested South China Sea.[148] The following detection triggers are likely to identify the features of a CPC escalation from 'light grey' political and informational warfare to 'dark grey' hybrid war in Australia and near region:

Phase 1 Escalation

- information warfare and coercive diplomatic messaging, sometimes called Wolf Warrior diplomacy, directed at governments, economies, institutions and the media;
- influence operations, such as cultivation and employment of influencers, corporate and political leaders with pro-CPC narratives, and through cultural engagement, media manipulation and social media;
- control of infrastructure, e.g. ports, airports, telecommunications networks, media outlets, principal real estate, transport and supply hubs, islands and remote locations;
- infiltration of civil society, such as sporting and entertainment sponsorships, donations to influential charities and not-for-profit organisations and association with culturally prominent organisations and individuals in civil society; and

148 Babbage, R, 2019, *Stealing a March*

- infiltration of education systems through influences on curriculum, academic discourse and donations;

Phase 2 Escalation

- the exploitation of political, religious, ethnic, regional, racial, class differences and social cleavages;
- economic pressure through embargos and restrictive trade;
- the exploitation of criminal networks, extremists and grievance groups;
- bribery, illegal donations and other corrupt practices to gain political and civil society influence; and
- cyber-attacks and further digital disruption.

Phase 3 Escalation

- recruitment, training and employment of members of grievance groups and criminals to intimidate leaders and citizens into deterring actions that are not in the interests of the CPC or orchestrating activities in the interests of the CPC; and finally
- the conduct of deniable and covert operations through proxies to apply violence, including terrorist acts, against institutions, groups and individuals and destroy property, accompanied by information actions, catastrophic cyberattacks and electronic warfare, and diplomatic pressure to negotiate political concessions.

Corroborating the CSBA analysis, David Carment and Dani Belo of the Canadian Global Affairs Institute suggest that the CPC might move through the shades of grey in the following phases:

- political action to promote favourable change in government policy and international norms;
- increasing economic pressure on allies and opponents;
- engagement in cyber and network warfare; and
- incorporation of non-state actors [criminal networks, extremists and grievance groups] into [concocted] conflicts.[149]

---

149 Carment, D & Belo D, 2018, 'War's Future', p. 6

The Rand Corporation's thorough analysis expresses the generic escalating phases of a grey zone campaign as Phase 1 Persistent [non-violent], Phase 2 Moderate [coercive] Phase 3 Aggressive [violent].[150] Arguably, Australia has already detected, and many sources have attributed CPC Phase 1 'light grey' persistent and competitive political warfare. The government has responded reflexively with stricter legislation and the formation of multi-agency task forces. Still, I will argue later that the government lacks agile multi-agency institutional machinery for decision-making and firmer deterrence and de-escalation options for responding to it. Should the CPC transition to 'darker grey' hybrid warfare, there will be strenuous efforts to avoid detection and attribution in its initial phases. I believe that arrangements must be in place to detect, deter and de-escalate in the 'lighter grey' persistent and moderate phases before it is too late to do so.

Notably, of the 14 grievances the Chinese Embassy leaked to the media in Australia in November 2020 explaining why China is causing billions of dollars of damage to the Australian economy with trade tariffs and embargos, only three refer to Australia's foreign policy actions. Eleven relate to Australia's hardening of its grey zone defences with legislation and enhanced institutional machinery to counter espionage, foreign interference, cyberattacks and foreign investment in infrastructure deemed not in the national interest.[151] Is this emphasis a sign that the main focus of the CPC's efforts to coerce Australia is in the grey zone? Is it also a sign that the CPC contemplates escalating to Phase 2?

Borrowing from the Russian playbook?

There is a growing concern in the literature that China will draw from Russia's 'playbook' for transitioning political warfare to include

---

150 Morris, LJ, Mazarr, MJ, Hornung, JW, Pezard, S, Binnendijk, A and Keep, M, 2019, *Gaining Competitive Advantage in the Gray Zone*, p. xvii

151 Kearsley, J, Bagshaw, E & Galloway, A, 2020, 'If you make China the enemy, China will be the enemy'

hybrid warfare.[152] The Russians deployed their Special Forces and intelligence agencies to recruit, arm, train, and employ grievance groups, 'patriotic' extremists, cyber militias, and criminals for their successful grey zone campaign in Crimea. They won the battle of the narratives by denying involvement while publicly supporting patriotic Russians and those sympathetic to Russia living there. Though their success in Crimea under favourable conditions may not be replicable elsewhere, the combination of military and non-military ways to annex territory is illustrative and instructive.[153] Arguably, the CPC has already employed a variant of this combination in the South China Sea with armed fishing vessels crewed by 'patriots', described more accurately as 'Uniformed, Navy-trained fishing militia', denying access to Vietnamese, Filipino and Indonesian fishing vessels and forcefully asserting Chinese control.[154]

There is evidence of increasing transfers of Russian military technology to China and vice versa.[155] Russian hybrid warfare that is now tested and proven for escalating grey zone campaigns could inform the CPC's grey zone campaign against Australia. Surprise and friction emerging from the grey zone fog could precipitate political concessions well before the Australian Government receives sufficient public support to mobilise a conventional military response, let alone an effective well-rehearsed multi-agency or hardened law enforcement response. It makes sense to deter escalation in the lighter shades of grey when tactics are non-violent and primarily political and

---

152 Bachmann, S, Oliver, V, Dowse, A & Gunneriusson, H, 2019, 'Competition Short of War', and Dibb, P, 2019, 'How the geopolitical partnership between China and Russia threatens the West'

153 Kofman, M, Migacheva, K, Nichiporuk, B, Radin, A, Tkacheva, O & Oberholtzer J, 2017, *Lessons from Russia's Operations in Crimea and Eastern Ukraine*

154 Kennedy CM & Erickson, A, 2016, 'China's Uniformed, Navy-trained Fishing 'Militia',

155 Bendett, S and Kania, E, 2019, 'A New Sino–Russian High Tech Partnership'; Bendett, S and Kania, E, 2020, 'The Resilience of Sino–Russian High-Tech Cooperation'; Kendall-Taylor, A, Shullman, D and MacCormick, D, 2020, 'Navigating Sino–Russian Defense Cooperation'; Kofman, M, 2020, 'The Emperor's League: Understanding Sino–Russian Defense Cooperation'; and Segal, A, 2020, 'Peering into the Future of Sino–Russian Cyber Security Cooperation'

informational. Failure to do so risks having to scramble in response to a range of non-violent and violent acts of coercion – friction – as the shades of grey get darker, and tactics and techniques become more violent and destructive.

To explore what Russian exemplars might inform a Chinese grey zone escalation, it is helpful to briefly describe the salient features of Russian hybrid campaigns in Estonia in 2007, Georgia in 2008 and Ukraine in 2014–15. The campaign in Estonia was 'light-grey' and limited in both duration and intensity, but there was a loss of life, disruption of computer systems and some property damage. The campaign in Georgia was 'darker grey' and accompanied a conventional invasion but was sudden, temporary and resolved quickly. The campaign in Ukraine was an example of an escalating grey zone campaign that resulted in a *fait accompli* 'takeover' of Crimea without military invasion. Russia incorporated Crimea under Russian control before the Ukraine Government, NATO, or the United States could react.

A lot has happened since 2007, 2008 and 2015 in both Russia and China. Cyberattack capabilities have improved, and counter-measures are in place to reduce the risk of the same effects occurring again. These campaigns are neither replicable in Australia nor examples of what an escalating CPC grey zone campaign might look like. Still, their characteristics serve my purpose with examples of cyber and electronic warfare-enabled pressure to coerce political concessions. They show how conventional electronic warfare and cyberattacks can combine to optimise disruption to ICT systems and what a mature hybrid warfare campaign achieved in 2014 in Ukraine under the noses of NATO and the United States.

None of these Russian attacks constituted acts of war. None prompted a conventional response from NATO, the Western military alliance charged with the collective defence of Western Europe. All were executed amidst multiple disruptive actions that applied pressure to governments and their populations with political objectives to impose the will of one nation on another. Key features of these campaigns are at least prototypes of what China and Russia are now capable of in the third decade of the 21st Century.

Estonia 2007 – subversion and economic disruption

The attack on Estonia was the first known cyberattack by a large nation on a smaller neighbour, though there is still inconclusive evidence of direct involvement of the Russian Government. For this book, the attacks over three weeks from late April to mid-May 2007 demonstrated 'how easily a hostile state can exploit potential tensions within another society.'[156] Internal tensions in Estonia and protests in Russia arose after an Estonian Government decision to move a bronze statue of a Russian solder built by Soviet Union authorities in Tallinn, the Estonian capital, in 1947 amidst a number of graves of Russian soldiers. The 'Monument to the Liberators of Tallinn' and its cemetery were prominent in the city's centre. This monument represented Russia's victory over Nazi Germany for Russian speakers in Estonia. For ethnic Estonians, it symbolised 50 years of Soviet occupation and oppression.[157]

Nearly 80 per cent of over 80 per cent of the Estonian population voted for independence from the disintegrating post-Cold War USSR in 1991 in a referendum. In 2007 the Estonian government decided to move the Bronze Soldier and the remains of Russian soldiers from the centre of Tallinn to a Russian military cemetery on the city's outskirts. Russian language media, stimulated by 'fake news' from the multiple Russian IP addresses, disseminated a narrative that the statue, as well as Russian war graves near its new location, were to be destroyed. The stories circulated on social media called for protests. Russian-speakers in Estonia accompanied by what an Estonian official described later as 'malicious gangs' 'took to the streets'. On 26 April 2007, Tallinn erupted into two nights of riots and looting. One hundred fifty-six people were injured, one person died, and 1,300 were arrested and detained. From 27 April, significant cyber-attacks tormented the computer systems of Estonian public and corporate institutions for three weeks.[158]

---

156 McGuinness, D, 2017, 'How a cyberattack transformed Estonia'

157 Ottis, R, 2008, 'Analysis of the 2007 Cyber Attacks against Estonia from the Information Warfare Perspective'

158 Maclellan, S and O'Leary, N, 2017, 'Doing Battle in Cyberspace: How an Attack on Estonia Changed the Rules of the Game' and McGuinness, D, 2017, 'How a cyber-attack transformed Estonia'

The attacks were a large-scale 'distributed denial of service'. The targets were the websites of government departments, banks, telecommunications providers and media companies.[159] The aim was to intimidate the Estonian Government to reverse its decision about moving the Bronze Soldier by crippling Estonian online infrastructure and unsettling the population. Almost 60 key websites were forced offline at once, automated teller machines, and government e-mail stopped working.[160] Internet trolls, 'bots,' and 'fake news' farms reinforced initial attacks. Tens of thousands of automated online requests and waves of spam swamped Estonian servers.[161]

The attacks silenced Estonia media. Newspapers and broadcasters could not upload articles or broadcast the news. The only communications to the public were pro-Russian 'fake news' agitating for more protests and falsely and profanely accusing the Estonian political leaders of a range of conspiracies. Estonians could not use cash machines or online banking, prompting a run on the banks. The riots, looting and arson, caused physical destruction. Hackers disrupted Estonia's networked public and corporate institutions.

Estonia's NATO allies watched but did not intervene. NATO's Article Five obligates NATO members to defend each other – the basis of alliance and conventional military deterrence.[162] But there was no act of war, no invading force and no significant loss of life. Failure to identify who was responsible for the attacks made NATO retaliation impossible. Attacks came from Russian IP addresses, and online instructions were in the Russian language, but there was no definite link to the Kremlin. The Russian Government ignored Estonian appeals for help against Russian-based hackers and denied any involvement.

All told, it is clear that the cyberattacks were linked with the overall political conflict between Estonia and Russia'.[163] In 2017 the BBC

---

159 Whitmore, P, 2016 'Current Cyber Wars', p. 52

160 Maclellan, S and O'Leary, N, 2017, 'Doing Battle in Cyberspace'

161 Paul, C and Matthews, M, 2016, *The Russian 'Firehose of Falsehood' Propaganda Model*

162 North Atlantic Treaty Organisation 1949, 'NATO Treaty'

163 Ottis, R, 2008, 'Analysis of the 2007 Cyber Attacks against Estonia', pp 163–168

reported, 'On condition of anonymity, an Estonian government official told the BBC that evidence suggested the attack:

> ... was orchestrated by the Kremlin, and malicious gangs then seized the opportunity to join in and do their own bit to attack Estonia.' ... [Furthermore] Hostile states often count on copycat hackers, criminal groups and freelance political actors jumping on the bandwagon.[164]

The street protests and cyberattacks did not cow the Estonian Government. A journalist wrote in 2017, 'Head bowed, one fist clenched and wearing a World War Two Red Army uniform, the Bronze Soldier stands solemnly in a quiet corner of a cemetery on the edge of the Estonian capital Tallinn.'[165] The Estonian Government learned from these attacks. A Cyber Defence Unit, comprised of anonymous IT experts trained by the Ministry of Defence, maintain 24/7 surveillance of the cyber domain. Members of this unit donate their free time defending their country online by practising what to do if a cyberattack brings down a significant utility or vital service provider. The BBC noted that 'It's the sort of private-sector talent the state could never usually afford to employ.'[166] Should Australia wait for a major cyberattack to establish a similar capability? Are the current arrangements sufficient to avoid strategic surprise?

Since 2007, Estonia has emerged as a leading cyber security state by integrating government, military and private sector capabilities.[167] One research study in 2017 concludes that despite this example of Estonia's recovery from strategic surprise, there does not appear to be any nation in the Western alliance that has a plan for resisting and responding to a significant cyberattack.[168] NATO has established the NATO Cooperative Cyber Defence Centre of Excellence in Tallinn to

---

164 McGuinness, D, 2017, 'How a cyber-attack transformed Estonia'
165 Ibid.
166 Ibid.
167 Estonian Government, 2020, 'Estonian Demographics: 2020 Population'
168 Maclellan, S and O'Leary, N, 2017, 'Doing Battle in Cyberspace'

leverage Estonia's capabilities and optimise regional engagement and cooperation.[169]

Georgia 2008 – cyber-attack

Thomas Rid, a researcher from Kings College, London, downplays the direct destructive effects of cyberattacks on Estonia in 2007. He opines that actions there were more akin to technically-enabled political protest than actions akin to war.[170] He acknowledges, however, that Russian information warfare and cyberattacks in support of a brief ground war with Georgia over a territorial dispute in South Ossetia in August 2008 was the first example of cyberattacks synchronising with a conventional military operation.[171]

Cyberattacks were a combination of denial of service, defacing Georgian government websites, distributing malicious software, and spamming e-mail services and websites akin to information warfare.[172] There were no lasting impacts on the economy or political system in Georgia.[173] Rid suggests that actions dubbed metaphorically 'cyber warfare' are criminal activities well below the threshold of acts of war. At best, cyberattacks fall into traditional sabotage, espionage and subversion.[174] He is right to caution about the lazy use of the term 'war', but sabotage, espionage and subversion are essential elements of an escalating grey zone campaign.

Crimea 2014 – fait accompli

Russia's conflict with Ukraine illustrates the use of electronic warfare and cyberattacks in the grey zone. The Russian Federation annexure of the Crimea region of Ukraine in 2014 after a *fait accompli* hybrid campaign set the benchmark. This grey zone campaign illustrates the

---

169 Estonian Government, 2017, 'How Estonia Became a Global Heavyweight in Cyber Security' and Czosseck, C, Ottis, R & Taliham, AM, 2011, 'Estonia after the 2007 Cyberattacks'

170 Rid, T, 2013, *Cyber war will not take place,* pp. 5–6

171 Ibid., p. 7

172 Hollis, D, 2011, 'Cyberwar Case Study: Georgia 2008', and Moses, A, 2008 'Georgian websites forced offline in 'cyber war''

173 Rid, T, 2013, *Cyber war will not take place*

174 Ibid., Preface pp. xv and xvi

convergence of cyberattacks and contemporary military electronic warfare designed to disrupt an adversary's communications by denying them access to the Electro-Magnetic Spectrum [EMS]. Russian cyber and electronic attacks paralysed Ukrainian military, law enforcement and civil command and control computer and communications systems. These operations were examples of traditional electronic warfare with enhanced cyber warfare attributes. Spot or barrage jamming of telecommunications denied Ukrainian access to portions of or the entirety of the EMS. Russian hackers jammed drone controllers and GPS signals to bring down uncrewed aircraft and disrupt GPS navigation systems. The Ukrainian armed forces lost their 'eyes in the sky' and technology to know where they were on the ground.[175]

Dependence on cellular technology exposed Ukrainian telecommunications networks. Cellular technology emits unique signatures and IP addresses to users.[176] Russian electronic warfare units detected all electromagnetic emissions and disrupted communications between Ukrainian vessels, land forces and aircraft, and headquarters and civilian Wi-Fi and personal cell phones.[177] Russians located 'everyone' through electronic 'signatures' and maliciously monitored and manipulated social media.[178]

Aftermath

Since 2014 Russia has become the nation to watch for the scale and mischievousness of their cyberattacks. Interference with the 2016 US Presidential elections is an example.[179] In 2020, one patient Russian cyberattack set a benchmark for other authoritarian nations

---

175 Smith, P, 2020, *Russian Electronic Warfare*, Karber, P and Thibeault, J, 2016, 'Russia's New-Generation Warfare' and Ackerman, RK, 2017, 'Russian Electronic Warfare Targets NATO Assets'

176 Trevithick, J, 2019, 'Ukrainian Officer Details Russian Electronic Warfare Tactics'

177 Freedberg Jnr, SJ, 2018, 'Electronic Warfare Trumps Cyber for Deterring Russia', Smith, P, 2020, 'Russian Electronic Warfare', and Ackerman, RK, 2017, 'Russian Electronic Warfare Targets NATO Assets'

178 Karber, P and Thibeault, J, 2016, 'Russia's New-Generation Warfare'

179 Central Intelligence Agency, Federal Bureau of Investigation, and National Security Agency 2017, 'Assessing Russian Activities'

to emulate for hurting ICT-dependent governments and economies. This time Russian hackers went global. The SolarWinds Orion cyberattack hacked the computer systems of 18 000 public and private organisations worldwide. This illustrated the capability to close down public and private sector institutions, economic activity and essential services. This attack was categorised as a 'supply chain attack' for its use of a trusted third-party vendor to install malware in multiple organisational networks. Reportedly, Russian hackers had access to sensitive databases in Australia's Defence, Finance and Home Affairs departments, and the Australian Securities and Investments Commission as well as Australian Radiation Protection and Nuclear Safety Agency, the Bureau of Meteorology, trade promotion agency Austrade and the Department of Education, Skills and Employment, NSW Health, Serco Asia Pacific, and mining giant Rio Tinto for several months that had the potential to set them up for catastrophic collapse at a future time.[180]

The SolarWinds Orion attack supports the warning issued in January 2021 by Francis Galbally, an Australian businessman and company director who has been involved in cyber security for the past 21 years:

> It is not rocket science to understand that a total attack by a rogue nation could decimate us [Australia] economically and render us instantly defenceless. ... Ransomware is perhaps the most known and the most prevalent form of cyberattack. It can be used for financial gain, an act of terrorism or by rogue nation states to create havoc. In 2017, a rogue group called NotPetya smashed thousands of corporate networks around the world, costing these organisations billions of dollars. This was not about financial gain, it was just to prove the ability to massively disrupt global digital networks. It was originally thought to be a ransomware attack, but was later traced to a Russian military unit.[181]

---

180 Packham, B, 2020, 'Cyber spy agency on high alert over hack'

181 Galbally, F, 2021, 'We must bolster our cyber war defences', p. 9

The question for the Australian Government is whether the CPC could emulate Russian expertise in cyber, electronic and information warfare? The CPC will not make it easy to find out. Evidence in 2019 and 2020 suggests a closer 'high-tech' collaboration between Russia and China.[182] There is also evidence that the CPC comprehends and could escalate to hybrid warfare in the grey zone. A US National Defense University report in 2020 analyses how Xi Jinping has 'remade' the Peoples Liberation Army [hereafter Chinese armed forces] since 2015.[183] It and other US and international reports warn of a new doctrine of 'informalionalised local warfare' and the capabilities of the Strategic Support Force [SSF] that 'combines assorted space, cyber, and electronic warfare capabilities from across the armed services and its former general departments. Understanding the primary strategic roles of the SSF is essential to understanding how China will practice information operations during escalations to hybrid warfare in the grey zone.[184] The creation of the SSF suggests that cyberattacks are now fundamental to CPC information warfare that has a global reach.[185] The Chinese armed forces have taken the opportunity to finally realign their sprawling space, cyber, and electronic warfare capabilities into one instrument.[186] A series of high-profile cyber intrusions since the mid-2000s have demonstrated both growing sophistication and the

---

182 Bendett, S and Kania, E, 2019, 'A New Sino–Russian High Tech Partnership', Bendett, S and Kania, E, 2020, 'The Resilience of Sino–Russian High-Tech Cooperation', Kendall-Taylor, A, Shullman, D and MacCormick, D, 2020, 'Navigating Sino–Russian Defense Cooperation', Kofman, M, 2020, 'The Emperor's League', and Segal, A, 2020, 'Peering into the Future of Sino–Russian Cyber Security Cooperation'

183 Kania, E, 2020, 'Innovation in the New Era of Chinese Military Power', Cordsman, AH, 2019 'China's New 2019 Defense White Paper', Costello, J and McReynolds, J, 2020, 'China's Strategic Support Force', and Burke, EJ, Gunness, K, Cooper, CA III, Mark Cozad MI, 2020, 'People's Liberation Army Operational Concepts'

184 Costello, J, and McReynolds, J, 2020, 'China's Strategic Support Force', p. 437

185 Valeriano, B and Maness, RC, 2015, *Cyber War Versus Cyber Realities*, Nye JS, 2017, 'Deterrence and Dissuasion in Cyberspace', Nye, JS, 2010, 'Cyber Power', essay from the Belfer Centre for Science and International Affairs, Harvard Kennedy School

186 Costello, J and McReynolds, J, 2020, 'China's Strategic Support Force', p. 441

rapid progress that Chinese forces had made in the span of a few short years.[187]

In light of the evidence presented in this chapter and Chapter 1, it is reasonable to conclude that the CPC can interfere with Australia's ICT-dependent public and private sector organisations and critical infrastructure. Imagine the impact on ordinary Australians of interference with food supply chains, power grids, hospitals, water and fuel supplies and online financial services. Chapter 1 highlights that the CPC included Australia in escalating cyber intrusions in 2020. Could these be probes before significant intrusions as part of an escalation from light to darker grey tactics?

Should the above-mentioned Russian examples of 'cyber-surprise' instruct Australia? In June 2020, the attacks on Australian public and corporate institutions described in Chapter 1 looked like probes. Suppose Australia has only defensive reflexive responses to probes and rehearsals. Could the CPC become emboldened to retaliate more forcefully after taking offence at Australian actions that its United Work Front deliberately exaggerates to launch a significant cyber-attack to achieve surprise and force political and economic concessions from the Australian Government?

Conclusions

The China threat debate in Australia varies. Is it real? Is it dangerous? Is it unstoppable? Corporations, groups and individuals sympathetic to CPC interests discredit those warning of the CPC's totalitarian intentions.[188] Some corporate leaders call for everyone to 'settle down' and continue a lucrative trading relationship.[189] Reputable experts have developed a new conciliatory and collaborative narrative for the Sino–Australian relationship, the outcome of a nationwide public debate and consultations with a diverse group of influential Australians from the public service, business and the university sector.[190] Other reputable experts advise Australia to increase its

187 Ibid.

188 Carr, B, 2018, 'Bob Carr replies to China critics'

189 White, N, 2020, 'Why two of Australia's richest men are backing China'

190 Jakobson, L, et al, 2021, 'A New China Narrative for Australia'

spending on conventional military deterrence, including acquiring more submarines, missiles and strike fighters, to oppose a Chinese invasion fleet in the Indonesian-Melanesian archipelago.[191] No one will ever know 'beyond a reasonable doubt' what Xi Jinping and the CPC's intentions are for Australia and its near region because the essence of CPC *modus operandi* is to disguise purposes and ways and means. Hindsight will be the 'exact science' for discovering the truth.

For me, the truth 'beyond a reasonable doubt' is that history is replete with nations, peoples and alliances who failed to heed strategic warnings about totalitarianism. Consequently, they were surprised and militarily and politically defeated as a result. Those who favour pragmatic and more soothing, nuanced and sophisticated engagement with the CPC to preserve commercial interests and garner goodwill should comprehend the brutal revolutionary history of the Peoples Republic of China. The ongoing suppression in Hong Kong, intimidation of Taiwan and domestic repression of Falun Gong and the Uighurs suggest that the CPC will ruthlessly and, when required, violently pursue its political objectives.

There are several geopolitical markers revealing CPC grey zone success and further intentions. The militarisation of islands in the South China Sea exemplifies unopposed grey zone strategic encroachment. Hong Kong has succumbed to a grey zone campaign without international intervention. The leasing of port facilities in Darwin and an attempt to lease an island in Solomon Islands suggest that the CPC is looking further afield for points of entry into Australia and the near region.[192] The PNG Government's Sustainable Development Program has identified a need for a deep international seaport on Daru Island to deliver a sustainable future for the people of the Western Province by attracting industry. China's Fujian Zhonghong Fishery Company signed a memorandum of understanding in November 2020 with the PNG government and the Fly River provincial government to build a $200 million 'comprehensive multi-functional fishery industrial park'

---

191 White, H, 2020, *How to Defend Australia* and Dibb, P, Brabin-Smith R & Sargeant B, 2018, 'Why Australia Needs a Radically New Defence Policy'

192 Barrett, J, 2019, 'Solomon Islands government says Chinese lease of island unlawful'

on the island.[193] Since then, a Hong Kong-based WYW Holding has pitched to invest $39 billion to build 'New Daru City', with plans for a port, industrial and commercial zones, homes and a resort.[194] Daru Island is in the Torres Strait that links the Coral and Arafura seas, close to Australia's northern sea and air trading routes, and just over 200 kilometres from the north tip of Cape York.

The CPC has launched a grey zone campaign in Australia and its near region to align Australia and its neighbours closely with China's strategic interests. This campaign is not traditional assertive statecraft. It is new, more technologically and informationally sophisticated and coercive, reminiscent of Cold War propaganda and espionage operations. But unlike the Cold War, contemporary grey zone campaigns escalate through coercive shades of grey until they achieve the same outcomes as conventional military campaigns.

Doomsday scenarios

So far, I have drawn on the literature on the grey zone and political, information, cyber and hybrid warfare to hypothesise what Australia should be afraid of and must deter and de-escalate. But what might an escalating grey zone campaign look like? What could be Australia's 'doomsday'? I now turn to two fictional scenarios. One offered by Linda Jakobson, the respected Founding Director and Deputy Chair of the Australian think tank China Matters about Taiwan and my variant scenario about Australia drawn from her insightful themes.

A takeover of Taiwan is on the CPC agenda for domination. Taiwan could be a strategic 'canary in the coal mine' exemplar of Phase 3 escalation, China's Crimea. Linda Jakobson argues that:

> a military attack on Taiwan is not the most likely route the People's Republic of China (PRC) will choose to achieve unification. Rather, the more probable scenario is *a strategy of 'all means short of war'*, [author's emphasis] in which the PRC would attempt to force Taiwan

---

193 Wall, J, 2020, 'China to build $200 million fishery project on Australia's doorstep'

194 Tillett, A, 2021, 'Chinese city plan on PNG island highlights concerns about Beijing'

> to the negotiation table through a mix of pressure tactics including military intimidation, dissemination operations, cyberattacks and covert actions [hybrid warfare]. The United States and others, including Australia, would find it extremely hard to counter these moves. No individual action by the PRC would warrant a military response. ... In an attempt to break the will of Taiwan, Beijing could adopt an aggressive mix of new technologies and conventional methods to apply pressure. These range from economic pressure or an embargo, via intimidation, cyberattacks, and covert actions and subversion, to assassination and the limited use of military force.[195]

While acknowledging that the relationship between China and Taiwan and China and Australia are very different and have no historical or cultural similarities, would China's incorporation of Taiwan foreshadow Australia's doomsday? Linda Jakobson provides a chilling grey zone scenario to ponder. The CPC's political objective for Taiwan is unification and acceptance of 'One China'. Its political objective for Australia appears to be for Australia to become a contemporary tribute state. Could ways and means applied for incorporating Taiwan be employed to coerce an Australian Government to negotiate for 'tribute state' status, presented as 'a partnership for peace and prosperity'? Linda Jakobson hypothesises that a CPC Phase 3 escalation in Taiwan might look like this:

> Scenario: 'All means short of war'
>
> In this scenario, the PRC would not invade Taiwan. Rather, Beijing would strive to create utter chaos in Taiwan and compel the government to accede to the PRC's demands. Initially, it would be impossible to credibly pinpoint who is behind many of the provocative actions. Few shots would be fired other than for possible political assassinations. Taiwan's armed forces would struggle to counter Beijing's actions. Barring strong condemnation of Beijing and imposing economic

---

195 Jakobson, L, 2021, 'Why should Australia be concerned about rising tensions in the Taiwan Straits?'

sanctions on the PRC, the US and others, including Australia, would find it difficult to assist Taiwan.

This scenario could start with PRC officials gathering major Taiwanese investors in the PRC and insisting that they sign a letter to Taiwan's government calling for cross-Strait political talks. Refusal to sign would result in business difficulties. Xi Jinping would also urge Taiwan's 'leader' [President] to immediately agree to consultations to collaboratively seek unification. Next, Beijing would suddenly cut Taiwan's air routes into PRC cities, stating that foreign airlines needed those routes. International airlines would be told to choose between flying to the PRC or to Taiwan. PRC combat aircraft would conduct incursions not only across the median line of the Taiwan Strait, as they do today, but over Taiwan itself. Would Taiwan's Air Force be directed to shoot down such intruders and risk all-out war?

Taiwan's stock market would presumably plunge. In this situation, the Democratic Progressive Party, the current ruling party that leans toward independence, would encourage legislators to insist on 'no preconditions for political talks'. PRC-backed media outlets in Taiwan would run scare campaigns. Protesters would take to the streets. Some groups would demand a declaration of independence; others would demand that the government open political talks with Beijing. Street gangs would attack independence supporters. Confrontations between opposing political groups could become violent.

The campaign's most intense Phase would include the PRC ramping up disinformation efforts and launching a barrage of sophisticated cyberattacks with the aim of first disrupting Taiwan's electricity and telecommunications and then shutting them down. ...

Rumours of the PRC's intentions would run rampant through Taiwan's darkened cities cut off from communications. The PLAN [Chinese navy] would start operations to impose a partial blockade of Taiwan's western harbours. Beijing would request governments to shut down their representative offices in Taipei. An editorial in the People's Daily would encourage Chinese compatriots in Taiwan to make the right decision, warning that the clock is ticking.[196]

196 Ibid.

It would appear to be far-fetched and ridiculous to apply this Taiwanese doomsday scenario to Australia. Surely the CPC would never find a group of Australian corporate leaders connected to trade with China, especially in Western Australia, to pressure the Australian Government to negotiate 'a partnership for peace and prosperity'? Surely the CPC would not impose more economic pressure on Australia, including closing Chinese ports and airports to Australian vessels and aircraft? Surely the Australian stock market would remain stable under renewed economic pressure? Surely the Australian people would remain strong and stoic in the face of state-of-art cyberattacks on Australia's critical infrastructure (energy, water, fuel and food supply) that coincided with a social media campaign warning that all bank accounts had been hacked and intermittent jamming of Australian television broadcasts, telecommunications and Internet access? Stampedes for toilet paper during the COVID 19 pandemic were no warning signs of fragility to contagion behaviour among the Australian population. To think otherwise is insulting!

Is this scenario ridiculous and far too pessimistic? Law enforcement agencies would cope easily with concocted civil protests in support of a new China–Australia partnership for peace and prosperity [PPP]. There would be no chance of a coalition of political opportunists, celebrities and civil leaders – the PPP Coalition – appearing at rallies seeking popular support for ending weeks of escalating civil unrest prompted by violence in supermarkets, interference in water and fuel supplies, runs on banks, night-time looting in blacked-out cities and an increase in crimes against persons and property. It is ridiculous to imagine a group of Parliamentary representatives from both parties and the crossbench joining the PPP Coalition in the interests of securing a better future for Australia. There is no chance of the PPP Coalition securing power after the Governor-General calls an urgent 'snap' election as a circuit breaker to help restore law and order.

I am more sanguine about this scenario. Following Linda Jakobson's lead, let's see what my three-Phase escalation of a notional CPC grey zone campaign might look like – a 'perfect grey zone storm'. For this scenario, the CPC pursues a grey zone campaign to coerce Australia, a significant source of mineral resources, agricultural produce, and a nation with substantial political influence in Southeast Asia and a middle power ally of the United States, to take actions in China's national interests. This campaign extends to the Pacific Islands and Timor Leste in a geopolitical manoeuvre to diminish Australian influence and dominate Australia's sea and air lines of trade and communication. The announcement of a Chinese proposal to invest $39 billion in building an industrial city and major port at Daru, the Capital of the Western Province of PNG less than 20 kilometres north of Thursday Island on the northern tip of Cape York is an example of this 'geopolitical and geo-economic squeeze'.[197]

Suppose we believe Hamilton, Joske, Fitzgerald and Hartcher and the US CSBA. In that case, Phase One might be CPC United Work Front operatives and their proxies infiltrating political institutions, corporations, universities and civil society in Australia and its regional neighbourhood. They intend to garner political influence and co-opt or compel individuals and groups. The Phase 1 objective is to undermine and shape the political and economic order and public narratives to favour CPC interests. A dominant narrative is that it is in Australia's national interests to establish a partnership for peace and prosperity with China. Anyone in Australia opposed to China's global aspirations is endangering a productive, mutually-beneficial trading relationship. Indeed, it would become un-Australian to question Chinese motives. The same tactics would apply in the Pacific Islands and Timor Leste, where it would be un-patriotic to criticise China and interfere with lucrative development projects.

A well-funded coalition of ex-politicians, corporate leaders, societal influencers, journalists and commentators provide a public platform for CPC narratives. This coalition registers as a political party, the Party for Peace and Prosperity [PPP]. It is anti-American and pro-China. It promotes the idea of American strategic decline and mocks its political and social divides. The PPP coalition calls for Taiwan to join the Chinese motherland. It claims to have unique leverage in China. It seeks credit for easing Chinese embargos on the Australian wine

197 Packham, B, 2021, China dangles $39 bn carrot to build city on our doorstep

industry to demonstrate that China wishes to partner with Australia, not pressure Australia.

In response to the Australian Government's assertion of sovereignty and affirmation of the US–Australian alliance, the CPC escalates to Phase 2. Institutional infiltration escalates to more severe cyberattacks to undermine public confidence in the Australian Government and its security arrangements. Economic embargos and other financial pressures increase. Behind the scenes, penetration of major Australian political parties continues apace. The intention is to create an uncertain environment to precipitate a change of a State or federal government to one more favourable to CPC interests. Drawing on the Russian playbook, there is increasing evidence of Chinese hackers manipulating Australian electoral and opinion poll processes manually and electronically.

The PPP facilitates the deployment of operatives among the Australian community of Chinese heritage and steps up its campaign to radicalise Australians of Chinese heritage to support China's plan for a partnership for peace and prosperity. There are protests supporting China and condemning the Australian Government's legislative actions to thwart the CPC's grey zone campaign. These protests attract counter-protests from White Supremacist and Far-Right activists, evoking patriotic Australians' need to stand up to Chinese bullying and an 'invasion'.

Political pressure on the government increases to appease China and negotiate an end to violent civil unrest. The PPP amplifies United Front Work narratives suggesting that the US alliance is unreliable and obsolete in light of China's inexorable rise and entitlement to influence in the Indo-Pacific Region. There are also concocted civil protests in cities in the Pacific Islands and Timor Leste calling for closer relations with China. New Zealand calls on Australia to recognise China's ascendency while boasting of its capture of Australian market share in the Chinese economy.

Taking advantage of destabilisation, sub-national extremist groups, independently or possibly in collaboration with the CPC, and even perhaps provoked by CPC agents and proxies, choose to commit or sponsor acts of terrorism in Australia and the near region. They employ enhanced technological capabilities for terrorists and cyberattacks to promote their religious or political creeds. This eruption of violence contributes to a CPC destabilisation campaign to force changes of governments to ones more favourable to CPC interests – the objective of unrestricted warfare.

Phase 3 escalation begins with several acts of terror, including bombing headquarters of law enforcement and intelligence agencies. Australia's law enforcement capabilities are stretched. In short order, Australia's counter-terrorism hunters become the hunted. Deniable terrorist acts and other disruptive acts of coercion and provoked public disorder escalate to a range of deniable coercive actions through proxies associated with the prosecution of hybrid war. The PPP blames the Federal Government for causing the deteriorating state of affairs and calls for an election to allow the people to decide on better policies for forging a new relationship with China. Factions in the Opposition party calls for a radical new approach to secure Australia's prosperous and peaceful future in partnership with China.

Australia faces this Phase 3 escalation alone. There is no military attack, so the ANZUS Treaty is irrelevant. No invasion fleet on the horizon. No ships, land forces or aircraft to fight. The government is left to call out the ADF to protect critical infrastructure and stand by if civil unrest overwhelms law enforcement agencies. Allies, such as the United States, assist Australia with intelligence support, public criticisms of the CPC, and promises of further help if things get worse. The United Nations Security Council is impotent. China vetos resolutions condemning their perceived involvement in destabilising Australia. Though Australia has participated in every 'coalition of the willing' since the end of the Cold War, there is no UN-sponsored coalition willing to help Australia counter a hybrid attack disguised as escalating political differences among Australians over the management of Australia's relations with China.

In an unprecedented surprise move, the Opposition splits. A rump of elected Opposition members affirms that Australia must negotiate an agreement with China or risk economic and societal collapse. They form a new coalition with the PPP advocating a snap election to decide Australia's relations with China. After a turbulent meeting of the

Federal Executive Council, the Governor-General-in-Council chooses to exercise his prerogative powers and authorises a dissolution of Parliament and an election under Section 28 of the Constitution.

In the most violent election in Australia's history, with claims and counter-claims of foreign interference in the form of cyber-attacks and concocted civil unrest, the PPP Coalition is elected. Suddenly, all violence ceases. China announces a return to the terms of its Free Trade Agreement and promises an enhanced agreement favourable to both countries. Statements and speeches affirm Australia's sovereignty and welcome Australia to the Belt and Road Initiative and new world order of peace and prosperity.

While this scenario is unthinkable, provocative and unpatriotic for some, ultimately, countering political and hybrid warfare is Australia's sovereign responsibility. The nation should neither presume assistance from allies nor rely on asking them to overcome Australia's lack of preparedness. My position is that Australia should signal to friend and foe alike and its regional neighbours that it comprehends grey zone strategies. The first narrative is that Australia is well prepared to defend its sovereignty and vital interests firmly and independently. The second narrative is that Australia is ready to partner with regional neighbours if they admire Australia's new 'fair but firm' approach and would appreciate support with their de-escalation strategies.

In the next chapter, I discuss what is being done to avoid an Australian doomsday and whether it is enough.

Part 2 – Responding to the Threat

CHAPTER 3

What is being done about it?

Introduction

For the first two decades of the 21st Century, international and homeland terrorism, border security, and managing an unprecedented bushfire season in 2019–20, a major pandemic in 2020–21, floods in early 2021 and another variant of COVID19 in 2022 have exercised, tested and sharpened Australia's national security arrangements. Responses have been both traditional and innovative. Australian military forces have participated in the War on Terror with the United States and other allies in the Middle East. Following tradition, Australian naval vessels, land forces, primarily Special Forces, and service aircraft served under American command. Counter-terrorism legislation and military call-out procedures sharpened reflexively in response to the Lindt Café and Brighton Motel 'lone wolf' sieges in 2014 and 2017, as well as international terrorist incidents. The government consolidated the Home Affairs portfolio and created the civil-military Border Force in an innovative and unprecedented way to bolster border security. In quick succession, the government called out the ADF to support national responses to fire, flood and pandemic hazards in 2020, 2021 and 2022.

The other significant challenge to Australia's national security in the 21st Century has been adapting to the competition between China and the United States – between Australia's most important trading partner and most important ally. Australia has spurned diplomatic and economic overtures from China in 2014–16 and affirmed its US alliance arrangements. In 2020 China issued 14 reasons why Sino–Australian relations had cooled. There were selective economic embargos on Australian exports to China in the same year. A CPC information campaign warning against Chinese students studying in Australia resulted in billions of dollars of lost revenue for Australia's economy.[198] ASIO warned of unprecedented increases in espionage and foreign interference, and there was a spike in cyberattacks on Australian computer systems and databases.

In Chapters 1 and 2, I have argued that Australia faces a CPC grey zone campaign that may escalate from non-violent espionage and political and economic coercion to hybrid warfare. I have painted a 'doomsday' picture. In this chapter, I discuss what is being done about it. I begin with the grey zone frontline and an overview of reflexive responses that have resulted in legislation and changes to institutional security machinery that responds to CPC espionage, foreign interference and cyberattacks. I then evaluate existing strategic guidance and discuss whether reliance on military deterrence is sufficient to deter escalation in the grey zone. I then discuss whether enough is being done for the time being both at home and in Australia's near region?

Noting gaps in existing deterrence and de-escalation arrangements in this chapter, I describe my proposed de-escalation strategy and the fourth form of power for national security, Response Power, in Chapter 4. It is essential to understand the big picture before getting into the ways and means of what should be done about countering an escalating grey zone campaign.

Homeland defence – the grey zone frontline

The establishment of the Department of Home Affairs on 20 December 2017 marked the consolidation of Australia's arrangements for homeland defence. This department aligns responsibilities, authority, accountability and resources for the Commonwealth's role in law enforcement, border security, counter-terrorism, cyber-security and social cohesion. The Home Affairs portfolio now brings together Australia's federal law enforcement, national transport security, criminal justice, emergency management, multicultural affairs, settlement services, and immigration and border-related functions to keep Australia safe.[199]

---

198 Dodd, T & Han, H, 2021, 'Fear unis are next in China trade war'

199 Functions are: National security and law enforcement policy, Emergency management, including crisis management and disaster recovery, Counter terrorism policy and coordination, Cyber security policy and coordination,

The Minister for Home Affairs has a range of policy, regulatory and enforcement agencies to secure the homeland from harm, coordinate emergency responses to hazards, such as bushfires and floods, and manage external aspects such as irregular migration and transnational crime. The Office of National Intelligence [ONI] provides assessments to the Prime Minister and National Security Committee of Cabinet (NSC) on matters of strategic importance. ONI also manages the intelligence enterprise, coordinates and evaluates Australia's foreign intelligence activities and leads the National Intelligence Community [NIC]. Under the direction of the Minister for Home Affairs, the flagship organisation for gathering national intelligence is ASIO. The Australian Federal Police [AFP] is the instrument for enforcing homeland security legislation.

Clarification of the CPC grey zone campaign in 2015 when John Garnaut reported to the Turnbull Government has resulted in the Australian Government hardening legislation and institutional machinery against espionage, foreign interference and investment as well as cyberattacks. Espionage is the theft of Australian information by someone acting on behalf of a foreign power or intending to provide information to a foreign power seeking advantage. Espionage can target defence, political, industrial, foreign relations, commercial or other information that is otherwise unavailable to the foreign power. Espionage is a crime in Australia, punishable by up to 25 years imprisonment. In contrast to legitimate influencing associated with statecraft, foreign interference is an activity that a nation or sub-national group conducts that is coercive, corrupting, deceptive, clandestine, and deemed contrary to Australia's sovereignty, values, and national interests.[200]

In December 2019, Prime Minister Scott Morrison announced the establishment of a new Counter Foreign Interference Taskforce in the Home Affairs portfolio that builds on an earlier investment in a Foreign Interference Threat Assessment Centre in ASIO and

---

Countering foreign interference, Critical infrastructure protection, Multicultural affairs, Countering violent extremism programs and Transport Security. Department of Home Affairs, website home page

200 Department of Home Affairs website Counter Foreign Interference

operationalises legislation passed in 2018.[201] These investments and institutional remedies and a Counter Foreign Interference Strategy are described diplomatically and euphemistically as responses to 'foreign interference'. In reality, they are countering Phase 1 'light grey' CPC political warfare. The crucial roles of the new task force are to 'discover, track and disrupt foreign interference in Australia.'[202] The Explanatory Memorandum does not mention political warfare, but its definition of the dangers illustrates that the threat is strategic, economic, societal and political:

> Activities undertaken by foreign adversaries, and those acting on their behalf can cause severe harm to Australia's national security, compromising Australia's military capabilities and alliance relationships, and can pose a grave threat to Australia's economic stability and well-being. By wielding undue influence on the Australian political landscape, foreign adversaries have the potential to undermine Australia's sovereignty and system of government.[203]

Hardening Australia against cyberattacks has been reflexive, like responses to espionage and foreign interference. It took disruptive cyberattacks on public and private sector institutions to prompt the establishment of the Australian Cyber Security Centre within the Australian Signals Directorate [ASD] as well as Cyber Command within the ADF in 2018, and for the nation's counter-cyber warfare policy-making and coordination to find its place in the Home Affairs portfolio. Though not publicly acknowledged, CPC cyber-attacks probably prompted the government to make a Defence Department asset, the ASD, a national asset and place the Australian Cyber Security Centre under its direction. This restructuring is another example of responding to incidents, developing capabilities and adjusting institutional machinery. There was public consensus that cyber

---

201 Morrison, S, 2019, 'Stepping Up Australia's Response Against Foreign Interference'

202 Ibid.

203 Australian Government, 2018, National Security Legislation Amendment, para 3

warfare is a real and present danger to Australia's national interests. Significantly, these arrangements and substantial investments did not deter a so-called 'sophisticated state actor' from conducting a major cyber attack on public and private sector institutions on 19 June 2020.[204]

In response to the June 2020 attacks, Prime Minister Morrison announced the 2020 Cyber Security Strategy as 'the largest ever Australian Government financial commitment to cybersecurity' on 6 August 2020.[205] He stated:

> The Government will introduce legislation to bolster the powers of the Australian Federal Police and Australian Criminal Intelligence Commission to identify individuals and their networks engaging in serious criminal activity on the dark web. Powers that allow offensive disruption capabilities will allow law enforcement to take the fight to the digital front door of those using anonymising technology for evil purposes. ... Agencies will be equipped to help address sophisticated threats, *particularly to the essential services all Australian's rely on – everything from electricity and water to healthcare and groceries* [author's emphasis].[206]

The CPC's grey zone campaign has engaged Australia's homeland defences, and the Australian Government has responded. The NIC has detected the campaign, and the Turnbull and Morrison governments have responded with legislation enabling the AFP to create some deterrence. But are these reflexive responses astute, anticipatory and hard enough? Arguably, CPC hardliners are counting on the Australian Government remaining one step behind in responding to escalations of political warfare to hybrid warfare – from light to darker grey.

Reflexive responses only when public opinion polls are favourable affords the CPC both the initiative and escalation dominance and optimise the chance of strategic surprise and success. An analogy would

204 Morrison, S, Reynolds, L & Dutton, P, 2020, 'Statement on malicious cyber activity against Australian networks'

205 Morrison, S & Dutton, P, 2020, 'Australia's 2020 Cyber Security Strategy'

206 Morrison, S, 2020, 'Australia's largest ever investment in cyber security'

be to give an opponent the first punch every time during a boxing bout. This advantage will be difficult to overcome unless politicians and the public heed warnings. A better option is to commit to a strategy that contains proactive protective legislation that hardens and rehearses institutional machinery and credible deterrent capabilities to pace escalation, deter further escalation and intensify responses in a timely way if deterrence fails.

The Australian Government released its first National Security Strategy in 2013. This, and other Federal Government strategy documents, aim to articulate the threats, focus national security efforts, and identify priorities.[207] The flagship strategy for the defence of Australian sovereignty is the 2016 Defence White Paper [DWP16], supported by the 2020 Strategic Update and 2020 Force Structure Plan. There are also several 'sub-strategies' to cope with single issues, including the Cyber Security Strategy (2020), Countering Foreign Interference (2020), Australian Disaster Preparedness Framework (2018), Critical Infrastructure Resilience Strategy (2015), and the Australian Counterterrorism Strategy (2015).

No National Security Strategy that includes the grey zone describes an 'all hazards' and 'all threat' approach to keeping Australia safe. This strategy would anticipate future hazards, such as the consequences of climate change, and threats such as a major war in the Indo-Pacific region and grey zone campaigns. It should guide legislation that puts arrangements in place to deal with them. I agree with Jim Molan and David Connery, experts on Australian national security, in their recent publication, *National Security: A National Perspective*, that there is an urgent need for a capstone National Security Strategy. Part of that strategy must be guidance and arrangements for countering grey zone campaigns.

Events rather than an anticipatory strategy have prompted legislation and adjustments to policies and institutional machinery since 2015. These responses are tactical rather than strategic and reflexive rather than forward-thinking. An analogy would be that emergency

---

207 Department of the Prime Minister and Cabinet, *Strong and Secure: A Strategy for Australia's National Security*, p. ii

wartime legislation and substantial investments in preparations for war do not occur without either a declaration of war or public consensus on the imminent approach of war. Geoffrey Blainey, an eminent Australian historian, wrote about Australia's preparedness for a war on the 75th anniversary of the end of the War in the Pacific in 2020, hinting at the CPC's grey zone campaign:

> Nevertheless, one thing is clear: democracies can often display dedication in fighting a war once a war occurs but still fall dangerously short when the time comes to prepare for tensions or *even for a cold war* [author's emphasis][208]

Hard enough?

While new national security legislation is beneficial and provident, it does not operationalise Defence strategic guidance for countering hybrid warfare. Defence and each Service compete for resources to prosecute a war against traditional existential threats, such as an invasion. That is Defence's core business. The recent 2020 Strategic Update's inclusion of the grey zone in strategic calculations and promises of capability development is timely:

> [Australia needs to develop] capabilities to hold adversary forces and infrastructure at risk further from Australia, such as longer-range strike weapons, cyber capabilities and area denial systems.[209] ... These capabilities will need to deliver deterrent effects against a broad range of threats, including *preventing coercive or grey-zone activities from escalating to conventional conflict.* [author's emphasis] ... The new policy will require force structure and capability adjustments focussing on responding to grey-zone challenges, the possibility of high-intensity conflict and domestic crises.[210]

Defence is only in the early stages of coming to terms with the grey zone.

---

208 Blainey, G, 2020, 'As the Pacific theatre opened, the nation was ill-prepared', p. 13–14

209 Australian Government, 2020, *2020 Defence Strategic Update*, para 2.23

210 Ibid., para 2.30

Its priorities for defending Australia against conventional military threats are paramount. The Services (navy, army, air force) have no incentives to collaborate with other government departments or agencies in the grey zone. Without clear Prime Ministerial and Cabinet direction, Defence cannot respond independently to internal threats to Australia's security that have traditionally been the responsibility of other Federal departments and agencies as well as State and Territory law enforcement agencies. Espionage, political warfare, information warfare, influence operations, cyber-attack and other forms of coercive tactics elevate and complicate threats for the Home Affairs portfolio, but not necessarily for Defence.

Hardening for hybrid warfare requires sophisticated whole-of-government arrangements. The NIC detects threats but cannot strike anywhere and anytime to retrieve intelligence forcibly, deal with a discovered threat, or respond firmly to a cyber-attack. As well, when adversaries disguise and carefully calibrate coercion to avoid a conventional military response and the attention of law enforcement agencies – a grey zone strategy – the deterrence of traditional military force no longer applies.

An enhanced strike capability anywhere and anytime has a better prospect of creating deterrence. Suppose deterrence accompanied by negotiations fail, and damage to life and property is imminent. In that case, Australia's strike capability has a 'warm start' for de-escalating the threat decisively because it has 'stared' at the threat for long enough. The Independent Intelligence Review warned that 'the proliferation of precision weapons will see more nations with the capability, and the temptation, to undertake 'surgical' strikes.[211] Arguably, in this instance alone, Australia should have the capability to strike first and not wait for a national or sub-national adversary to give in to temptation. Australia is vulnerable now because it is figuratively giving an adversary escalating a grey zone campaign the first punch every time.

Building on existing legislation for the shades of grey

New 'grey zone' legislation must distinguish between traditional

---

211 Australian Government, 2017, 2017 *Independent Intelligence Review*, para 1.20

statecraft and contemporary political and hybrid warfare. Australia's existing laws protecting its sovereignty and the formation and empowerment of the Home Affairs portfolio constitute a foundation for countering illegal Phase 1 'light grey' political warfare. This foundation already includes legislation authorising ultimate sanctions for terrorist acts. The difference between a criminal act and a political act determines both the jurisdiction and the response. In effect, Australia treats a terrorist with a political motive who is committing a violent act as a combatant. Legislation that keeps pace with the shades of grey through to hybrid warfare should categorise parties committing a violent act sponsored by a nation or a sub-national group as a 'grey zone' combatant.

Though not meant to support my line of argument, George Williams of the University of New South Wales observes that Australia's counter-terrorism legislation is a product of reflexive responses that were intended to be transient but have become more enduring:

> In the decade since September 11, the Federal Parliament has enacted 54 anti-terror laws, with many more made by the States and Territories. This has given rise to a large and remarkable new body of legislation providing for powers and sanctions that were unthinkable prior to the 2001 attacks. Indeed, the rhetoric of a 'war on terror' reflects the nature and severity of the laws enacted in response to the threat. While these laws were often cast as a transient response to an exceptional set of events, it is now clear that the greater body of this law will remain on the Australian statute book for the foreseeable future.[212]

For this book, counter-terrorism legislation is provident.[213] So are laws enacted in 2018 to counter treason, treachery, espionage, sabotage and foreign interference. The proposed amendments to the *Intelligence Services Act 2001* and new Foreign Relations Bills, and the promised establishment of a Counter Foreign Interference Taskforce are steps in

---

212 Williams, G, 2011, 'A Decade of Australian Anti-Terror Laws', Conclusion, Australian Government, 2020, *Counterterrorism Laws*

213 Attorney-General's Department 2020, 'Australia's counter-terrorism laws'

the right direction for anticipating the darker shades of grey.[214] These laws and institutional proposals constitute a foundation for a fair, firm and lawful de-escalation strategy. They set the scene for developing hardened capabilities along the spectrum of the shades of grey, from law enforcement countermeasures to the ultimate sanctions of lethal military force.

Unarmed foreign principals, or 'malicious insiders' and proxies acting on their behalf, already conduct 'light grey' non-violent political warfare in Australia – Plato's informal war. The shades of grey align with offences covered in the existing body of legislation. In conjunction with the NIC, the Home Affairs portfolio and Australia's law enforcement agencies respond to parties involved in these non-violent coercive activities. Offences include foreign interference, giving false and misleading information, interference with political rights and duties, treason and related crimes, treachery, espionage and related offences, encouraging mutiny and urging violence and advocating terrorism or genocide.

Custodial sentences apply to some of them. For example, espionage is a crime in Australia, punishable by up to 25 years imprisonment.[215] Alternatively, foreign interference is a broader, more nuanced concept about covertly shaping decision-making to the advantage of a foreign power and, left unchecked, becomes highly corrosive. There are no custodial sentences for foreign interference to deter foreign principals from prosecuting political warfare.[216]

Darker grey tactics are violent and destructive. Existing legislation applies custodial sentences to actions that can involve violence and destruction using weapons and explosives, as well as malicious software to disrupt and destroy IT systems. Examples of violent and

---

214 Australian Government, 2018, 'National Security Legislation Amendment (Espionage and Foreign Interference)' and Morrison, S & Dutton, P, 2019, 'Stepping up Australia's response against foreign interference'. and Australian Parliament, Australia's Foreign Relations (State and Territory Arrangements) Bill 2020 and Australia's Foreign Relations (State and Territory Arrangements) (Consequential Amendments) Bill 2020

215 Australian Security and Intelligence Organisation, 2020, 'Counter Espionage and Foreign Interference'

216 Ibid.

destructive activities are political violence, military-style training, cyberattacks, terrorism and sabotage. There is legislation for Special Forces and some specialist ADF engineers to respond to terrorism and terrorist-like actions such as sabotage and possession of WMD. Still, there is less clarity about responding to other acts of violence, disruption and destruction.

I recommend extending existing counterterrorism, espionage and foreign interference legislation by expanding categories of illegal activities to include warlike actions related to hybrid warfare and then specifying offenders as enemies of Australia who can become military targets. Additional categories should include hostile, unlawful and warlike activities such as cyberattacks intending to disrupt and destroy; recruitment, training and employment of members of grievance groups, criminals and others to intimidate leaders and citizens violently for political purposes. Finally, the conduct of deniable and covert operations personally or through proxies to apply violence, including terrorist acts, sabotage and military-like actions, against institutions, groups and individuals.

This extension of legislation that permits the application of military force on Australian soil will attract the interest of the Law Society and human rights groups. Their reasonable question will be, 'Are cyber-attacks acts of warlike violence if they intend to cause 'disruptive or destructive effects'? When does a hacker become a grey zone combatant who can be killed if apprehension is too risky? Arguably, their political and violent credentials, as well as their *modus operandi*, make them cyber terrorists.

The question for me is, 'Would legislation declaring cyber terrorists as targets for counter-terrorism assault teams deter attacks like those of 19 June 2020?' Arguably, hackers contemplating a destructive attack might have second thoughts if they thought that armed Australian operatives had discovered them and were 'staring', awaiting their next move. A history of reflexive responses to homeland threats suggests that Australia will only have the political will to target cyberterrorists with ultimate sanctions after a devastating cyberattack on an essential service that results in loss of life and severe economic disruption. Why should Australia wait for strategic surprise and hastily respond to this type of catastrophe before passing hardened legislation? Legislation is a reasonable precautionary measure for a liberal democracy based on the destructive possibilities of cyber-attacks and hybrid warfare.

Precautionary legislation is not a declaration of war. It is intended to prompt second thoughts among those conducting disruptive cyberattacks and deter them from authorising other types of destructive attacks. Laws that allow a Special Forces-like AFP Response Force to participate with departmental and agency partners against terrorism, destructive cyberattacks and other forms of sabotage, and the violent intimidation of Australian citizens, are crucial for a de-escalation strategy.

In summary, grey zone campaigns rely on liberal democracies making reflexive responses to incidents. This advantage leaves Australia one step behind each Phase of a grey zone campaign that maintains one punch ahead of a counter punch until the time is right for a 'king' hit. The government has enacted counter-terrorism laws, laws to counter foreign interference and muscled-up counter cyber warfare capabilities after incidents stimulated enough political will to do so. Reflexive responses leave the initiative and escalation momentum with CPC hardliners. Precautionary grey zone legislation will retake the initiative and create deterrence and de-escalation capabilities.

Current options for doing something more about it

What can be done under current national security arrangements? The 2016 Defence White Paper follows a traditional geographic prescription. Australia's priorities are to defend the continent first, defend the near region to defend the homeland and its trade routes, and contribute to a rules-based global order to mitigate risks to the immediate region and the homeland.[217] I agree with these traditional priorities that focus on conventional warfare capabilities – fighting ships, stealthy submarines, armoured vehicles, artillery, missiles and strike aircraft.[218] The Australian people expect the defence of their territorial sovereignty to be the Australian Government's priority,

---

217 Australian Government, 2016, *Defence White Paper*, paras 1.15–1.17

218 Ibid., para 4.4

the near region next, and the world after that. These priorities justify a strong navy, army and air force to defend the homeland from invasion by an adversary deploying their navy, army and air force. They accommodate the use of the same military power to secure the approaches to Australia – vital sea and air trade routes – as part of securing the regional neighbourhood. They also give Australia the capabilities for supporting the US-led Western alliance in maintaining a rules-based global order.

Australia has and continues to rely on its relationship with the United States to create 'extended deterrence' against conventional attacks from a powerful adversary. The ANZUS Treaty is the formal declaration of mutual defence interests, but those interests are defined by assistance when there is a direct military attack.[219] Grey zone campaigns avoid a direct military attack that constitutes an act of war. The ANZUS Treaty does not cover the grey zone. Still, it encourages the parties to 'consult together whenever in the opinion of any of them the territorial integrity, political independence or security of any of the Parties is threatened in the Pacific.'[220] Presumably, the Australian and US governments have begun discussions on grey zone threats and countermeasures as part of annual Australia–US Ministerial talks about each nation's security. However, the emphasis would still likely be on conventional military deterrence and cooperation.

Huth and Russett examined an 'expected-utility' model of extended deterrence.[221] This is the deterrence that Australia's alliance with the United States is intended to provide. It means that powerful authoritarian nations will not attack Australia because they fear an American military response. Taiwan and Japan rely on extended deterrence to remain independent of China. Both have treaties roughly equivalent to the ANZUS Treaty. Article 3(c) of the Taiwan Relations Act states:

---

219 Department of External Affairs, *Security Treaty between Australia, New Zealand and the United States of America [ANZUS]*, Australian Treaty series 1952

220 Ibid., Article III

221 Huth, P and Russett, B, 1984, 'What Makes Deterrence Work? Cases from 1900 to 1980', pp. 496–526

> The President is directed to inform the Congress promptly of any threat to the security or the social or economic system of the people on Taiwan and any danger to the interests of the United States arising therefrom. The President and the Congress shall determine, in accordance with constitutional processes, appropriate action by the United States in response to any such danger.'[222]

Article V of Japan's treaty states:

> Each Party [the United States and Japan] recognizes that an armed attack against either Party in the territories under the administration of Japan would be dangerous to its own peace and safety and declares that it would act to meet the common danger in accordance with its constitutional provisions and processes.[223]

Hutt and Russett tested whether extended deterrence worked on 54 historical cases from 1900 to 1980. Though they did not contemplate the grey zone, their findings suggest that neither Australia's alliance with the United States nor Australia's conventional military deterrence will dissuade the CPC from pursuing its grey zone campaign against Australia. Though outside my scope, Taiwan and Japan will most likely have to face the CPC alone in the grey zone as well. Indeed, extrapolating their findings strengthens my conclusion that the CPC's grey zone strategy already bypasses US extended deterrence afforded to its allies as well as Australia's substantial conventional military deterrence that is still more than a decade away. In the meantime, Australia has to deal with the CPC in the grey zone alone. The next ten years are a window of vulnerability.

The Department of Defence 2020 Strategic Update mentions the grey zone for the first time in Australian strategic guidance with a definition and a one-paragraph observation that there are grey zone

222 US Congress 1979, Taiwan Relations Act, Public Law 96–8, 96th Congress

223 Ministry of Foreign Affairs of Japan, 1960, 'Treaty of Mutual Cooperation and Security between Japan and the United States of America'

activities in the Indo-Pacific region.[224] The Update cites Special Forces as the option for countering grey zone activities, emphasising that they are, 'increasingly important to countering the grey-zone threats Australia is likely to face *in the future* [author's emphasis].'[225] The Update emphasises non-geographic domains for warfare – information, cyber and space.[226] There is a promise of 'increased investment in capabilities to respond to grey-zone activities, including improved situational awareness, cyber capabilities, electronic warfare and information operations.'[227] Commendably, there is also a focus on growing 'the ADF's self-reliance for delivering deterrent effects.'[228] But additional deterrence is primarily confined to longer-range missile systems. Still, the 2020 Update mentions expanding 'Defence's capability to respond to grey-zone activities, working closely with other arms of Government.' – a promise, but not yet a strategy.[229]

The Update does harden Australia's strategic posture [capabilities and intentions]. Prime Minister Scott Morrison announced his government's commitment to upgrading Australia's defensive conventional capabilities and reminded the nation of the 1930s.[230] He focussed on Australia's immediate region and put adversaries on notice that Australia would project military hard power further from the homeland if needed. He emphasised:

> The first objective is to shape Australia's strategic environment. The Indo-Pacific is where we live – and we want an open, sovereign Indo-Pacific, free from coercion and hegemony, ... We want a region where all countries, large and small, can engage freely with each other, guided by international rules and norms. Where countries can pursue their own interests peacefully and without external interference. ...

224 Australian Government, 2020, *2020 Defence Strategic Update*, para 1.1 and Forward

225 Australian Government, 2020, *2020 Defence Force Structure Plan*, para 7.15

226 Ibid., paras 1.20, 2.5–6

227 Australian Government, 2020, *2020 Defence Strategic Update*, para 3.3

228 Ibid., para 2.13

229 Australian Government, 2020, *2020 Defence Strategic Update*, para 2.13

230 Benson, S, 2020, 'Scott Morrison shoulders arms to China in 10 year $270 bn plan'

> We need to hold our potential adversaries to a greater distance. Part of our repositioning is to hold them further away and to work with multiple partners to achieve our goals of regional stability, peace and security. ... These new objectives [shape, deter, respond] will guide all aspects of Defence's planning, including force structure planning, force generation, international engagement and operations.[231]

The new concepts of 'shape, deter and respond' add a layer of sophistication and flexibility to Australia's traditional geographically focused military strategic guidance. Shaping is proactive, collaborative and anticipatory. It marshals diplomatic, informational, military and economic power to pursue Australian national interests that align with maintaining peace and prosperity in the Indo-Pacific region. For shaping, Australia should leverage all tools of statecraft proactively to improve its relative position in the grey zone while controlling risks of escalation. This proactive approach should involve aligning and supporting like-minded regional neighbours to recognise that the CPC's grey zone campaign is part of its broader regional ambitions to create tribute states in its perceived historical and entitled sphere of influence.

Deterrence is commendable because its focus is on having and communicating credible and forceful consequences for adversaries coercing or committing violent acts against Australia. It is a concept for precipitating 'second thoughts' about escalating coercion and contemplating military action. Traditionally, Australia relies on conventional military deterrence in the form of extended deterrence from its alliance with the United States and its own traditional military power. Likewise, Australia's conventional responses to external coercion are to turn to its armed forces.

The question is how relevant conventional military deterrence and responses are for countering an escalating grey zone campaign that deliberately seeks to avoid military retaliation and ignores geographical borders? An evasion rather than an invasion strategy. For deterrence, Australia must have credible and well-communicated

---

231 Ibid.

military and non-military response options to coercion and more aggressive violent actions that pace rather than risk escalation. For response, response forces should have capabilities to detect and 'stare' at grey zone threats in the making. At the same time, the Australian Government cautions threat sponsors to 'cease and desist' and then respond quickly and decisively if cautions are ignored, and there is a threat to life and property.

The Australian Government has recognised the non-geographic dimensions of grey zone coercion. Prime Minister Morrison announced Australia's largest-ever investment in cybersecurity called the Cyber Enhanced Situational Awareness and Response package in June 2020.[232] His emphasis on 'providing greater capacity to take the fight to cybercriminals offshore and neutralise and block emerging [nation-sponsored] cyber threats to Australia' indirectly acknowledges the grey zone. His focus on shaping the capacities and capabilities of Australia's regional neighbourhood and engaging adversaries further from Australia's homeland accords with my recommendation of 'upstream' engagement for a de-escalation strategy (discussed later). In short, my proposals build on Scott Morrison's strategic prescriptions and complement investment in conventional military deterrence rather than replace them.

I support the tone and messaging of the Update. It is logical and provident to arm Australia conventionally for more self-reliant defence against a significant Asian power like China that is developing conventional military capabilities apace. Arguably, Australia could face a Chinese invasion fleet in the future. Still, the CPC would not invade unless it assessed the Chinese armed forces could defeat or negotiate the withdrawal of the United States' conventional military power in the Indo-Pacific region. Arguably, the initial test of strength and resolve for the United States and its allies would have been the incorporation of Taiwan. But, in my view, that incorporation will be achieved through a grey zone campaign, possibly escalated to hybrid warfare, well before any declaration of war.

Ultimately, the 2020 Update is a $270 bn investment over ten years

232 Morrison, S, 2020, 'Australia's largest ever investment in cyber security'

in 'more of the same' conventional military power to deter a significant Asian nation from employing traditional military power against Australia. Identifying the grey zone as a future threat is a welcome step in the right direction but not an announcement of a proactive strategy. Understandably, the Update is mindful of Australia's major trading partner. It communicates firmly and indirectly. It does not acknowledge explicitly that Xi Jinping and CPC hardliners are already prosecuting a light grey political campaign in Australia and its near region.

The worst-case scenario for Australia could be the CPC incorporating Taiwan and forcing Japan and South Korea to remain neutral. At the same time, the United States, troubled by its own domestic political and social instability, stands by, dithering about its treaty obligations and reluctant to provoke a Third World War. In this new reality, the United States could agree with China on spheres of influence and withdraw militarily from North and Southeast Asia to maintain its strategic defence perimeter closer to home. In effect, the world's post-Cold War policeman figuratively puts away his baton. Australia would stand alone with its armed forces continuing to stare at the air-sea gap and no strategy or prepared responses for defending itself in the grey zone.

Is it safe to only rely on more conventional military deterrence?

The ADF stands ready to defend Australia and its national interests, but is upgrading Australia's military hard power the complete answer to countering an escalating grey zone campaign? Is it safe to rely only on more conventional military deterrence? Influential and respected voices are calling for substantial Australian investments in more deterrence. For Hugh White, Emeritus Professor of Strategic Studies at the Strategic and Defence Studies Centre of the ANU, Scott Morrison's update does not promise enough conventional military deterrence. He has called for a massive increase in Australian military hard power to deter and counter hard-line CPC strategic ambitions. He began the journey to his recent book, *How to Defend Australia,* with his book, *The China Choice.*[233] He followed with *Without America: Australia in*

233 White, H, 2013, *The China Choice: why America should share power*

the New Asia in 2017.[234] He contends that China's rise to a military superpower is inexorable and America's decline in the Asia-Pacific region inevitable. He opines that Australia should not rely solely on the United States to defend Australia's national interests in a more contested Asia.[235] He highlights the risks of both entrapment in America's wars, especially with China, and abandonment by America if China threatens Australia.[236] Finally, he alerts his readers to a tipping point where a more heavily armed Australia increases threats from more formidable regional neighbours and attracts the malevolent attention of America's enemies, presumably China.[237] Eminent colleagues at the ANU support White's departure from the current DWP16 strategic guidance.[238]

White puts a case for Australia to adopt an independent strategic posture. He calls for a 32-strong submarine fleet and more strike aircraft and consigns the Army to defend the homeland and engage in guerrilla warfare if necessary after an invasion. He assigns the RAAF to support the RAN in attacking an inbound invasion armada in the Indonesian-Melanesian archipelago, presumably after achieving air superiority – Australia's future battle of Midway, probably without the support of the US navy and air force.[239] White offers a 'defence from invasion' grand strategy through 'sea denial'.[240] He is silent about responding to political and hybrid warfare in the grey zone, dismissing cyber warfare as neither a decisive strategy nor a viable warfare domain because of its mutually-assured destructive effects.[241]

White is right to question the utility of Australian conventional land force projection. Enhanced Australian air force and maritime force projection will carry more strategic weight in a contested Asia-Pacific region. Inconveniently, Australia's new fleet of nuclear-powered

---

234 White, H, 2017, 'Without America: Australia in the New Asia'

235 White, H, 2020, *How to Defend Australia*, p. 296

236 Ibid.

237 Ibid., p. 289

238 Dibb, P, Brabin-Smith R & Sargeant B, 2018, 'Why Australia Needs a Radically New Defence Policy'

239 White, H, 2020, *How to Defend Australia*, Chapter 12

240 Ibid., Chapters 16 & 18

241 Ibid., pp. 27–28

submarines is more than a decade away from delivery, though there are proposals to lease UK or US subs in the interim. There are uncertainties about the US Global Support Solution for reliably and affordably sustaining Australia's F35 Joint Strike Fighters.[242] More particularly, White did not include unconventional land force projection that can enhance targeting and precise application of Australian maritime and air power. He is right about using Australia's geographic advantage to attack an inbound invasion fleet closer to the Australian mainland rather than further north. He is silent on disrupting and mauling shipping in home ports and cutting supply lines and communications by employing unconventional warfare capabilities, including cyber. This oversight echoes the failure of imagination of Australian civilian and military leaders concerning the Japanese shipping in 1942 that was molested briefly in Singapore Harbour. Australian leaders did not develop capabilities to attack Japanese ships in port and elsewhere or cut fuel and other supply lines.[243]

John Blaxland, one of Hugh White's colleagues at the ANU, offers a sobering and realistic assessment of Australia's conventional deterrence over the next 10 to 15 years:

> ... while the ADF is a capable force, should Australia ever face a challenge from a nation with advanced weapons systems, this force may be inadequate for the task. A one-division regular-army force of three combat brigades and some special forces, a navy of a dozen or so warships and a handful of submarines, and an air force of only 100 fighter aircraft, means Australia has little if any ability to sustain significant attrition in case of a substantial conflict. *In effect, the ADF is only a one-punch force* [author's emphasis].[244]

I do not challenge deterring China or other major Asian powers with conventional armed forces. Still, I am concerned about the affordability,

---

242 Australian National Audit Office 2020, *Future Submarine Program – Transition to Design*, and Australian National Audit Office 2020, *Joint Strike Fighter*

243 Horner, D, 1982, *High Command: Australia and Allied Strategy*, Horner, D, 1996, *Inside the War Cabinet:* and Horner, D, 1998, *Blamey: Commander in Chief*

244 Blaxland, J, 2020, *Developing a new Plan B for the ADF*

impact and timeliness of relying only on more traditional military deterrence. The danger is that massive investment may still not create sufficient ADF punching power against significant Asian military forces. Let alone China's. It just might become too expensive to deter in this way. Too little investment in countering grey zone strategies, combined with delays with new submarines and uncertainties about US logistic support for new F35 strike aircraft, might create incentives for CPC hardliners to escalate their current grey zone campaign. Assuming that the objective is creating a 21st Century version of a tribute state, CPC hardliners may argue that it is better to increase the pressure on Australia in the grey zone soon rather than face enhanced conventional military power later. Australia cannot afford to cede the grey zone to the CPC and hope its enhanced military deterrence strategy will work 'down the track'. Scott Morrison was prescient to evoke the 1930s and wise to assess that Australia has no more strategic warning time left.

I do not advocate a replacement strategy for conventional military deterrence. Participation in a traditional military conflict cannot be ruled out. However, trying to contain China militarily may gift the CPC with a narrative that the United States and its allies are not only denying China's destiny aggressively but also preparing for war. It is better to precipitate second thoughts and create dilemmas. Why not remain engaged and constrain rather than attempt to isolate and contain? I argue later that aggregating regional de-escalation strategies gives Australia and the Western alliance a sophisticated strategic option that not only counters grey zone campaigns directly but can also curtail escalation to war. There is still sufficient time to de-escalate in a way that complements and strengthens Australia's longer-term conventional hard power deterrent strategy, with or without the United States. It is an 'and/and' rather than 'either/or' strategy, or, for that matter, a third way.

My scope for this book does not include discussing how much money to spend on conventional military deterrence in light of the perceived demise of the United States and the inexorable rise of China. It is focused squarely on offering an affordable option for countering a 'light grey' campaign that the CPC has already begun with Australia and its regional allies. Its premise is that the CPC wants to succeed strategically but avoid conventional warfare. Accordingly, another option is to de-escalate the CPC's political warfare and deter the possibility of escalation to hybrid warfare. Others are welcome to marshal the political will to spend billions of dollars to defeat an invasion fleet.

What about just adapting the ADF to meet changed circumstances?

There appears to be an assumption in DWP16 that the ADF can adapt quickly to changed circumstances and operational environments, such as counter-insurgency and peace support operations.[245] Why not political and economic coercion escalating to hybrid warfare? The danger of assuming that conventional forces will adapt to escalations in violence in the grey zone is that it negates equitable investment in other capabilities for firmly countering grey zone campaigns now. It is a myth that conventional forces have inherent skills to adapt quickly. Conflict in the Middle East and Afghanistan and terrorist attacks in Australia's near region over the past 15 years suggest that conventional forces have lost some relevance to meeting several existing and emerging unconventional threats to Australia's national interests. They cannot find adversaries who fight conventionally after declarations of war. They train and are equipped for warfighting, but what if warfighting is not on the adversary's 'main game? The world is now replete with authoritarian nations and sub-national groups who fight asymmetrically and do not declare war. They do not want to fight a war. They want to win in the grey zone.

The CPC will not push its grey zone campaign to a military threshold with an act of war. Consequently, the Australian Government is unlikely to deploy and employ combat troops against Chinese groups and their proxies operating in the grey zone, especially on home soil. Firstly, mobilising the Army for this purpose could be interpreted as an act of war. Secondly, the ADF trains and authorises Special Forces to go after violent terrorist groups and individuals, not regular troops. Small

245 Australian Government, 2016, *Defence White Paper*, paras 4.4, 4.9

teams of regular infantry forces are not trained to collaborate with law enforcement agencies to hunt and neutralise opposing Special Forces and specialist armed operatives on home soil or in the near region.

More generally, conventionally-trained single Service headquarters, units and personnel are not capable of global operations to disrupt and complicate an adversary's contemplation of military action against Australia or strike at imminent threats in the grey zone. Counter-hybrid, counter-terrorist, counter-cyber, counter-information and counter-political warfare capabilities, as well as counter-WMD proliferation operations, should be new core security capabilities that underpin a de-escalation strategy. Modalities like these are not natural subsets of RAN, Army or RAAF capabilities. One Army analyst opines that the Army in the grey zone would be 'punching at air' ... 'like a punch-drunk prize-fighter: swinging at shadows, wasting energy, resources and reputation'.[246] He is right; the Army is not suited to landing a punch in the grey zone.

American commentators, Matisek and Bertram, describe the limits of conventional military power in the US context:

> Moreover, the US and its allies face the problem of how to conceptualize 21st-century war, because most adversaries engage in fringe activities to weaken American influence and power and undermine US-built narratives. This [approach] effectively neuters the perception of US military power, rendering it practically irrelevant in stopping the attainment of political objectives by Russia, China, and others. It is almost as if Edward Luttwak's paradoxes of strategy are showing empirically now as America's greatest strength – conventional military dominance in the ground, sea, and air domains – is evaded by hostile state and non-state actors, making the US look like a lumbering giant that lacks the nimbleness, energy, or long-term willingness to deal with insurgents, terrorists, and gray-zone conflicts initiated by near-peer states.[247]

---

246 O'Neill, M, 2020, 'Punching at Air'

247 Matisek, J & Bertram, I, 2017, 'The Death of American Conventional Warfare'

Alan Dupont comments in a similar vein in the Australian context:

> Authoritarian states and political movements have developed three main strategies for countering [conventional] Western military superiority. The first is by conducting 'threshold' warfare. Its central idea is to seize territory or attack opponents opportunistically without triggering an overwhelming [conventional] response. Doing so quickly, in plausibly deniable operations that don't directly threaten core Western interests, makes it politically difficult for democracies to respond militarily. ... Second, authoritarian states have become adept at using proxies to help achieve strategic objectives. ... A third tactic that has caused particular problems for Australia is the manipulation of our democratic processes and institutions for political gain.[248]

But is there another Catch 22 for Australia? How much conventional military deterrence is enough? Will Australia ever reach a deterrence threshold for CPC hardliners to cease pressuring Australia to act in its interests because Australia can project potent military hard power? Spending on Australia's defence in the 21st Century is unprecedented.[249] The Prime Minister, Scott Morrison, announced an additional $274 billion over the next ten years when launching the 2020 Strategic Update in 2020. On 28 April 2021, he announced an additional $747 million to upgrade four key training areas and ranges in the Northern Territory to enable the Australian Defence Force to conduct simulated training exercises and remain battle-ready.

Australia's updated 'shape, deter and respond' strategy is insufficient. It implies conventional retaliation if deterrence fails. Arguably, Australia will never be able to afford the projection of sufficient 'credible military force' to deter a significant Asian military power like China in a more contested Indo-Pacific region.[250] A bolder escalation or retaliation strategy in response to a CPC grey zone campaign is also problematic. These responses equate to a middle

---

248 Dupont, A, 2019, 'A New Type of War at Our Door'

249 Hellyer, M, 2020, *The Cost of Defence 2020–2021*, Part 1: ASPI, 2020–2021 Defence Budget Brief

250 Australian Government, 2020, 2020 *Defence Strategic Update*, paras 2.25–2.26

power provoking an unwinnable conflict with a significant Asian military power and an important trading partner.

David Kilcullen points to Qiao Liang and Wang Xiangsui's 'side principal rule'. In the context of this book, the rule suggests that Australia may be exhausting itself in its traditional conceptual comfort zone of further investment in conventional military force projection. This deterrent preference may give insufficient attention to the possibility of 'an unconventional side stroke from an unexpected direction', such as political and hybrid warfare explicit in *Unrestricted Warfare*.[251] I accept that conventional deterrence is necessary, but it should be accompanied by a strategy for de-escalating grey zone threats. A grey zone campaign is a clear and present danger to Australia's interests now and, as a possibility, constitutes a softening up Phase before traditional warfare.

Is there enough being done about it for the time being?

One could argue that enough is already being done to counter the escalations of economic pressure, espionage, cyber-attacks and foreign interference. Legislation is in place, and several strategies are guiding the work of multi-agency taskforces. I can't entirely agree because the initiative remains with the CPC, and there is insufficient deterrence. Deterrence will always be ineffective if there are no credible and potent means for responding to escalations. During the Cold War, an eminent American strategic theorist, Thomas Schelling, described deterrence as the 'art of coercion and intimidation'. It involves communicating the power to hurt. It is based on what nations know other nations can do to hurt them. Deterrence is a form of firm communication, backed by a credible forceful capability, that can also be a form of bargaining power that underpins negotiation for reconciliation.

The challenge is to identify focal points, not only to optimise the timing and nature of 'hurt' but to open up lines of conciliatory communication immediately in a hostile environment if deterrence has failed and a 'hurtful' response is required.[252] One analogy would

---

251 Kilcullen, D, 2020, *The Dragons and the Snakes*, p. 223

252 Schelling, TC, 1966, *Arms and Influence*

be that a person who persists with malicious actions and is unwilling to communicate or negotiate can choose to ignore a person who has a guard dog on a lead. That person would most likely pay attention and communicate after the dog has bitten them once. That same hostile bullying person can be forced to pay attention and communicate after a jab to their nose or a sting to their ear. Bites, jabs and stings are hurtful and annoying but not sufficient justification to kill someone because the reasons for hurtful responses are explained and warned about in the spirit of 'Look at what you have forced me to do. Let's see if we can work things out now.'

British strategic thinker, Colin Gray, opined that deterrence without the capability to 'hurt' is futile.[253] He agrees with Schelling that the prospect of coercive force must be real and credible for deterrence to work. Schelling in his seminal work, *The Strategy of Conflict*, elaborates by observing, 'We [the Western alliance] have learned that the threat [of coercive force] has to be credible to be efficacious and that its credibility may be dependent on its cost and risks associated with the fulfilment made by the party making the threat.'[254] Put more simply, for Australia to create sufficient deterrence in the grey zone, it has to have a well-communicated capability to 'hurt' with affordable capabilities that mitigate the risk of disproportionate retaliation. I would add that Australia's credible de-escalation capabilities, if deterrence fails, have to be lawful, proportional and justifiable to the community of nations and the political leadership and people of the targeted adversary. In short, Australia has to make it clear that it wishes to get along with the CPC but can stand up to the CPC firmly and hurtfully if bullied.

Thomas Schelling's most important ideas for me are that most conflict situations in international relations are bargaining situations.[255] Bargaining with hurtful deterrent capabilities in the grey zone is feasible because the threat of conventional warfare is metaphorically 'off the table' even when a major power like China is bullying a middle power like Australia. Put simply; the CPC will

---

253 Gray, CS, 2010, 'Gaining Compliance', pp. 278–283

254 Schelling, TC, 1980, *The Strategy of Conflict*, p. 6

255 Ibid., p. 5

not contemplate a conventional or a nuclear response to Australia establishing a deterrent response capability in the grey zone that is calibrated to persuade the CPC to negotiate rather than continue bullying to force political and economic concessions.

Is enough being done in Australia's near region?

The 2014 visit to Fiji by Chinese President Xi Jinping and bilateral meetings with leaders from Samoa, Vanuatu, Niue, Tonga, Papua New Guinea and the Federated States of Micronesia, and a round-table discussion with all the Pacific leaders confirmed increasing Chinese strategic interest in the Pacific Islands. Xi Jinping conducted another Pacific Islands leaders' roundtable before the APEC meeting in Port Moresby in November 2018.[256] Professor Anne-Marie Brady and Cristian Talesco, and others have made it clear that the CPC is conducting a 'silent invasion' of the Pacific Islands and Timor Leste.[257]

In 2018 a Harvard University assessment of CPC 'Debtbook Diplomacy' described the nature of the threat in the Pacific Islands from a US strategic perspective:

> Over the past decade, Chinese loans have financed a construction boom in Oceania. As the grace periods begin to expire, these countries are finding themselves financially distressed. While these smaller PICs [Pacific Island Countries] may not yet be able to offer strategic assets of significant concern to the US, their deep ensnarement in China's debt trap raises long-term concerns about potential Chinese naval facilities in the Second Island Chain and beyond – staging points that could help the PLAN [Chinese navy] cover key trading routes and US lines of communication and supply.[258]

---

256 Riordan, P, 2018, 'China to host Pacific Islands meeting ahead of APEC'

257 Brady, AM, 2019, 'China's Activities in the Island States of the South Pacific, Case Study #4', pp. 27–36, Milhiet, P, 2017, 'China's Ambition in the Pacific: Worldwide Geopolitical Issues', Zhang D & Lawson, S, 2017, 'China in Pacific Region Politics', pp. 197–206, McCarthy, J, 2016, 'China extends its influence in the South Pacific' and Talesco, C, 2020, 'Foreign Aid to Timor-Leste and the Rise of China'

258 Parker, S & Chetfitz, G, 2018, *Debtbook Diplomacy* pp. 42–47

From an Australian strategic perspective, its economy relies on these same trading routes and lines of communication and supply through the Indonesian and Melanesian archipelagos. Though the Harvard report recommends actions for the United States to take in Australia's near region, Australia's responsibility is to comprehend and respond to the CPC's assertive Wolf Warrior diplomacy and its development aid entrapment strategy. The increasing presence of Chinese commercial interests and aid programs leaves Australia with the task of maintaining its neighbourhood influence as both a preeminent strategic and trading partner. The challenge is to do this without friction that could complicate Sino–Australian diplomatic relations and trade or intrude on the Pacific Islands or Timor Leste's sovereignty.

The Morrison Government's response to CPC influence in the near region is its 'Pacific Step Up' policy.[259] The Department of Foreign Affairs and Trade emphasises a 'shared agenda' for security and prosperity with the Pacific Islands and Timor Leste.[260] But is diplomatic goodwill and trying to match China's development aid enough? While there are contrary views, including a spirited denial that Timor Leste was succumbing to Chinese influence by its foreign minister in 2019, there is sufficient evidence of CPC political warfare.[261] The CPC employs debt trap aid to leverage obligations to its interests that undermine the sovereignty of Australia's neighbours. This close arch of islands was formerly known pejoratively as the Arch of Instability in the late 1990s and first decade of the 21st Century. For me, the preference is Professor Joanne Wallis's optimistic title, 'the Arch of Opportunity'.[262] The opportunity is to partner with neighbours in a unique regional de-escalation strategy (discussed later).

---

259 Australian Government, 2020, *Australia's Pacific engagement, Stepping Up Australia's Engagement*

260 Australian Government, 2017, *Foreign Policy White Paper, Opportunity, Security Strength*, pp. 99–107

261 Mulyanto, R & Tobin, M, 2019, 'East Timor's China friendship won't compromise its national interests: foreign minister'

262 Ayson, R, 2007, The 'arch of instability' and Australia's strategic policy', and Wallis, J, 2015, 'The South Pacific: arch of instability of arch of opportunity?', pp. 39–53

Conclusion

Australia has sufficient detection capabilities in place but still does not have deterrence based on having sufficiently hurtful responses to de-escalate an escalating grey zone campaign at home and abroad. The NIC is the frontline of detection. The government has enhanced the NIC's capabilities in response to reforms in the United States and Britain.[263] The NIC now has over 7,000 employees and an annual budget of over $2 billion. It is comprised of the Office of National Intelligence, the Australian Secret Intelligence Service [ASIS], ASIO, the ASD, the Australian Geospatial-Intelligence Organisation, the Defence Intelligence Organisation, AFP, the Department of Home Affairs, the Australian Criminal Intelligence Commission and the Australian Transaction Reports and Analysis Centre.[264] Attentiveness to the future is explicit:

> We consider that Australia is well served by its intelligence agencies. But the challenges they face are significant, and over coming years, their capabilities, as well as the effectiveness of our intelligence community as a whole, will be significantly tested.[265]

There is a suite of laws aimed at detecting and countering foreign espionage, interference, and international investments that are not in Australia's national interests.[266] The NIC meets these threats by strengthening integration across Australia's national intelligence enterprise. The evolution of these ways and means suggests that the detection function for de-escalating political and hybrid warfare is already capable and 'always-on'.

What about deterrence? Deterrence arrangements are working

---

263 Australian Government, 2017, *2017 Independent Intelligence Review*, para 1.15
264 Australian Government, 2020, *Australian National Security website*
265 Australian Government, 2017, *2017 Independent Intelligence Review*, para 3.0
266 Australian Government, 2018, *National Security Legislation Amendment (Espionage and Foreign Interference) Act, amendment to Criminal Code Act 1995 (Cth)*, Commonwealth of Australia, Canberra and Australian Government, 2019, *Foreign Influence Transparency Scheme Amendment Bill amendment to Foreign Influence Transparency Scheme Act 2018*

well if one measures success by the rarity of successful terrorist attacks and the number of terrorist, espionage and foreign influence plots uncovered and plotters arrested and brought to justice.[267] This success suggests that Australia's counter-terrorism arrangements are a foundation for building deterrence and response capabilities for countering an escalating grey zone campaign, at least at home.

The critical point about deterrence is that hurtful responses to bullying must be real and ready. The 2020 Strategic Update mentions the connection between Special Forces and countering grey zone activities in the future.[268] Legislation and institutional machinery to deter escalation in the grey zone are needed now, not in the future. The Australian Government cannot afford to wait for a destructive or fatal incident or a catastrophic cyberattack to respond forcefully. The success of deterrence depends on adversaries understanding the risks they will take if they are detected planning for or executing violent acts against Australia's national interests. They must inspect legislation that targets them and comprehend the hurtfulness of responses available to the Australian Government. An analogy would be householders putting a sign on an entrance gate, 'Beware of the dog that we are planning to buy' rather than 'Beware of the dog'.

The questions for me are whether Australia should have a military or a police guard dog at home for the grey zone, including counter-terrorism? Should the same guard dog operate regionally and internationally in the grey zone? My first concern is that it is possibly provocative and retaliatory to employ military forces, such as Special Forces, on Australian soil when the CPC grey zone campaign has not reached a Phase 3 military or warlike threshold. Australia and the CPC are at one on avoiding this threshold. The CPC game plan is not to escalate unless early phases are unsuccessful. Australia's game plan should pace any escalations and deter, not provoke or inadvertently justify escalation. Employing Special Forces too early risks escalation rather than achieving de-escalation. The CPC has decided to conduct

---

267 Australian Government, 'Counter-Terrorism Legislation Amendment Bill (No. 1)', para 19

268 Australian Government, 2020, *2020 Defence Force Structure Plan*, para 7.15

a grey zone campaign in the Australian homeland and its regional backyard. Hence, a more sophisticated Strike Force that operates overseas is needed to create deterrence in China's backyard.

Part 3 – Dealing with the threat

CHAPTER 4

De-escalation Strategy and Response Power

Introduction

The most prominent contemporary example of a liberal democracy hardening its security arrangements and chasing adversaries in the grey zone after a surprise attack on its sovereignty is the United States. The unprecedented 9/11 attacks stunned the US Federal Bureau of Investigation [FBI], Central Intelligence Agency [CIA], Federal Aviation Agency, and Department of Defense.[269] The US Government and its agencies had not expected this type of attack. To 'harden' for the future, the 9/11 Commission Report recommended that:

> long-term success [against terrorism] demands the use of all the elements of national power: intelligence, diplomacy, law enforcement, covert action, economic policy, foreign aid, public diplomacy, and homeland defense.[270]

While not declaring a strategy, the report acknowledged the requirement for the coordinated use of 'all elements of national power'. It recognised that the US homeland had become a battlespace. The implication was that countering their adversaries required hardened, agile and well-coordinated responses at home and abroad. Though not declared in this way at the time, the United States was enhancing its detection, deterrence and response capabilities to prosecute the War on Terror in the grey zone. Notably, the United

269 Kean, TH, Hamilton, LH, Ben-Veniste, R, Kerrey, B, Fielding, FF, Lehman, JF, Gorelick, JS, Roemer, TJ, Gorton, S, & Thompson, JR, 2004. *The 9–11 Commission' Report*, p. 346

270 Ibid., p. 96

States combined 22 different federal departments and agencies into a unified, integrated Department of Homeland Security [DHS] in 2002. In 2005 the government simplified the DHS to comprise Border and Transportation Security, Emergency Preparedness and Response and Information Analysis and Infrastructure Protection.[271]

The United States sharpened its instruments for both creating deterrence and striking at terrorist networks at home and abroad. The US Government enhanced the capabilities of the FBI and the CIA, and Special Forces to ensure that there were 'ultimate sanctions' for terrorism at home and abroad. In effect, the United States created sufficient deterrence and de-escalation capabilities at home with the Department of Homeland Security and the FBI and abroad with Special Forces and the CIA to counter terrorist networks and insurgents in the grey zone.

Australia has not endured a galvanising attack like 9/11 or horrific bombings like those in Britain and Europe in the 2010s. Australian Governments have responded reflexively and incrementally to micro-9/11s, such as the 2014 Lindt Café Siege and the 2017 Brighton Motel Siege and other 'lone wolf' incidents in Melbourne and Sydney and the deaths of Australians in overseas terror attacks in Bali, London and Bagdad.[272] Australia's legislative and institutional responses to people smuggling and border security prompted its own consolidation of security agencies into the Department of Home Affairs. Australian Special Forces joined their American and British counterparts in the Middle East for the War on Terror in 2001 and were still serving there in 2021.

I am not advocating following American precedents for the War on Terror for an Australian de-escalation strategy in the grey zone. Australia does not need national security instruments akin to the FBI and the CIA. Australia can enhance existing Departmental and agency structures to align authority, responsibility, accountability and resources astutely to strengthen institutional law enforcement,

---

271 US Department of Homeland Security, 'Organisation Chart', DHS website

272 Turnbull, M, 2017, 'National Security Statement', and Turnbull, M, 2017, 'A Strong and Secure Australia', transcript

intelligence and military machinery. I propose a whole-of-government de-escalation strategy for a bullied middle power to stand up to a bullying superpower but avoid war. It is a strategy for returning China and Australian relations to mutual respect and free and fair trading arrangements.

De-escalation

The counter-grey zone strategy I propose is de-escalation – a fair and firm assertion of Australia's sovereignty and values, and a means for enabling regional allies to develop capabilities in the grey zone as well. The concept of de-escalation is not new. It is pro-active firm behaviour to prevent the escalation of competition to conflict. Generically, a de-escalation strategy is about proportional and lawful pre-emptive responses to coercion. The aim is to thwart escalation from non-violent political pressure to violent, disruptive and destructive intimidation and possibly war. More particularly, it is proportional and lawful employment of civil-military detection, deterrent, information and de-escalation capabilities to anticipate and counter the three phases of grey zone campaigns at home and abroad. It comprehends Australia's middle power capabilities, existing instruments of national power, Australian values and traditions and a foundation of mature counter-terrorism arrangements, both at home and in the near region. It is mindful of Australia's trading relationship with China and the mutual obligations of its alliance with the United States, and relationships with regional neighbours.

My de-escalation strategy aims to cause CPC hardliners to have second thoughts and encourage CPC moderates and China's corporations to argue for ending the so-called Wolf Warrior statecraft and returning to fair, respectful and equal relations with Australia based on mutually beneficial trade. This strategy contributes to Scenario 4 of CSBA's predictions for Chinese strategic trajectories, Macro-Singapore:

> a future where economic, social and political difficulties mount, but Xi Jinping moves decisively to alter the country's direction. He institutes far-reaching economic and social reforms, reduces the country's

> military and international footprint, and negotiates a genuinely co-operative partnership with the West.[273]

My de-escalation strategy comprehends one of the CSBA's conclusions:

> The Western allies need a planning system that can accommodate marked changes in China's trajectory. The need is for a mechanism [*de-escalation strategy*] that can detect and assess strategic changes in China promptly and link them directly to rapidly-paced Western countermeasures [*pacing*]. Devising and implementing such an alert and agile system [*Response Power*] is a primary 'front-end' challenge for allied defense and security planning.[274]

This new approach is not a replacement strategy. Australia's strategic posture based on geography, traditional priorities (homeland, region, world), and conventional deterrent military power is viable, albeit its full array of deterrent capabilities is more than a decade away. A de-escalation strategy counters grey zone campaigns while still complementing conventional military deterrence and supporting traditional military campaigns.

Detection and deterrence precede de-escalation. The tools for detection, deterrence and de-escalation are multi-agency civil-military taskforces. The strategy at home and in the near region extends counter-terrorism, counter-espionage and foreign interference arrangements. The need is for anticipatory grey zone legislation that authorises covert surveillance and forceful action on home soil. Australia would also partner with neighbours, who are uncomfortable with CPC grey zone coercion, to apply de-escalation customised to their circumstances and preferences. The ultimate deterrence and de-escalation dimensions of this strategy are simple. Australia must have the capabilities to take forceful action anywhere in the world and at any time to de-escalate threats in the grey zone. Intense political, diplomatic and informational engagement seeking rapprochement

---

273 Babbage, R, 2020, *Which Way the Dragon*: p. iii

274 Ibid., p. vi

accompanies the de-escalation process. It disappoints rather than provokes.

I propose a new mode of Australian national power to underpin this strategy. Imagining Australia's defence strategy as a chair, the advent of political and hybrid warfare in the grey zone leaves it with only three legs – maritime, land and air power. The fourth leg of Australia's defence strategy chair should be Response Power [see below]. It incorporates counter-cyber warfare and counter-information warfare capabilities and optimises civil-military security machinery for counterterrorism and counter foreign interference. It develops detection, deterrence and de-escalation capabilities to counter grey zone operations anywhere and anytime.

This de-escalation strategy builds on the Morrison Government's 2020 Strategic Update and Force Structure Plan. It complements promised enhancements to Australia's conventional military power and optimises precise and effective employment of those enhancements. Promises about meeting dangers in the grey zone are welcome. Still, they do not constitute a strategy. They are not prominent or specific enough to initiate empowering legislation, strategic guidance, capability development, changes to institutional machinery and doctrine for response options. My de-escalation strategy fills that gap.

This strategy responds to the current CPC grey zone campaign in Australia and its neighbourhood in the first instance. This campaign is not traditional statecraft. It is illegal, coercive and unacceptable. Hopefully, moderate CPC factions and China's corporate leaders will recognise, understand and grow to respect Australia's measured and lawful response. There can be a new era where Australia and China can deal with each other on equal and fair terms for mutual benefit. CPC hardliners must concede and accept Australia's separate existence as a liberal democracy and entitlements to its sovereign rights and alliance choices.

The strategy removes CPC's incentives or temptations to escalate darker grey hybrid warfare. While understanding that Australia must communicate carefully and diplomatically with one of its major trading partners, cyberattacks and espionage, political interference and intimidation of Australian citizens warrant more than firm condemnation. Australia must warn the CPC that there are hurtful consequences for bullying Australia. The messaging tone is disappointment, not anger, and intends to dissuade those seeking inappropriate influence. Australia seeks rapprochement, not retaliation. Ultimately, there is no point in being disappointed and issuing warnings without the capability to back them up with potent deterrent actions that hurt.

Intentions

The strategy defends against threats to national diplomatic, economic and political interests in whatever form they may take at home and abroad. Its Response Power dimension provides the ways and means for acquiring intelligence, enabling precise targeting and conducting preliminary disruptive operations and de-escalation actions if deterrence fails. It maintains Australia's non-nuclear policies for military capabilities while at the same time defending Australia against nuclear and other WMD threats by responding to them before they reach dangerous thresholds or imminent use.

This strategy's front line is 'anywhere', and the readiness level is 'anytime'. The aim is to engage threats 'upstream' overseas rather than risk surprises 'downstream' at home. Detection, forward deterrence and de-escalation modalities apply. It offsets reliance on the projection of conventional military force or dependence on allies to respond to international threats similar to Australia's. In effect, it gives Australia a sovereign option to shape, understand and influence operating environments across the competition, conflict and warfare spectrum overseas where threats are in different stages of development. This approach accords with the 2020 Strategic Update's emphasis on shaping and enhancing deterrent capabilities further from Australia's homeland.

This strategy complements collaboration with allies. It enables Australia to join partners in operations below the threshold of limited war in the grey zone to protect the rules-based global order and de-escalate potential conventional or nuclear war threats. In effect, it gives a proper strategic context to Australia's Special Forces and RAN and RAAF participation with the United States and other allies.

Most importantly, it gives authority and direction for developing and employing unique whole-of-government capabilities to counter grey zone campaigns, hopefully before they escalate from light grey to darker grey violent and destructive hybrid warfare tactics.

Force is the last resort. Australian legislation, the Laws of War, the Geneva Conventions and human rights conventions bound this strategy. Australia is a liberal democracy founded on respect for human life and the rule of law. Lethal and destructive force is not the first or the only option. The emphasis is on prevention, protection and deterrence. It is a graduated response process that 'paces' the shades of grey lawfully. Intense diplomatic and political engagement to find peaceful consensus as a better alternative accompany each step towards the possibility of applying lethal force. While regretting the requirement to develop Response Power, it is a strategy that does not shirk from forcefulness. The intention is to detect and disrupt threats in the making. If deterrence and disruption fail, de-escalation will hurt.

This strategy's hardening of Australian society against all forms of illegal coercion does not require ethical compromises. But Australian governments must take decisive action in response to coercive intentions and activities. It is a firm response to 'rude and nasty' behaviour, such as espionage, political interference and intimidating Australian citizens in their own country. It will involve lethal force if those seeking to dominate Australia show that they are taking things further and considering violent and destructive options, including softening up before war.

Instruments and modalities

The strategy hardens Australia's multi-jurisdictional security arrangements to counter foreign espionage, interference, and terrorism. It requires the extension of current security legislation to authorise multi-agency teams from several levels of government to meet complex grey zone challenges, especially those appearing on Australian soil. A coalition of government departments and agencies, already working together for counter-terrorism, will conduct military, law enforcement, cyber and informational operations anywhere and anytime simultaneously or sequentially.

The aim is to generate strategic pressure and opportunity. The means are sophisticated asymmetric methods that are more politically, diplomatically and culturally astute than conventional military action. This multi-domain pressure de-escalates a nation's or sub-national group's coercion as well as their threatened use of more intimidation, such as terrorist actions, civil disorder and cyber-attacks. Consequently, the strategy minimises casualties, provocation and other negative consequences of conventional military action.

De-escalation closer to the threshold of war includes intimidatory, disruptive, and coercive action domains. Traditional law enforcement and military operations at sea, on land and in the air are no longer sufficient. Australia must have the ways and means to counter the CPC's asymmetric and technological capabilities for the grey zone. These modalities include cyber, space and all information technologies and forms of information operations, and the employment of autonomous and remote-controlled weapon systems as they evolve and are suited to de-escalation contingencies.[275]

Cycle and modalities

The de-escalation cycle includes detection, 'staring', analysis, decision, communication and action. The detection instrument is the NIC. Depending on the level of danger, Special Forces, law enforcement agencies and intelligence services then 'stare' at existing and emerging threats via covert surveillance and reconnaissance at home, near region and internationally. The deterrence instrument is the existence of 'always-on' sophisticated and ominously described coercive and strike capabilities. Deterrence modalities are well-crafted political, societal and diplomatic communications and negotiations to influence the attitudes of adversaries and create dilemmas, wicked problems and Catch 22s for them.

Modalities are intelligence-led and carefully calibrated forceful actions. They aim to achieve surprise, shock and strategic de-escalation

---

275 Strawser, BJ, 2010, 'Moral Predators', pp. 342–68, Sparrow, R, 2011, 'Robotic Weapons and the Future of War', pp. 117–33, and Taft, E, 2017, 'Outer Space: The Final Frontier or the Final Battlefield?'

effects. Importantly, they are always accompanied by intense political and diplomatic engagement seeking mutually beneficial agreement. De-escalation is about constraint, not containment, and diplomatic and political engagement, not exclusion or isolation.

Information operations are integral modalities for de-escalation. The ability to gain the initiative and win in the grey zone rests upon quickly achieving information dominance. This dominance, in turn, requires the ability to collect, manage, and exploit accurate information more rapidly than anyone else. This modality must 'outpace' competitors and adversaries inside the international system. There are two dimensions. The first is to enhance and support 'hurtful stings' with rapid information dissemination. The second is to degrade and constrain an adversary's information dissemination capabilities. The 'battle of the narratives' and for the Electro-Magnetic Spectrum is about understanding, shaping and influencing the decisions of governments and the attitudes of populations. The nation that can change international public opinion and perceptions has an enormous advantage.

De-escalation ways and means are pre-meditated, carefully-calibrated 'stings' rather than expedient conventional military retaliation that could be interpreted as acts of war. There will be political pressure to placate an angry electorate after provocations, such as a damaging cyberattack, a suspicious death or a terrorist incident, but conventional military retaliation risks miscalculation and severe escalation. Stinging is about surprise and deception, but stings only occur after fair warning about uncomfortable consequences for unreasonable behaviour. Stinging hurts adversaries and bolsters deterrence in the first instance. Initial stings may be the public exposure of a plot, arrest and detention of operatives or a raid on a facility accompanied by publicity to optimise the exposure of illegality. As a last resort, a sting may cause loss of life and destruction. Still, it must always come after an adversary is about to take, or has taken, Australian lives and destroyed Australian property. Even in these circumstances, there should be a fair warning and an invitation to negotiate unless surprise and safety are paramount.

De-escalation in Australia's near region

Continuing the idea of hurtful 'stinging' to get attention and return to negotiations, de-escalation in the near region has its own 'stinging' concept. The Singaporean statesman Lew Kuan Yew's prescriptions in the mid-20th Century for deterring larger Asian powers from interfering in Singaporean affairs and seeking to annex the tiny island state can apply to Australia and its neighbours in the 21st Century. Ironically he drew on a Chinese proverb when he said at a conference in 1966 that:

> In a world where the big fish eat small fish, and small fish eat shrimps, Singapore must become a poisonous shrimp. ... There are various types of shrimps. Some shrimps stay alive...Species in nature develop defence mechanisms. Some shrimps are poisonous: they sting. If you eat them, you will get digestive upsets.'[276]

An attendee at the conference asked what he meant in the context of Singapore's dependence on commercial relations with its 'big fish' neighbours, China, Malaysia and Indonesia. He replied, '... our separate existence having been accepted and conceded, we then deal with them on equal and fair terms'.[277]

My de-escalation strategy has the objective of Australia and its neighbours dealing with China on equal and fair terms as long as China respects their sovereignty. Arguably, this would be a position the CPC would be comfortable with if its intentions for Australia and its neighbourhood were benign. If the CPC persists with grey zone strategies for intimidating neighbours to become tribute states, Australia and its regional allies should develop defensive capabilities to become 'poisonous shrimp'. Their military-civilian taskforces would challenge and stand up to CPC interference and intimidation figuratively with 'stings' and 'unpalatable digestive processes'. Governments would calibrate stings to get attention and invite more effective dialogue for rapprochement. The aim is to avoid sufficient

---

276 Singapore Government, 'Transcript of a talk given by the Prime Minister'
277 Ibid.

provocation for retaliatory conventional military action. Once again, the objective is to disappoint and dissuade, not retaliate and provoke. In short, the CPC is prosecuting a grey zone strategy. It is logical and understandable for those nations the CPC is coercing to have a counter-grey zone strategy.

The conceptual framework for regional de-escalation

I am attracted to Ross Babbage's strategic prescriptions of 'partnership and leverage' and former DFAT Secretary Peter Varghese's policy guide rails of 'engage and constrain' for implementing a regional de-escalation strategy.[278] Babbage states,

> At its core, the strategy of partnership and leverage would also substantially enhance deterrence and defensive capabilities against any attempt to coerce or attack … [It] offers powerful leverage to deter regional bullying and force any aggressor to cease operations and quickly come to reasonable terms.[279]

Peter Varghese opines,

> [The question is] how to deal with a China that is not interested in reaching mutually agreed rules. What do we do then? That is why I think we cannot have an honest narrative which does not also canvass the need to constrain China's unacceptable behaviour through some *new balancing arrangement* [author's emphasis] which sits side by side with [continuing] engagement. To think we can leave it with striving for mutual agreement on rules leaves us open to being seen as naïve.[280]

My de-escalation strategy combines Babbage's and Varghese's

---

278 Babbage, R, 2015, *Game Plan: The Case for a New Australian Grand Strategy*, pp. 66–71 and Varghese, P, 2020, 'How to best manage our relationship with Beijing', p. 20

279 Ibid., p. 71

280 Varghese, P, 2019, 'A new China narrative for Australia Submission by Peter Varghese'

realistic deterrence prescriptions with existing Australian efforts to strengthen political, economic, defence and border security relationships with regional neighbours. The focus would be on enhancing regional capabilities to resist external interference and coercion. This prescription would build on the mutually beneficial partnerships the AFP have formed with neighbours for thwarting terrorism and transnational crime, such as drug, arms and people trafficking. The RAN cooperates with neighbours for border protection and surveillance of Economic Exclusion Zones, and there are other Defence regional engagement programs. These engagement programs are a foundation for de-escalation – a complementary strategy, not a replacement.

Modalities for regional de-escalation

Australia's strengthened partnership arrangements would include a range of modalities. They would consist of specialised consulting services related to countering political and hybrid warfare, the supply of critical technologies and systems interoperable with Australia's security and intelligence agencies, assistance with education and training and many other activities.[281] This de-escalation strategy echoes Varghese's prescription:

> Constraining the PRC [People's Republic of China] is not a call for a grand anti-PRC military alliance. Indeed, some of the members of this group [of Australia's regional neighbours] are allergic to the very idea of alliances. Rather, it is a means of managing the PRC's ambitions in a way that puts constraints on how far Beijing is prepared and allowed to go. It signals that leverage is a two-way street. .... Constraining the PRC will require a new strategic equilibrium in the Indo-Pacific. It will take time to construct. It will operate in the space between alliances and consultation. Collective pushback – when needed.[282]

---

281 Babbage, R, 2015, *Game Plan*, pp. 66–67

282 Varghese, P, 2019, 'What should Australia do to manage risk in its relationship with the PRC?'

Babbage focuses on an aggregation of regional conventional military power to deter the CPC from applying traditional military force. Varghese emphasises collective demonstrations of military resolve and diplomatic effort. I posit that CPC hardliners wish to win without fighting and take offence at an aggregation of conventional military power in its desired sphere of influence. Moreover, they will use this approach to justify more expenditure on traditional military capabilities – a possible arms race to war.

The imaginative development and employment of regional Response Forces trained by and partnered with the Australian Response Force will create potent de-escalation forces for deterring the CPC's light grey Phase 1 and Phase 2 campaign. If a Phase 2 escalation occurs, Australia's Strike Force can assist. Figuratively speaking, the Chinese big fish swimming in the Indo-Pacific region will find it uncomfortable to digest schools of unpalatable stinging shrimps.

My recommendations for regional engagement are not new. The idea of responding anywhere and anytime in the company of allies originated in Australia's initial National Counter-Terrorism Plan in 2001 and is present in the 4th Edition 2017 Plan:

> The AIC [Australian Intelligence Community] and the AFP maintain overseas liaison channels to gather intelligence and to pursue investigations. ASIO and the AFP also maintain a 24-hour monitoring and alert unit. Relevant Commonwealth agencies provide the interface with overseas security, intelligence and police agencies as part of international counter-terrorism efforts. Defence contributes to the prevention of terrorism through its overseas operations by disrupting a primary source of, and inspiration for, terrorist activities worldwide.[283]

It specified a targeted and deliberate enabling plan with regional counter-terrorism forces. It also committed Australia to liaison and burden-sharing with countries that reluctantly host trans-national terror groups due to a lack of adequate or capable security services

283 Australian New Zealand Counter-Terrorism Committee 2017, p. 19, pp. 23–24

to eject them from their sovereign territory. In effect, the Australian Government has always authorised its Special Forces to target terrorist groups in their foreign sanctuaries in conjunction with allies and local civil and military authorities. This authorisation was an essential precedent for countering terrorists 'up-stream' rather than 'down-stream' at an endpoint in Australia where their destructive plans might be too late to stop. How Americans would have rejoiced had their Special Forces intercepted and neutralised those who perpetrated 9/11 ' upstream'.

Australia should continue its 'upstream' approach to countering terrorism anywhere and anytime by assisting regional neighbours to harden up against grey zone campaigns. The answer is to export Australia's de-escalation strategy. It follows traditional strategic prescriptions of affording Australia's neighbourhood a high priority for Australia's defence after defending the homeland first. The logic is that countering a grey zone campaign in the near region protects Australia, and what defends Australia in the grey zone should assist in defending its neighbourhood.

Ethical Responses

Solid moral and ethical messages accompany the de-escalation strategy. It is incumbent on a liberal democracy like Australia to declare its intentions to de-escalate coercive and illegal threats against its national interests with force. Australia is employing its armed forces and law enforcement and intelligence agencies lawfully in compliance with international laws on armed conflict and human rights.[284] The Attorney General must scrutinise all actions under the Human Rights (Parliamentary Scrutiny) Act 2011.[285] The Laws of Armed Conflict incorporated into the 1949 Geneva Conventions, especially Common Article 3 that covers situations of non-international armed conflicts, must apply. Also applicable is the International Covenant on Civil and Political Rights and the

---

284 International Committee of the Red Cross, *The Geneva Conventions of 1949 and their Additional Protocols*

285 Australian Parliament 2011, 'Human Rights (Parliamentary Scrutiny) Act 2011'

Convention Against Torture and Other Cruel, Inhuman or Degrading Treatment or Punishment.[286]

The strategy is carefully calibrated to be below the threshold of war. It is like a cocked fist. Its stinging jabs are a last resort in the face of the threat of force or other warlike actions. It responds to coercive acts that will cause harm to Australian citizens directly or indirectly through the destruction or disruption of essential services and economic activity. Before and after every jab, there is an invitation to talk. It admires the boxer Muhammad Ali's boast, 'Float like a butterfly, sting like a bee. The hands can't hit what the eyes can't see.'

Response Power

Response Power underpins the de-escalation strategy structurally with detection, information, deterrence and de-escalation pillars. The National Intelligence Community (NIC) is the detection pillar. Home Affairs and DFAT are the national and international information and negotiation pillars. Response and Strike forces [see below] are the deterrence and de-escalation pillars. Response power is ready for action anywhere and anytime.

Pillars of Response Power		
Detection	Information Negotiation	Deterrence De-escalation
National Intelligence Community	DFAT Home Affairs	Response Force Strike Force
Anywhere and Anytime		

Response Power is a spectrum of responses to detect, pace and counter an escalating grey zone campaign through the three generic phases of a grey zone campaign. It has law enforcement, diplomatic and military instruments that rely on the NIC to detect threats. It is founded on

286 Australian Human Rights Commission, 2020, 'International Covenant on Civil and Political Rights', Australian Human Rights Commission 2020, 'Convention against Torture and Other Cruel, Inhuman and Degrading Treatment or Punishment'

prevention rather than provocation and de-escalation rather than retaliation. Response Power integrates with Australia's diplomatic, informational, military and economic power. It intends to give firm and fair consequences for coercive behaviour against Australia's sovereignty and national interests. It upholds liberal democratic values and the rule of law but is potent if negotiation and deterrence fail and forceful de-escalation is required.

The instrument for deterrence and de-escalation for Phase 1 is a Home Affairs AFP Response Force to counter a light grey zone campaign operating well below the military threshold of coercion. A called-out Special Forces begins collaboration and rehearsal with Response Force as threats and actions transition to darker grey tactics in Phase 2. Now called out and engaged, Special Forces counter a Phase 3 dark grey zone campaign that is about to escalate to and possibly exceed a military, warlike threshold of coercion. Response Power coalesces with Australia's military maritime, land and air power should the Australian Government deem an adversary's coercive action is an act of war requiring the mobilisation and employment of military force in defence of Australia and national interests.

Response Power, underpinned nationally and regionally by Response Force and internationally by a new Foreign Affairs Strike Force, is the practical extension of the 2020 Strategic Update's concepts of shape, deter and respond. They add hardened law enforcement, diplomatic and military capabilities in the grey zone for Australia's national security. Response Power both paces and responds to Phase 1, 2 and 3 of an escalating grey zone campaign. What needs to be done?

Phase 1

Australia already has Phase 1 Response Power in place. A required enhancement is establishing a Special Forces-like Home Affairs AFP Response Force that integrates Counter-Terrorism and Special Investigations Command with Specialist Protective Command and builds on the existing AFP Special Response Group.[287] Response

287 See Australian Federal Police website, www.afp.gov.au/about-us/our-organisation

Force would collaborate with Border Force and the NIC, particularly ASIO, to detect grey zone threats on Australia's sovereign territory and near region and maintain surveillance. It would deter threats to lives and property, arrest and detain suspects, and de-escalate threats forcefully if deterrence fails and violence is imminent. This realignment of Home Affairs responsibilities, authority, accountability and resources for countering Phase 1 of a grey zone campaign includes taking over responsibilities for Australia's counterterrorism responses on home soil.

The NIC, especially ASIS, detects and can disrupt light-grey, non-violent threats overseas with intelligence diplomacy. Australian intelligence officers overseas are armed for self-defence but are prohibited from armed response operations. Consequently, ASIS can only deter and de-escalate Phase 1 threats overseas non-violently.

Phase 2

Phase 2 Response Power is about clenching and cocking the Special Forces fist if a grey zone campaign escalates towards political violence for the homeland and near region. The government would call out Special Forces for interdepartmental planning and joint operations with Response Force. This call-out does not begin liaison and cooperation; it builds on habitual collaboration and rehearsal between the two forces that comply with Constitutional prescriptions. Enhancing the AFP's Specialist Response Group to become a Response Force for homeland duties in conjunction with Special Forces in Phase 2 extends current counter-terrorism arrangements.

While there is an option for ASIS to detect and for Special Forces to deter and de-escalate in Phase 2 overseas, the use of military force during this Phase risks provocation and further escalation. There is also an appearance of retaliation rather than de-escalation accompanied by invitations to negotiate. Also, giving Australia's Special Forces more to do overseas in Phase 2 is an expedient solution that repeats past mistakes. The time has come for creating an ASIS Strike Force that integrates intelligence diplomacy with painful consequences for contemplating escalation to violence and destruction.

Phase 3

If Phase 2 deterrence fails in the homeland and near region, Response Force and Special Forces conduct forceful Phase 3 countermeasures against grey zone combatants in a final effort to deter war. Ultimately, if the de-escalation strategy fails and war is imminent, Australia will mobilise and deploy the ADF, including its Special Forces, hopefully in the company of powerful allies.

For Phase 3, Strike Force will refocus its operations on optimising strategic effects and deter sponsors of grey zone campaigns overseas. The stakes are high because Phase 3 hybrid warfare can be a precursor to conventional warfare. Phase 3 strike operations forcibly gather intelligence, arm third parties and pre-position strike teams that will now include Special Forces in anticipation of ultimate lethal sanctions for an adversary's political elite and their economic interests.

Conclusions

In one of the more eventful weeks in Australia-China communications at the end of April 2021, 'the Morrison Government terminated Victoria's controversial Belt and Road Initiative deal with China, Defence Minister Peter Dutton declared that a war with China over Taiwan 'should not be discounted', Homeland Security Secretary, Mike Perzullo delivered a resonating speech [on Anzac Day] about the 'beating drums of war', and Prime Minister Scott Morrison announced an upgrade of the Northern Territory's training ranges in a move widely viewed as a response to China's military build-up. Alan Dupont opined, 'Feigned indignation, authoritarian self-righteousness and threatened retribution were China's all too familiar responses, underlying the depths to which the relationship has sunk and the difficulty of engaging a regime that relentlessly asserts its secular infallibility.'[288]

The common thread for me is that Australia has no strategy or plan except to increase conventional military deterrence and rely on the US alliance amidst this steady decline in Sino–Australian relations and talk

---

288 Dupont, A, 2021, 'China strategy: Get a bigger stick with which to protect ourselves'

of war. Metaphorically, Australia cannot afford a bigger stick to protect itself and should not rely entirely on America's big stick or 'shouting' at China's actions or inactions indignantly. Arguably, the CPC response to every Australian escalation of its conventional military power provokes the CPC and leaves CPC hardliners in a stronger position than moderates. Australia will always be 'out-escalated' by China in a conventional war. Australia has no war prevention strategy to get the attention of the CPC hardliners and force them to have second thoughts. Australia can only express disappointment without a de-escalation strategy if the CPC escalates its grey zone campaign with more severe actions than trade embargos and Wolf Warrior intimidation.

My proposed de-escalation strategy is a war preventer rather than a war provoker. International relations in the 21st Century oscillate between cooperation, competition and conflict. China and Australia have enjoyed decades of economic collaboration in the past. The challenge is to deter escalation from competition to conflict and return relations between Australia and China to pre-2014 cooperation. Australia's sovereign responsibility in the grey zone is not for the United States to broker.

There is a need to go back to the drawing board to develop ways and means that are affordable and depend on more ingenuity rather than more Australian firepower. Australia already has the foundations to build a de-escalation strategy to pace and counter the three phases of an escalating grey zone campaign. It is not a strategy for taking a knife to a gunfight. It is a strategy for making the gunfight unnecessary.

The gap in Phase 3 Response Power is that Australia does not have 'joined-up' whole-of-government capabilities to oppose hybrid warfare. There is no integrated force for countering Phase 3 hybrid operations. This challenge is new and complex. Australia has no history or institutional arrangements to deal with coercion that astutely manifests between Home Affairs and Defence department jurisdictions and their responsibilities for national security. Australia has no strategy or practised capabilities to counter a range of military and non-military actions orchestrated in unison to undermine the Australian population and coerce political concessions. The time has come to create a new Strike Force in the Foreign Affairs portfolio customised for de-escalation overseas and a Home Affairs Response Force for de-escalation at home and in the near region.

Let's look at the ways and means for building Response Force and Strike Force on current legislative and organisational foundations.

Part 4 – New national security instruments for the grey zone

CHAPTER 5

The ways and means of de-escalation

Introduction

Peter Mattis, a former CIA analyst and Fellow at Jamestown University, summarises the challenge for Australia and its allies in the grey zone thus:

> The key issue is political will. Knowledge [of a CPC grey zone campaign] may be present, and a number of individuals or bureaucracies may be building their understanding. Creating the tools for countering CPC interference are one thing; using them effectively is something completely different.[289]

Robert Mark, the founding father of the AFP and Australia's counter-terrorism arrangements capabilities, was right in 1978 to advise that there is a critical choice. Liberal democracies have to decide 'sooner or later' when to apply 'the ultimate sanction of force' against 'attempts ... to prevent government by consent or to usurp the function of government'.[290]

Part 1 The Threat (Chapters 1 and 2) explains what Australia should be afraid of and why. Part 2 Responding to the threat (Chapter 3) discusses what is being done about it and identifies a gap in Australia's deterrence and de-escalation capabilities. Part 3 Dealing with the threat (Chapters 4 and 5) outlines a de-escalation strategy and underpinning Response Power to close these gaps. In this chapter, I argue for an AFP Response Force and an ASIS Strike Force pacing and de-escalating the three phases of an escalating grey zone campaign, in

289 Mattis, P, 2018, 'Testimony before the U.S.–China Economic and Security Review Commission'

290 Department of Administrative Services, Mark, R, 1978, *Report to the Minister for Administrative* p. 19

addition to the traditional roles of the ADF's Special Forces at home and abroad. In Parts 4 and 5, I will describe the attributes of these new national security instruments and the steps required to build them.

Horses for courses – AFP Response Force and an ASIS Strike Force

The saying 'horses for courses' alludes to an aphorism that horses will perform more effectively on courses they are familiar with and suited to their attributes. Another maxim is 'Stick to the knitting' that Tom Peters and Robert Waterman popularised in their best-selling book on management *In Search of Excellence*.[291] These aphorisms instruct that organisations perform well when optimised for specific and well-defined roles. I will make 'horses for courses' and 'stick to the knitting' arguments for optimising arrangements for deterrence in the grey zone based on having credible, ready and 'always-on' 'hurtful' de-escalation response capabilities.

I hypothesise that the AFP and the NIC, the Home Affairs instruments for a Response Force, are the 'horses for courses' for the homeland and near region grey zone operations. The new requirement is for a secret ASIS Strike Force designed to create sufficient deterrence internationally to deescalate before the military threshold for war is reached. Special Forces, Defence instruments, are the 'horses for courses' as an ultimate deterrent and sanction 'anywhere and anytime', but only when the military threshold is approaching, and war is inevitable.

In my opinion, the immutable separation of Federal and State and Territory jurisdictions and creating the Home Affairs portfolio means that it is more efficient, effective, and less provocative to assign the deterrence and de-escalation of Phases 1 and 2 grey zone escalations to Home Affairs. It is more effective and efficient for Home Affairs to enforce grey zone legislation related to espionage, foreign interference, and counterterrorism legislation. This consolidation of homeland responsibilities, authority, accountability and resources leave Strike Force and Special Forces free to counter a Phase 3 grey zone escalation anywhere and anytime. The creation of an intelligence-led Strike Force

291 Peters, T and Waterman, R, 2006, *In Search of Excellence*

deters in the grey zone. It enhances Special Forces capabilities to support ADF joint operations after war is declared, in the tradition of Special Operations Australia during the Pacific War (discussed later).

The legislative basis for Response Force and Strike Force

There is an immutable separation of powers and jurisdictions for national security in Australia. The Commonwealth of Australia is a federation of States and Territories with a constitution that assigns its sovereignty against military attack to the Federal Government and the Department of Defence. It entrusts homeland security and domestic law enforcement to collaboration between the Federal Government and State and Territory law enforcement agencies. The NIC works with all jurisdictions to detect threats to national security. In particular, ASIO works with Home Affairs to secure the Australian homeland and territories, and ASIS works with Foreign Affairs to protect national interests overseas. The Defence Intelligence Organisation supports Australian military operations before and after declaring war.

Response Force

The time has come for establishing a Response Force, built on the existing ASIO-AFP partnership, to take responsibility for counter-terrorist operations and deal with grey zone combatants operating in Australia and its territories. For three reasons, Robert Mark's 1978 prescriptions for employing SASR for counter-terrorism on Australian home soil are obsolete. The first reason is that Mark recommended establishing Australia's first national police force in 1978. There was no mature law enforcement option for counter-terrorism. In 2022 the AFP has Counter-Terrorism and Special Investigations Command, Specialist Protective Command, and the Specialist Response Group [SRG].[292] The SRG has the following role:

> The SRG provides the AFP with a professional, flexible and dynamic capability across three distinct operational areas. This includes

---

292 Australian Federal Police, 'Australian Federal Police Organisation Structure', AFP website

> assisting ACT Policing within the community, national support of the AFP's responsibilities and international support with capacity building missions and regional stability operations. The unique skills and flexibility of the SRG enables the AFP to maximise its response to diverse operations by tailoring deployments to meet a range of operational requirements.[293]

In 2022 the SRG has a full suite of specialist tactical responses to incidents: search and rescue and crisis, hostage and negotiation operations supported by a bomb response team and a maritime team backed by command, coordination and planning, extended capabilities, and communications response, logistics and tactical intelligence teams.[294]

The second reason is that Robert Mark was an Englishman influenced by the troubles in Northern Ireland in the 1970s. The British Government deployed regular Army units to occupy and protect Northern Ireland against the Provisional Irish Republican Army [IRA] and assist local police forces.[295] At the same time, the British SAS conducted clandestine and covert operations against the IRA in conjunction with intelligence agencies.[296] Mark wrote in his report:

> The soldier, in contrast to the policeman, is the embodiment of the ultimate sanction of force which is necessary to every government, even the most democratic, for protection from external attack or for dealing with revolutionary activities for which *the machinery of government by consent is inadequate* [author's emphasis]. A minority which attempts by armed force to prevent government by consent or to usurp the function of government is engaging in revolutionary activity no matter what euphemisms it employs to describe its activities. If that minority is sufficiently large, sooner or later, it will be necessary to

---

293 Australian Federal Police, 'Specialist Response Group', AFP website

294 Ibid.

295 Dewar, M, 1985, *British Army in Northern Ireland*

296 Urban, M, 2012, *Big Boys' Rules: The SAS and the Secret Struggle Against the IRA.*

> decide whether the ultimate sanction of force rather than the ordinary democratic process of law is necessary to contain or suppress it.[297]

The Australian Government has enacted legislation to counter the 'external threat' of the CPC's grey zone campaign. The Department of Home Affairs has adequate 'machinery' for detecting 'revolutionary activity'. Arguably, the AFP's Counter-Terrorism and Special Investigations Command, Specialist Protective Command, and the Specialist Response Group [SRG] constitute deterrence and are more than just the beginnings of de-escalation capabilities. These are the capabilities for a Response Force to operate effectively in the Australian homeland and near region to deter and de-escalate an escalating grey zone campaign.

Strike Force

Legislation relevant to call out of the ADF under the provision of the Defence Act of 1903, understandably, does not mention terrorism, the grey zone or a Strike Force. The Australian Constitution authorises the employment of military force on Australian soil, in sovereign air space and on and underwater after a call-out to defend sovereign territory and 'domestic violence' exceeding the capabilities of State and Territory authorities. In all cases, the context of call out in the spirit of the Constitution is to deal with domestic security situations beyond the capacity of civil authorities – a two-step process. A military attack, terrorism and civil disorder are three contexts for this support. These contexts apply in the grey zone. Thus, this body of legislation can be enhanced to include Strike Force but apply for International operations.

Australia had a body of legislation related to counter-terrorism, counter-espionage, foreign influence, and counter-cyber. The blending of this body of legislation and the Intelligence Services Act 2001 governs the roles of ASIS that provides the legislative basis for Strike Force. Hybrid warfare is steeped in the doctrines and techniques of terrorism. I equate terrorists with grey zone combatants. Their

297 Mark, R, 1978, *Report to the Minister for Administrative Services*, p. 54

objectives are to attack national interests through a range of violent acts. The Commonwealth Criminal Code Act 1995 facilitates the call out of military forces for employment against terrorists.[298] This Act is particularly relevant to the grey zone because it defines a 'terrorist act' and then uses this definition as the basis for codifying terrorism offences, proportional responses, and ADF call-out. This Act provides three criteria for defining a terrorist act:

> [an act must] include violence or the threat of violence; have the intention of advancing a political, religious or ideological cause; and be intended to coerce or intimidate a government as well as the public; or seriously disrupting trade, critical infrastructure or electronic systems.[299]

The Act also provides the authority for law enforcement to exercise specific coercive powers when dealing with terrorism offences.[300] Other Australian jurisdictions – such as New South Wales in the *Terrorism (Police Powers) Act 2002* and Victoria in the *Terrorism (Commonwealth Powers) Act 2003* – use the same definitions to provide additional police powers.[301] Section 119 of the Australian Constitution provides the context by which the Commonwealth may provide security assistance to States and Territories when requested by the latter 'against domestic violence'.[302] Part III AAA of the Australian Government's *Defence Act 1903* contains a mechanism for a 'call-out' of the ADF for domestic security operations in two contexts: protection of Commonwealth interests; and protection of States and self-governing Territories.

---

298 Parliament of Australia, 1995, 'Criminal Code Act 1995, Australian Government, Canberra', p. 183

299 Ibid., p. 183

300 Parliament of Australia, 1995, Criminal Code Act 1995, Australian Government, Divisions, pp. 104–05

301 New South Wales Government, 2002, *Terrorism (Police Powers) Act 2002 No 115* and Western Australian Government, 2008, *Billing v The State of Western Australia*, State of Victoria 2010, *R v Vinayagamoorthy & Ors. VSC 148*, 31 March, Melbourne and State of Victoria 2012, *R v O'Brien and Hudson*

302 Parliament of Australia, 1901, The Constitution, Australian Government

Call out gives coercive powers to mobilised military forces. The same legislation should give coercive powers to Response Force and Strike Force, organisations designed for national and international defence in the grey zone. Response Force enhances the existing partnership between ASIO and the AFP and for the future with Strike Force, which gives ASIS additional capability to de-escalate forcefully in the grey zone 'anywhere and anytime', but primarily overseas. These powers may include authority to recapture locations/things, end acts of violence and protect persons; powers to protect designated critical infrastructure; and general security area powers including search, control of movement and detention. The Defence Amendment Bill 2018 streamlined these call-out mechanisms.[303] This amendment facilitates more proactive Commonwealth support to States/Territories, among other modifications. Defence call-out arrangements are provided in Defence Regulation 2016, although these are mainly consistent with Part III AAA of the Defence Act 1903.[304]

State and Territory authorities should still rely on Special Forces to respond to hostile groups' coercive and destructive actions and their planning for and then prosecuting a hybrid war. In this context, State and Territory law enforcement agencies would be first responders to politically motivated coercive and destructive acts. Even with heavily-armed special weapons assault squads, lightly-armed law enforcement agencies may not be a match for armed grey zone combatants that may include another nation's Special Forces. Indeed, those adversaries may target law enforcement agencies to unsettle the public and erode their confidence in the government's ability to protect them. But this level of threat will have reached or is about to reach a military intervention threshold that triggers the employment of Special Forces anyway. Well before this threshold, Response Force will have been at work deterring and de-escalating threats to enable more substantial negotiations for de-escalating the CPC's grey zone campaign.

My argument is that employing Special Forces against grey zone combatants that may behave like terrorists is too much too early if

---

303 Parliament of Australia, 2018, *Call Out of the Australian Defence Force Bill 2018*

304 Australian Government, 2016, *Defence White Paper*

the intention is to de-escalate a grey zone campaign in the Australian homeland or overseas. Let's do a 'reality check'. Firstly, it was never beyond law enforcement agencies to de-escalate terrorist attacks in Australia in recent years. If they were trained for the counter-terrorist role, law enforcement agencies could handle the 2014 Lindt Café Siege in Sydney and Brighton Siege in 2017. In collaboration with State and Territory police, the AFP has pre-emptively neutralised the number of terrorist threats with raids and arrests.

The Lindt Café Siege, which occurred over two days in December 2014, is Australia's most notorious contemporary example of a 'lone wolf' barricade hostage terrorist act. It was not the first 'lone wolf' incident in 2014. Three months before, on 23 September 2014, an 18-year-old Australian of Afghan descent, Abdul Numan Haider, a Daesh/ISIS devotee, attacked several police officers with a knife outside a police station in Sydney before police killed him in self-defence. No need for Special Forces. Haider's frenzied attack during a pre-arranged meeting did not attract enough public interest to warrant a more specific investigation into counter-terrorism arrangements.

This passing interest was not the case for Man Haron Monis, another Daesh/ISIS devotee and the perpetrator of the Lindt Café siege. Andrew Shearer, the former National Security Adviser to Prime Minister Tony Abbott, observed in December 2014, 'What we saw that night [at the Lindt Café] was that the seam between the Commonwealth response and the State response was a critical point of weakness'.[305] He was right up to a point. The fundamental weakness was that NSW Police commanders and their special weapons assault squads trained and rehearsed to de-escalate domestic siege incidents. They did not train for acting decisively against a terrorist, albeit a 'home-grown-self-made' one, who was not a proficient armed member of a terrorist organisation. There is no point in offering a 'What if' argument. The reality was that the NSW squad did not have the technology, training and rehearsal regime for a terrorist incident because Special Forces had that responsibility.

There has been sufficient political will after each terrorist attack to

305 Snow, D, 2018a, 'Abbott offered Army Commandos to help resolve Lindt Siege'

harden counter-terrorism laws and enhance institutional machinery that began after the 1978 Hilton Hotel bombing in Sydney. The Turnbull Government initiated a review of Defence's support to national counter-terrorism arrangements in 2016 for the first time since 2005 in response to the Lindt Café siege and the changing nature of the threat demonstrated in recent terrorist attacks around the world.[306] Commendably, Australia's counter-terrorism arrangements had detected and ended several terrorist plots, but not before another Daesh-inspired lone wolf incident occurred in 2017. Again, this incident demonstrated that a two-step process did not work well when the threat to life was immediate. This time the Victorian police did not have the command-and-control system, or an assault team trained and equipped to take down terrorists.[307]

On 5 June 2017, two and a half years after the Lindt Café Siege, Somali-born, Yacqub Khayre, took a female escort hostage in a Brighton serviced apartment complex. He was on parole for an armed robbery offence but had been tried and acquitted of complicity in terrorist activities. He killed a clerk at the complex before police arrived. During the subsequent stand-off, he made references to al-Qa'ida and Daesh. He was shot to death by Victorian police during an exchange of fire that wounded three officers. There was speculation that Khayre's purpose had been to lure police into a siege situation and attempt to kill police in a suicide shoot-out – a tactic promoted by Daesh on social media.[308]

Might the Brighton siege outcome have been different, and risks mitigated had the incident been identified as a terrorist act earlier and Special Forces called out? After four inquiries, an expert panel made pertinent recommendations. It recommended 'reforms necessary to enhance the ability of relevant agencies and institutions to prevent,

306 Turnbull, M & Payne, M, 2017, 'The Hon Malcolm Turnbull Prime Minister & Senator the Hon Marise Payne Minister for Defence joint media release- Defence support to domestic Counter-Terrorism arrangements'

307 Australian Government, *Counter-Terrorism Legislation Amendment Bill (No. 1)*, para 19

308 State of Victoria 2017, 'Victorian Coroner's Inquest into the death of Yacqub Khayre'

investigate, monitor and respond to terrorist attacks.'[309] This panel called for expanding the legislated definition of a terrorist act beyond political, religion and ideology. It broadened the definition considering 'the changing nature of the terrorist threat – a threat which ranges from highly organised and structured major criminal organisations to the lone, disaffected, [fixated] but potentially deadly actor'.[310] It put less emphasis on determining motive, i.e., political, religious or ideological, to more focus on calibrating lethal force's use on intentions and imminent risk to life and property.

This broadening of the definition of a terrorist act to violent extremism had two effects in the grey zone. It theoretically enhanced the timeliness of having Special Forces stand-by at an incident site. It simplified the rules of engagement for applying lethal force to resolve an incident where the motives of the perpetrator or perpetrators were not apparent at the beginning.[311] This broadening of the definition thwarted deliberate efforts to disguise the perpetrators' motives and origins by a nation-state sponsoring terrorism as part of a deniable grey zone campaign.

In the wake of the Brighton Siege, there has been a renewed examination of Australia's counter-terrorism capabilities. There has also been a focus on the role of the ADF, primarily Special Forces, in these security crises instead of the AFP, State and Territory police forces.[312] In reality, Special Forces would not have resolved the Brighton Siege because the nearest Special Forces Terrorist Assault Team was in Sydney, not in Melbourne. The Victorian Police at the motel would still have had to go up their chain of command to the Police Minister, who would have had to ask the Minister of Home Affairs to approach the Minister for Defence to authorise the call out of Special Forces. The call-out would have required Prime Ministerial

---

309 State of Victoria 2017, 'Justice Assurance and Review Office's review of Corrections Victoria's management of Khayre (JARO Review)', Executive Summary

310 Ibid.

311 State of Victoria 2017, 'Expert Panel on Terrorism Report 2: The second report', Recommendation 14

312 Australian Federal Police 2014, *Annual Report, 2014–15*, p. 42

authorisation. Though there was ample time for Special Forces to be on the scene for the Lindt café Siege, the NSW police decided not to use SAS snipers for technical reasons and to execute their assault without Special Forces.

The ISIS-inspired attacks in Orlando, Brussels and Nice in 2016, as well as in London, Stockholm, Manchester, Paris, and New York in 2017, prompted Prime Minister Scott Morrison to announce in July 2017 that 'the Australian Defence Force will expand its role in assisting the States to respond to terrorist incidents.' As a part of this enhancement, the Government introduced legislation into the Federal Parliament to amend the Defence Act, 1903 to strengthen the types of support that the ADF can provide in the event of a call out to significant acts of 'domestic violence' [including terrorism].[313] This legislation facilitates the earlier deployment of Special Forces into terrorism scenarios such as those that prevailed at the Lindt Café and the Brighton motel.[314] This legislation did not assume that Special Forces should conduct an assault every time or as a first resort. But from then, both Federal and State officials had legislation to enable them to work with Special Forces on-site when presented with a future crisis. Notably, the Attorney-General explained in his second reading speech, '[It] removes any potential delay in seeking ministerial authorisation to act once an incident has taken place and enables the ADF to already be on the scene, ready to assist the police response.'[315]

These enhancements attempt to overcome the immutable separation of the Australian Constitution and Federal, State and Territory legislation and jurisdictions for timely responses to politically motivated violence and destruction. But the two-step process, geographic challenges for timely response, and the cultural and organisational separations of military and law enforcement remain. Defence may only assist civil authorities in emergencies under Defence Assistance to the Civil Community arrangements and Defence Force Aid to Civilian Authorities. This action only occurs when a specific

313 Parliament of Australia, 2018, *Call Out of the Australian Defence Force Bill 2018*

314 Australian Government, 2018, *Introduction of the Defence Amendment (Call Out of the Australian Defence Force) Bill 2018*

315 Porter, C, 2018, 'The Hon, Attorney-General, 'Second Reading Speech', p. 6

crisis is beyond the capabilities of the State and Territory authorities to resolve.[316]

Call out will always be a two-step process that must cross a cultural and operational military and law enforcement divide. Any perceived sub-optimal responses by NSW and Victorian police to 'lone wolf' terrorist acts in 2014 and 2017 had more to do with the unique and unexpected nature of those incidents and the police forces' lack of rehearsed roles and tasks for counter-terrorism than competence. Arguably, if the AFP and State and Territory police forces had responsibility, authority, accountability and resources for counter-terrorism, these incidents may have been resolved without police and civilian casualties. If the AFP had a forceful Response Force to counter any form of politically motivated violence and destruction in the grey zone, two-step processes would disappear.

Finally, it is better to employ the AFP that already works with ASIO and other members of the NIC routinely to deal with grey zone threats in the homeland and the near region during Phase 1 and 2 escalations. Building on this foundation is a proportional response for deterrence and de-escalation. The AFP and State and Territory police have similar cultures, training backgrounds and structures and collaborate habitually to maintain law and order. For the grey zone, they would come together for a common purpose with a clear understanding of their responsibilities, authority, accountability and resources. But they need harder 'grey zone' legislation to empower them for their new roles.

Law enforcement options are better for Phase 1 and 2 deterrence and de-escalation

Strike Force is Australia's answer to creating deterrence and de-escalation capabilities in the international grey zone. All grey zone threats come from overseas. The Foreign Affairs portfolio and ASIS are the 'horses for courses', and they can 'stick to the knitting' because they operate overseas routinely. Strike Force's priority would be to deter the use of Weapons of Mass Destruction [WMD] and cyber-attacks

316 Australian Government, 2017, *National Counter Terrorism Plan*, p. 35

against Australia. Preventing the use of WMD is an obvious priority, but deterring cyber-attacks is complex. The government identifies those who perpetrate cyberattacks designed to threaten the integrity, availability or confidentiality of digital information and their potential impacts thus:

> Nation-states and state-sponsored actors seek to compromise networks to obtain economic, policy, legal, defence and security information for their advantage. Nation-states and state-sponsored actors may also seek to *achieve disruptive or destructive effects* [author's emphasis] against their targets during peacetime or in a conflict setting. These actors tend to be sophisticated, well-resourced and patient adversaries, whose actions could impact Australia's national security and economic prosperity.

Arguably, illegal activities that aim to 'achieve disruptive or destructive effects' are akin to terrorist acts. If they are connected to a grey zone campaign, they could also be 'warlike' and politically motivated. It would seem reasonable for existing legislation that categorises terrorists based on their violent intent to extend to the grey zone. Political motives should also classify those perpetrating cyberattacks in the same way, i.e. politically motivated and destructive cyber terrorists. Following this logic, cyber terrorists, like their bomb-making kin, should become Strike Force targets overseas and Response Force targets if they operate maliciously on Australian soil.

The time has come to fully empower the Home Affairs portfolio to defend the homeland with an extension and integration of counter-terrorism, espionage and foreign interference legislation. The critical enhancement is to define what constitutes acts that warrant the application of proportional levels of detection, deterrence and forceful de-escalation. These definitions become the basis for identifying organisations and persons for surveillance and, if deterrence fails, targets for de-escalation.

AFP and ASIO raids in 2020 on the offices of a politician and one of his staff mentioned in Chapter 1 to gather evidence for possible action in the Courts is an appropriate response under new legislation against 'light grey' foreign interference. Existing legislation gave the AFP and ASIO the authority to intervene. For the grey zone, there needs to be legislation that articulates appropriate responses that pace light grey to dark grey tactics, from non-violent to violent. It would be reasonable for this 'grey zone' legislation to specify that organisations and persons preparing for, planning and executing cyberattacks intended to 'achieve disruptive or destructive effects' – arguably forms of terrorism – should become lawful targets for de-escalation.

Conclusions

In the future, an Australian Prime Minister can warn of severe consequences for not respecting Australia's sovereignty and the rights of its citizens. Currently, the Australian Government and its intelligence agencies can only express concern about cyberattacks, espionage and foreign interference, and intimidation of Australian citizens through malicious proxies living and working in Australia. In the future, Prime Ministers can refer to legislation and capabilities that anticipate and pace escalation of shades of grey from light to dark and authorise forceful responses if deterrence is not enough to compel China to return to cooperative mutually beneficial diplomatic and trade relations.

The enhancement and hardening of the Home Affairs portfolio with an AFP Response Force streamlines Australia's response to Phase 1 and Phase 2 escalations. These measures acknowledge the Federal, State and Territory jurisdictions and optimise Constitutional arrangements for the call-out of military forces only when State and Territory resources risk being overwhelmed during a Phase 3 escalation before war.

A Home Affairs Response Force paces grey zone threats and has the capability and capacity to strike decisively anywhere and anytime in Australia and the near region in conjunction with neighbours to get the attention of adversaries and persuade them to cease their escalation. A Response Force enhances homeland and near region deterrence with sufficient 'hurt' to de-escalate threats below the military threshold. It is an instrument for enacting grey zone legislation that targets grey zone combatants such as those responsible for cyberattacks launched from Australian soil to cause disruption and destruction. While enhancing the AFP's Specialist Response Group for the grey zone is straightforward, establishing a new Strike Force is more complicated. It is not a matter of giving Australia's Special Forces more to do overseas, an expedient solution repeating past mistakes.

CHAPTER 6

Strike Force Attributes

Introduction

Strike Force is not an instrument for battle. It is an instrument for using intelligence, diplomacy, information actions, deterrence and de-escalation to renew and maintain mutually respectful cooperation with China. While it is an armed force, it should be for bargaining, not as a destructive instrument *per se*. Strike Force has to be credible and potent to create meaningful deterrence. If deterrence fails, its operations have to be calibrated carefully to cause sufficient hurt to persuade an adversary to return to negotiation and bargaining for agreement, but not constitute an act of war.

Special Forces in their present form with their current culture should not be Australia's automatic 'force of choice' for the grey zone unless it is clear that de-escalation has failed and war is imminent. To automatically turn to Special Forces for extra duties in unfamiliar international operational settings requiring diplomacy and nuanced use of force and information actions would repeat past mistakes that led to elitism, estrangement, expedient over-employment and lawlessness incidents. I argue for a new Strike Force that draws on the ethos of Special Operations Australia in the Pacific War, enabled with 21st Century technology, bounded by ethics and displaying ingenuity befitting Australia's sovereignty and values. I prefer to draw on Australian creativity and lessons and legacies from the past than recommend emulating the armed intelligence services of other countries, like Israel's Mossad, Britain's Secret Intelligence Service or America's Central Intelligence Agency.

Fourth Fighting Force 1942–1945

Initially, Australia copied British precedents for special operations behind enemy lines for the Pacific War 1942–1945.[317] Both Britain and Australia founded their capabilities urgently after being unprepared, strategically surprised and defeated in the initial battles of the European and Pacific theatres of the Second World War. In both countries, navy, army, and air force chiefs resented supporting special operations, preferring conventional warfare against opposing navies, armies and air forces.[318] After several years of development, mature special operations capabilities emerged. Special operations were conducted too late to make a significant difference in the first years. Still, they did assist in shortening the duration of the Second World War in the European and South-West Pacific theatres.

In Britain, leadership for the development of the Special Operations Executive [SOE] came from Prime Minister Winston Churchill in July 1940 because none of the Service chiefs was either interested in or made responsible for hurting the German war effort in occupied Europe by employing intelligence agents and conducting enabling operations with local armed resistance groups.[319] SOE was a national asset with separate government funding. The RAF resented supporting special operations, calling SOE 'Churchill's Secret Army' and 'The Bureau for Ungentlemanly Warfare'.[320] The hurried hybrid structure of SOE and its independent mission 'to set Europe ablaze' quickly gathered detractors who were reluctant to allocate aircraft and vessels to insert strike teams and agents into Europe. By the war's end, SOE had a staff of 13 000 personnel. 'After the war, SOE's work was widely praised by Allied generals, who believed its operatives had helped shorten the conflict.'[321]

In Australia, leadership for establishing special operations also came from the top. The Australian Government raised the Inter-Allied Services organisation that later became Special Operations Australia [SOA] in March 1942, four months after the Japanese attack on Pearl Harbour, under the command of General Thomas Blamey, Command-

---

317 Davies, W, 2021, *Special and Secret*, p. 44

318 Ibid., p. 32–33

319 Ibid., p. 28

320 Ibid., p. 32–34

321 Ibid., p. 40

in Chief, Australian Military Forces. Prime Minister Curtin kept the SOA separate from the Services and set aside significant funds for its establishment.[322] But this organisation and its successors soon came under American command. They were beholden to American approval processes and resource managers to allocate submarines and aircraft for strike team and agent deployment.

From the end of 1942, General MacArthur's General Headquarters took control of all US, Australian and allied special operations. He suspected that those proposing them, mainly the British and the Dutch, were more interested in resuming their colonies than supporting his plans for Japan's defeat. He did not accord them a high priority.[323] In April 1943, SOA disguised as the Services Reconnaissance Department [SRD] reported to Controller, Allied Intelligence Bureau, an Australian with an American deputy responsible for managing resources.[324] All operations had to receive General MacArthur's approval.

Even after the tactical success of Australian commandos in Timor and Z Force in Singapore Harbour in 1942 and 1943, there were no innovative minds above the tactical level capable of turning tactical experience into more substantial operational and strategic success. With the benefit of hindsight, senior Australian leaders did not recognise that an investment in commandos, intelligence agents and small strike teams was affordable because they would depend on ingenuity, not firepower. Australia did not have the time, expertise or resources to build more ships, raise, train and equip more land forces or construct more attack aircraft in the first year of the Pacific War. Still, there was time to draw on Australia's human capital and invest in ingenuity and unconventional warfare capabilities.

Independent commando companies' and SRD 'M' and 'Z' special units conducted over 116 missions behind Japanese lines in Southeast Asia. Most operations came too late to impact the outcome of the war. During the Pacific War, the mindset for SRD employment was a British-

---

322 Official History of the Operations and Administration of Special Operations Foreword, p. 1

323 Davies, W, 2021, *Special and Secret,* p. 47

324 Ibid.

inspired concept of operations; small teams deploying by sea, land, and air covertly gathering intelligence and/or raiding and destroying enemy personnel and assets.[325]

Analysis of the official history of Australian special operations during the Pacific War reveals that operations soon adapted to suit Australia's near region. Commando activities in Timor against the Japanese and raids against Japanese shipping in Singapore began a unique tradition of innovation, boldness, and resilience at the tactical level. There were also losses and terrible hardships at the hands of the Japanese after capture. In his 2021 book *Special and Secret*, Will Davies wrote about the scope and impact of commando operations. Between late 1942 and October 1945, Z Special Units undertook a total of 84 operations across a wide area of Southeast Asia, including New Guinea and New Britain, Timor, Borneo, the Celebes and Moluccas, Singapore and even at the end of the war, Vietnam, known then as French Indochina. By the war's end, the SRD had approximately 2250 men and a few women. In total, their casualties were: Killed 18, executed while POW 11, died while POW 2, died of illness 1, missing 2, missing believed killed 36, missing believed drowned 4. Total 74. Add to this number were Portuguese, Timorese and other attached troops fatalities bringing the total to 119. Against this, enemy casualties were 1846 killed and 249 captured. Their operations included sabotage and subversive activities, the training of local guerrilla groups, surveillance and the reporting of Japanese shipping and aircraft movements, the coordination of airdrops and the distribution of arms and supplies, even the extraction of a Sultan and his family.

Despite their impact, bravery, and endurance, commandos, agents, and coastwatchers were minor to conventional Allied campaigns against the Japanese. Post operations reports testify to a lack of higher command imagination, innovation, and sub-optimal arrangements for special operations that increased risk. Aside from sporadic tactical level cooperation between US submarine commanders and Australian commandos and coastwatchers, there is no evidence of operational

325 Official History of the Operations and Administration of Special Operations

or strategic level encouragement of more potent commando raids on Japanese military leaders and their headquarters, shipping, aircraft and infrastructure.[326]

According to David Horner's Australian and US higher command histories in the Pacific War, the Australian Army did not increase the tempo of strikes on Japanese lines of communications, such as railways, harbours and airfields, in Japanese-occupied territory to distract and tie-down Japanese forces. The objectives of most operations were limited to intelligence gathering. Senior Army officers did not contemplate innovative surgical strikes on Japanese headquarters to paralyse command and control capacity and kill or capture senior Japanese officers. The killing of Admiral Isoroku Yamamoto, commander of the Combined Fleet of the Imperial Japanese Navy in 1943 and architect of the Pearl Harbour attack in 1941, had a significant impact on the morale and strategic planning capacity of the Japanese Navy.[327] This one success illustrated the possibilities of intelligence-led strike operations against senior Japanese officers. This strike against a senior Japanese leader was an innovative American operation. Based on David Horner's analytical histories of higher Australian command and biographies of General Sir Thomas Blamey and Sir Fredrick Shedden, there was no equivalent level of innovation or ingenuity among Australian military planners, commanders or Defence officials.[328]

A combination of Julius Caesar and Aldous Huxley's adages that 'Experience is the teacher of all things, but only the teachable learn from experience' summarises the lost opportunities of the Pacific War for SRD operations. Australian politicians and senior military leaders were not teachable or imaginative. They were indebted to British and American imagination for defending Australia and defeating Japan. The Japanese were operating in unfamiliar territory among hostile populations in Australia's regional neighbourhood. Australian politicians and their military advisers did not know how to turn this

---

326 Ibid.

327 Haulman, DL, 2003, 'The Yamamoto Mission'

328 Horner, D, 1982, *High Command: Australia and Allied Strategy*, Horner, D, 1996, *Inside the War Cabinet* and Horner, D, 1998, *Blamey: Commander in Chief*

Japanese disadvantage into Australia's strategic advantage using special operations and enabling populations in South East Asia to rise against cruel Japanese occupiers.

Lessons for Strike Force

There are lessons for establishing Australia's 21st Century Strike Force from the Pacific War. The first was that Australia started developing its so-called 'Fourth Fighting Force' to hurt the Japanese war effort too late. Though there were years of warning in the 1930s of the possibility of a southern thrust from Japan, Australia did not develop a complementary self-reliant strategy. There was no sovereign hedging strategy against the dominant British Singapore Strategy that promised that the British Navy and the fortress of Singapore would thwart any Japanese encroachment into Southeast Asia and Oceania.[329] In reality, Australia had no deterrent force in the 1930s to cause Japan, a significant trading partner, to have second thoughts about attacking Australian sovereign territory after capturing Singapore.

The second lesson is that creating a potent Strike Force takes years and not months and should not be thought about and acted on only after strategic surprise. It took over 18 months to raise and train commandos companies, Z Force and M Force covert strike units to conduct raids and enabling operations among local populations in Southeast Asia. Australia's first successful raid on Singapore Harbour occurred in late September 1943, two months short of two years after the surprise Japanese attack on Pearl Harbour. 'The raiders were credited with the sinking of seven ships weighing about 40,000 tons total and the shattering of the Japanese myth of invincibility in the port of Singapore.'[330] By any assessment of investment return, this was a strategic level triumph. The investment was 14 specially selected and trained commandos, one fishing boat, several canoes and a couple of dozen limpet mines.[331] By the time SRD had an approved operation, sufficient technology and resources to attack Japanese shipping in

329 Hamill, I, 1981, *The Strategic Illusion*

330 Ibid., p. 89

331 Silver, L, 2001, *Krait, the Fishing Boat that went to War*

several ports in Southeast Asia and conduct a raid on the Japanese main headquarters and infrastructure in Rabaul, it was 1945. The war was almost over.

The third lesson was about lost opportunities. By January 1944, the commander of the Singapore raid had developed a larger-scale plan called Operation Hornbill, a series of SRD operations in the South China Sea targeting the ports of Singapore, Saigon, Hong Kong and inserting groups of agents to gather intelligence, enable resistance movements and conduct 'small, annoying pin-prick raids'.[332] This plan was mayhem in the making. If Churchill had inspired the SOE with the order to 'set Europe ablaze', Hornbill promised 'disruption and distraction in Southeast Asia.' The Japanese would have lost ships, oil refineries, supply depots, airfields and other critical infrastructure. They would have had to tie down forces to protect themselves from hostile locals, spies and raiders. Operation Hornbill depended on the construction of 'Country Craft', a fleet of specially-constructed vessels identical to junks operating at that time in the South China Sea. Trade union stoppages in Australia stalled their construction, and lack of high-level support postponed Hornbill until 1945. In its place in 1944 was an improvised, under-resourced Operation Rimau that ended in disaster at Singapore Harbour a year after the successful first raid on Japanese shipping there.[333]

The fourth lesson was that specialist technology and training bases with optimum curricula, instructors, resources and training infrastructure for strike operations take time to develop. High command postponed Operation Hornbill because specialist 'Country Craft' could not be built in time. It took two years for British inventors to develop small submersibles, called Motor Submersible Canoes, suited to transporting commandos into harbours and ports covertly.[334] It took 18 months to fully establish a range of SRD training centres, technical support schools and other infrastructure in Australia.[335]

The fifth lesson is that special operations must have their own means

---

332 Davies, W, 2021, *Special and Secret*, p. 290

333 Ibid., p. 291 and Chapter 15

334 Ibid., p. 157

335 Ibid., pp. 51–59

for rapid, covert movement and resupply. Several SRD operations were cancelled because there were no submarines or aircraft available. Initially, Australian SRD operations had to rely on US submarines and service aircraft. The RAAF finally established a secret and separate unit, No. 200 Flight, to support SRD operations in June 1944. Still, it was not fully operational until March 1945, six months before the war's end.[336] The RAN reluctantly enhanced its small boats unit for training SRD personnel in 1944.

In summary, Australia only began thinking about sovereign capabilities to hurt the Japanese war effort with special operations after the strategic surprise of Pearl Harbour in December 1941 and the fall of Singapore in February 1942. It took over 12 months to conduct strike operations and another two years before SRD was a capable 'Fourth Fighting Force'. The three Services were not appropriate sponsors for developing an innovative, unconventional 'Fourth Fighting Force' like a Strike Force. From the beginning, SRD was a national asset with separate funding. Still, US and Australian Service priorities and control over submarines and aircraft limited the potential of SRD operations to make an early and significant impact on Japanese forces operating in Southeast Asia and the Pacific Islands.

Reprise

Let me reprise conclusions from earlier chapters before discussing countering dark grey escalations. In 2021 the CPC's grey zone campaign against Australia was still in Phase 1 'light grey' political and economic pressure and coercion. If objectives cannot be achieved in Phase 1, the CPC might escalate to Phase 2 and Phase 3 darker grey tactics akin to Russia's successful hybrid warfare model. The CPC strategy would avoid a Third World War but achieve similar ends by different means in the grey zone. Taiwan will be the test case, as Ukraine was the test case in 2022. Australia would stand alone countering increasing light grey economic and political pressure. Where will the capacity and the capability come from for opposing Phase 2 and 3 escalations?

In 2016 Australia began hardening legislation against espionage,

336 Ibid., p. 59

foreign interference, cyber-attacks and muscling up intelligence and counter cyber capabilities with legislative support. In my view, these reflexive responses are not enough. The CPC escalation from light grey Phase 1 political and informational subversion to darker grey economic coercion in 2020 demonstrates that the CPC seeks an escalation momentum that will increase tempo and disruptiveness. Are the ADF's Special Forces the answer for de-escalating this momentum?

The answer is 'Yes' and 'No'. Yes, enhanced Special Forces capabilities are required to counter a dark grey zone escalation to hybrid warfare. But 'No', Australia needs a new national security instrument that operates overseas within the Foreign Affairs portfolio to detect and pace threats in the grey zone, such as cyber-attacks, and create sufficient deterrence to obligate negotiation, and if threats continue, to de-escalate forcefully. Australia needs to raise, train and develop a new multi-domain Strike Force with the best people, a new culture, the latest technology and ways and means to conduct operations anywhere and anytime. New command and control arrangements and force projection capabilities are required to achieve these capabilities.

A sovereign Australian approach

It is politically, ethically, and morally uncomfortable for a liberal democracy like Australia to 'harden up' for the grey zone. But strategic guidance, capability development priorities and tactics for the defence of the Australian homeland and near region to counter Phase 3 escalations of a grey zone campaign must change. It is even more uncomfortable to plan for and maintain a presence in someone else's homeland when an adversary, like the CPC, does not respect the sovereignty of other nations and has grey zone operatives located in Australia and throughout Australia's near region. It would be easier if a state of war permitted wartime legislation and the employment of conventional military forces. But that has not, and will not happen in the 21st Century if the first 20 years are instructive.

The first step to taking a sovereign approach is to enhance Australia's strategic guidance to direct national security capability development to deal with existing and emerging threats in a world of continuous 'grey zone' conflict. Traditional national security threats, such as those posed by authoritarian Communist nations during the Cold War, have evolved into China and Russia's ongoing asymmetric and oscillating competition and conflict with their neighbours and the world. Russia is achieving its expansionist strategic objectives through hybrid warfare. The annexation of Crimea in 2014 and the domination of Ukraine in 2022 measure recent success. Interventions into Syria and northern Iraq testify to ongoing Russian mischief in international affairs. China's militarisation of the South and East China Seas is a grey zone campaign. Arguably, Australia's cooperation with the United States and regional allies to defend the rules-based global order against China and Russia's new way of coercion increases the strategic risks of escalating grey zone campaigns.

The second step is also about strategic thinking. More nuanced and sophisticated strategic thinking would generate whole-of-government capabilities to project influence and force anywhere in the world in a rapid response, as well as pre-emptively when time allows. Australia could employ these unique capabilities, either unilaterally and self-reliantly or as a coalition member. The new Australian Strike Force will continue to operate in the international grey zone with the armed and potent US and British intelligence services.

These two enhancements of strategic guidance and thinking create a new mindset that comprehends asymmetric threats and specifies capability development priorities. But new strategic perspectives will not be enough. There is an urgent need for a conceptual framework for Australian Strike Force operations based on surgical strike, electromagnetic spectrum and enabling operations. This new framework would mitigate against improvising traditional strategy or acting reflexively to incidents.

My analytical history of Australian military force projection in the late 1990s and 2000s should inform new concepts and theoretical frameworks.[337] The concept of an island nation requiring national, regional and international force projection capabilities and the theoretical framework of 10 functions of force projection (generic

337 Breen, B, 2006. 'Australian Military Force Projection in the late 1980s and the 1990s', and Breen, B, 2008, *Struggling for Self-Reliance*

and specific force preparation, command, deployment, protection, employment, sustainment, rotation, redeployment, reconstitution) would help identify the capabilities required for Strike Force operations anywhere and anytime.[338]

It is essential to be precise about Strike Force attributes. Precision will come from applying lessons from the past, understanding the nature of an escalating grey zone campaign and identifying requirements. Special Forces will engage in the homeland when called out and in anticipation of escalation to the operations and tactics of hybrid warfare. This Phase 3 escalation could be sudden, so Special Forces need to have a 'warm start' through collaboration with Response Force. Hopefully, rigorous surveillance of developing threats overseas and pre-positioning contingency Strike Force teams will deter escalations in the Australian homeland. Sponsors of grey zone campaigns may test Australia's resolve overseas, and Strike Force may have to apply lethal and destructive force there to re-establish negotiations. DFAT will always complement international Strike Force operations with information operations and negotiation.

What might a Strike Force look like for new roles in the grey zone to counter Phase 3 escalation overseas? I believe that fundamental attributes must build on current Special Forces roles and characteristics. However, there is a need to 'go back to the drawing board' and examine the roots of the Special Operations Australia tradition in the Pacific War, contemporary Australian military and strategic literature, and Australia's strategic circumstances that obligate self-reliance in the grey zone. There is no point in emulating the Special Forces or armed intelligence agencies of significant allies like the United States and Britain. Their traditions, legislation and operating protocols are different. Their capabilities in the grey zone are more than what a middle power like Australia can afford.

Finally, Australia should not wait for a Hilton bombing, a 9/11 terrorist attack, or the slaying of political leaders, police and innocent civilians to develop future capabilities for protection against hybrid operations employing terrorist tactics. Authoritarian nations and sub-

---

338 Breen, B, 2008, *Struggling for Self-Reliance*, pp. 2–3, Conclusion

national groups have already stolen a day's march on the Western alliance to conduct successful political and hybrid campaigns in the grey zone. Australia is already experiencing political warfare with unprecedented espionage, foreign interference and intimidation of citizens. The urgency to act is immediate. While Response Force should de-escalate grey zone threats 'downstream' at home, Strike Force must de-escalate threats 'upstream' anywhere and anytime overseas. China has metaphorically begun invading Australia 'silently' and already conducts cyber-attacks with impunity. It is time for Australia to assert its sovereignty with more than rhetoric, deter rude and nasty behaviour, and de-escalate forcefully if deterrence does not work.

Strike Force attributes

Who should be in the Strike Force, and how should they operate? In 2014 an Army monograph *Australian Special Operations: Theory and Practice,* articulated and discussed the distinctive nature of Australian Special Forces.[339] It defined them as:

> specially selected, trained and equipped personnel who conduct special operations. They are characterised by 'their composition of selected personnel with specialised individual competencies who use rapidly acquired and technologically advanced equipment and possess elevated levels of training and education'.[340] ... they are exceptional individuals who receive sophisticated training to enhance their complex problem-solving attributes. They operate in small teams, guided by the law and specific rules of engagement, but are dependent on other agencies to provide intelligence, mobility, firepower and sustainment.[341]

The monograph defined a distinctively 'Australian' special operation as:

> ... generally undertaken to achieve or support significant political or military objectives in support of national security and foreign

339 Langford, I, 2014, *Australian special operation*
340 Ibid., p. 16
341 Ibid., p. 29

> policy objectives. Special Operations are conducted throughout the operational spectrum and employ unique forms of tactical techniques, equipment and training.[342]

In a 2014 analysis, the Australian Strategic Policy Institute [ASPI] discussed optimum attributes.[343] ASPI chose the US Joint Special Operations doctrine for describing special operations:

> ... requiring unique modes of employment, tactical techniques, equipment and training often conducted in a hostile, denied, or politically sensitive environment, and characterized by one or more of the following: time-sensitive, clandestine, low visibility, conducted with and/or through indigenous forces, requiring regional expertise, and/or a high degree of risk.[344]

Two fundamental attributes emerge from the papers mentioned above; a direct and indirect approach. The direct attribute focuses on 'small-unit precision lethality' or surgical strike. In contrast, the indirect feature enables third parties, usually local military, law enforcement, and other countries' national security forces, to conduct effective special operations. These enabling Strike Force operations disable an adversary's capabilities to prosecute a coercive grey zone campaign against their country's national interests.

These two attributes of 'precision lethality' and 'enabling third parties' fit with the essence of Response Power and inform both Response and Strike Force operations. They resonate with the two attributes of the stern end of Australia's Response Power when deterrence is not sufficient to stop escalating coercive behaviour.[345] One attribute is an ultimate sanction to 'hurt' that establishes credible deterrence. The other denotes enabling collaboration with allies to

---

342 Ibid., p. 12

343 Davies, A, Jennings, P & Schreer, B, 2014, 'A versatile force: the future of Australia's Special Forces'

344 US Special Operations Command, JP 3–05, 2013, *Special Operations*, p. xi

345 Petit, B, 2013, *Going Big by Getting Small*, p. 44

empower them to establish credible deterrence through having their own ultimate sanctions that 'hurt'.[346]

Borrowing from US doctrine, I am defining Surgical Strike as 'the execution of activities anywhere and at any time in a precise manner that employs strike teams in hostile denied, or politically sensitive environments to seize, destroy, capture, exploit, recover or damage designated targets or influence threats'.[347] Enabling Operations are 'the execution of activities that involve a combination of lethal and non-lethal actions taken by specially trained and educated teams that have a deep understanding of cultures and foreign language, proficiency in small unit tactics, and the ability to fight with and alongside allied security agencies and Special Forces in permissive, uncertain, or hostile environments'.[348]

Anywhere and anytime?

What does 'anywhere and anytime really mean? American and British Special Forces have struck terrorist and insurgent networks anywhere and around the world since 9/11.[349] They operate against targets within malevolent organisations, including leaders and their lieutenants in their sanctuaries, whenever and wherever threats are identified.[350] Australia does not have equivalent capabilities or legislation for independent 'upstream' strikes at grey zone adversaries. The traditional strategic orthodoxy of cooperation and interoperability with Western allies belies Australian aspirations for self-reliance for its security in the grey zone. Failure to develop 'upstream' surgical strike attributes implies that allies will deal with mutual adversaries regionally and internationally. Australia needs a world-class Strike Force with 'anywhere and anytime' detection,

---

346 Petit, B, 2013, *Going Big by Getting Small*, p. 44

347 United States Army 2011, *Army Doctoral Publication 3–05 Special Operations*, p. 10

348 Ibid., p. 9

349 Neville, L, 2015, *Special Forces and the War on Terror*

350 UK Government, 2014, 'The situation in Iraq and Syria', United States Department of Defense 2014, *Strategy for countering weapons of mass destruction*, and United States Government, 2018, *National Strategy for Counter-terrorism*, October 2018

deterrence, information and de-escalation capabilities that will gain the respect and admiration of allies and cause concern for adversaries.

Australian Special Forces support conventional military operations with special operations; Strike Force supports the Australian Government's efforts to counter grey zone campaigns. Strike Force is about Australia having a sovereign capability to strike anywhere and anytime in its national interests because, figuratively, the world is already at war when there is no war. A Strike Force simultaneously mitigates reliance on allies while consolidating partnership with them. It can join traditional and new national, regional and international partners in the grey zone. Strike Force operations encompass the domains of cyber-warfare, information operations and space while countering political and hybrid warfare.

My recommendations for striking 'upstream anywhere and anytime' are not new. Phase 3 Response Power was an Australian aspiration in 2003, though the term was not used then. The then Chief of the Defence Force, General Peter Cosgrove, outlined his strategic aspiration, *Future Warfighting Concept* that built on his predecessor's *Force 2020* vision:[351]

> Our future adversaries will come in different forms, have different goals and employ different methods, but they all have a common thread: the will to fight. ... Multidimensional Manoeuvre is based on the Manoeuvrist Approach, which is already present in our current warfighting doctrine. This approach seeks to apply strength against weakness. It values surprise and deception. It requires an ability to act fast, to reach out to the critical place at the right time and create simultaneous problems that an adversary cannot resolve. In order to fight this way, the ADF will need the ability to be deployed and sustained at home and at a distance.[352]

I am particularly interested in Cosgrove's vision of applying strength against weakness to achieve surprise and deception at a distance.

---

351 Department of Defence, 2002, *Force 2020*

352 Department of Defence, 2003, *Future Warfighting Concept*, p. 2

He committed the ADF to develop attributes 'to act fast, to reach out to the critical place at the right time, and to create simultaneous problems that an adversary cannot resolve.' Response Power realises Peter Cosgrove's *Future Warfighting Concept* and his predecessor's *Force 2020* visions of network-centric seamless force projection, nearly 20 years after their prescriptions. Arguably, Peter Cosgrove would have been even more emphatic about developing a Strike Force had he known about political and hybrid warfare in the grey zone in 2003.

Strike Force will have to employ unconventional methods beyond the scope, remit and capabilities of the three ADF Services or Federal, State and Territory law enforcement agencies. Australia does not have an FBI or a CIA with legislation authorising a Strike Force to underpin Phase 3 de-escalation. It is time to put that legislation in place.

Always on

Strike Force must address threats anywhere and at any time. In effect, it is 'always on', monitoring threats with their departmental and agency partners as early as possible to deter or prevent their development or de-escalate them before they come to fruition. If a threat is imminent and dangerous, it ensures that strikes are customised to surprise and optimise deterrence. The aim is to create operational dilemmas for adversaries that prevent, slow or stop threatening behaviour. The particular threat is a build-up of capabilities for hybrid or, in the worst case, conventional warfare. It includes deciding on teachable moments where a sudden and decisive strike can sufficiently de-escalate an adversary to renew negotiations or at least 'back-off'. It intends to create optimum conditions for deterrence in the first instance. If deterrence fails, strike again to disrupt darker grey operations in the making and encourage further negotiations.

Rapid deployment

Special Forces are currently dependent on RAN, Army and RAAF at the strategic, operational and tactical levels to deploy into, manoeuvre inside, and re-deploy from areas of operation. Strike Force will not succeed without reliable capabilities to project and operate without detection to the right place at the right time, especially in contested environments. The RAN, Army and RAAF are not reliable when amidst competing priorities.

Many international and Australian organisations operate aircraft, watercraft, and vehicles to suit their rapid, routine, and discrete movement needs. At the strategic level, ASIS requires the means to move individuals, groups, and strike teams by air, sea, and land discreetly in Australia, regionally, and worldwide. At the operational and tactical levels, Strike Force fixed, and rotary-wing aircraft must form the core of the fast and discrete movement in areas of operation, especially for contingencies such as WMD capture and surgical strike missions. Deployable submersibles move underwater, stare and strike. A fleet of military and modified commercial vehicles constitute the means for covert and clandestine movement.

Clandestine strategic surveillance – 'staring'

The capability to 'stare' secretly at detected threats is essential for Strike Force. The aim is to get Australia in front of emerging threats. This attribute is about secret planning, preparation, deployment, employment and re-deployment without public announcements or traditional declarations of hostilities. Clandestine strategic surveillance and reconnaissance enable early warning in concert with DFAT and its information-gathering networks and allied intelligence agencies that inform the Australian Government. A forward-deployed, 'always on' Strike Force surveillance capability, moving seamlessly into and out of Australia's areas of strategic interest, delivers two dividends.

The first dividend is an inter-generational presence overseas that is extremely sensitive to change and variation in emerging and existing threats to Australian national interests. This permanent secret presence would inform Australia's sovereign intelligence system and consistently complement allied intelligence sources. The forward deployment of Strike Force teams to remain in place on rotation in both contested and uncontested environments and governed and ungoverned spaces provide the right kind of strategic early warning system. This presence is a human-generated strategic 'radar' for political and hybrid warfare threats, especially terrorist acts involving WMD.

The second dividend is the enhanced capability for forward-based strike teams to provide a 'warm start' and immediate action in response to sudden changes in strategic circumstances or an unforeseen threat. This rapid response can have two effects. The first is to de-escalate an emerging security crisis quickly and decisively before it becomes dangerous. This 'nip in the bud' capability can have a deterrent or a compulsion effect. Suppose an initial warning and possibly an informational or cyber sting fails. In that case, personnel and resources are in place to execute a pre-emptive, surgical strike across all domains – a firmer signal that 'enough is enough'.

Secret strategic reconnaissance creates 'escalation dominance' in the grey zone. In effect, the government retains the initiative in the face of a darker grey hybrid threat; usually, one vigorously denied and secretly pursued by its sponsor, or other dangers and political sensitivities constrain conventional forces' employment. It can maintain the initiative and de-escalate well before there is talk of war or risk of miscalculation. Ultimately, having a Strike Force that can operate in the air, land, maritime, space, cyber, and information domains give Australia early dominance over emerging threats. It can mitigate the rate of coercive escalation without committing conventional forces that risk miscalculation, an act of war or escalation that leads to war.

With de-escalation in mind, the future Strike Force must be capable of conducting surveillance and intelligence operations with an 'always on' information collection and target development posture. These attributes give Australia the political, diplomatic, military and informational advantage necessary to underpin its competitive, forward deterrence approach for operating in the grey zone. No longer will Australia wait for a grey zone adversary's next move. Strike Force will detect the next move and have rehearsed response options.

In partnership with diplomats and ASIS intelligence agents, Strike Force must provide understanding and insight into emerging regional and international threats. Strike Force would conduct covert and clandestine surveillance that detects and 'stares' at threats to understand them and identify, analyse and rehearse response options. This attribute incorporates cunning and deception as well as covert and clandestine infiltration. It encompasses collaboration with international proxies and partners to infiltrate and undermine inimical political, religious, military, racist, extremist, and criminal groups – political and hybrid warfare tools. It is capable of sufficient technological intrusion to retain the strategic initiative.

Covert and clandestine strike and enabling operations

Strike Force must be capable of covert and clandestine operations, both in collaboration with allies and autonomously. Covert means a military operation intended to conceal the identity of, or allow plausible denial by, the sponsor and intended to create a political effect that can have implications in the military, intelligence, or law enforcement arenas – affecting either the internal population of a country or individuals. Clandestine means an operation sponsored or conducted by governmental departments or agencies in such a way as to assure secrecy or concealment. A clandestine operation differs from a covert operation in that emphasis is placed on concealment of the operation rather than on concealment of the sponsor's identity. An activity may be covert and clandestine for strike operations and may focus equally on operational considerations and intelligence-related activities.

Strike Force must target an adversary's terrorist, hybrid warfare and proxy leaders. A terrorist network or a hybrid campaign deprived of its core leadership group is almost certain to fail. Leaders will be challenging to recruit when they know of their vulnerability. This attribute enables close cooperation and interoperability with significant allies seeking to defeat hostile terrorist organisations and hybrid task forces 'upstream'. Strike Force would join allies in the grey zone wherever threats arise, and leaders are detected and identified.

Strike Force must deny sanctuaries as well as pace and stare at threats. It is better to deter and de-escalate inimical groups in the homelands of other nations and an adversary's homeland rather than in Australia and its regional neighbourhood. In Clive Hamilton's assessment, the CPC is conducting a 'silent invasion' of Australia and is the 'hidden hand' in the silent invasions of other countries. It does not make sense to curtail surveillance operations in other countries and China when Australia's sovereignty is routinely breached.

It makes sense to declare that breaching Australia's sovereignty has consequences in the homelands of perpetrators. Doing nothing and providing no deterrent message with credible ways and means to 'hurt' encourages further coercion.

In the first instance, Strike Force would deny sanctuaries outside Australia and conduct de-escalation operations with regional and international partners. Partner nations and their security forces would welcome this approach. This special operations approach includes support to armed forces and local law enforcement agencies and the use of technical and human intelligence capabilities, and the prosecution of cyber offensive and defensive operations. Defeating these groups 'up-stream' stops their toxic narratives radicalising and inspiring adherents in Australia, or worse still, to appear on Australian soil to conduct terrorist acts. Should there be signs of planning and preparations of operatives and capabilities for prosecuting hybrid warfare in Australia and its near region, de-escalation strikes are warranted.

In the Information Age, a political dimension to military operations goes all the way down to the tactical level. Politics permeate all aspects of Strike Force operations. Strike Force commanders at all levels must have a deft and adroit awareness of politics and socio-political, ethnic and cultural influences, such as tribalism, ethnicity, corruption, and parallel structures, also known as 'shadow governments', as well as organised criminal networks. They must improvise, innovate, and apply language skills, cultural awareness, and understanding of local politics. They should also expand, fuse, and decentralise intelligence functions and targeting while developing proficiency in the assertive use of influence, information and public affairs. Strike Force must be the force of choice for partnering with nations' security forces in Australia's near region to protect their nationhood from political warfare escalating to hybrid warfare because of their political and cultural acumen.

The Western notion of Mission Command, 'the exercise of authority and direction by commanders to enable disciplined initiative within the commander's intent to empower agile and adaptable leaders in the conduct of unified operations.' [353] Adaption and trust are crucial. Mission command sits comfortably with Strike Force operations against those prosecuting political and hybrid warfare. Well-trained junior leaders and small teams, enabled by intelligence and technology, can detect, and deter threats with sudden strikes to unsettle antagonists. The intention is to create 'friction' for adversaries and 'escalation dominance' rather than allow them to do so.

Enabling operations rely on technical inter-operability/intra-operability. Strike Force and most Western alliance armed intelligence agencies and Special Forces will be interoperable and trust each other with information. The Western alliance operates with sophisticated command and control and communications systems, fusing intelligence and precision targeting. Other partners may be less technologically compatible and more cautious about sharing information. These constraints will complicate optimising transparency, intelligence sharing and technical interoperability. Strike Force will need to quickly adapt to partner capabilities and requirements to achieve technical inter-operability/intra-operability.

Interoperability will be crucial for collaborative multi-agency efforts in Australia, the near region and internationally to oppose political and hybrid warfare. It makes no sense for Strike Force to have incompatible command and control, intelligence surveillance and information technology with departments and agencies at home and abroad. A priority for capability development should be a standard secure telecommunications system for collaborative civil-military operations.

Enabling operations depend on trust and mutual respect. It takes time to build trust and open the flow of information to facilitate collaboration. Accordingly, both Response Force and Strike Force teams need to be co-located with counterpart partners in the near region and internationally all the time.

One of the most affordable but deadly weapon systems fielded by asymmetric belligerents worldwide are Improvised Explosive Devices [IED]. These devices are placed and detonated to cause maximum

---

353 US Army 2017, *Multi-Domain Battle: Evolution of Combined Arms*

psychological and physical impact. Some bombs are large enough to blow up buildings and cause mass casualties in a marketplace, while others are small enough to remove limbs, leaving horrific wounds. Suicide bombers are a potent threat. Some bombers strap IEDs to themselves for personal detonation, while others drive cars and trucks packed with explosives into their targets.

In the context of developing a Strike Force attribute, it is deeply concerning that adversaries, inspired by the impact of bombings such as those in Bali in 2002, London in 2005, at the Boston Marathon in 2013, at the Manchester Arena in 2017 and Sri Lanka in 2019, could contemplate placing and detonating IED in Australia and its near region as a tactic of hybrid war. The lesson is that adversaries must know that Response Force and Strike Force have the latest counter-IED capabilities. As part of a detect, deter, and de-escalate strategy, they need to know there are dire consequences for being discovered planning to employ IED.

Hostile groups may occupy parts of a city or town as a hybrid warfare tactic to force political concessions. Until the Malawi Siege in the Philippines in 2017, few experts would have predicted that an ISIS-inspired sub-national group would seize and occupy a city in Australia's near region. The Armed Forces of the Philippines were surprised and unprepared for an urban fight in their nation's only Muslim city or the sustained information operations its occupiers prosecuted against them and the Philippines Government.

The jihadi's concept of operations in the Philippines was to seize the city, defy the nation's security forces and discredit the Philippines government into allowing a caliphate in the southern Philippines, the location of decades of a separatist insurgency.[354] A culminating masterstroke for a Phase 3 escalation of a grey zone campaign in Australia could be the sudden appearance of armed proxies who overwhelm local law enforcement agencies and occupy a town or several suburbs of an Australian city. The aim would be to compel an Australian Government to negotiate or force a government to resign in favour of a political coalition promising to negotiate a partnership for

---

354 Knight, C & Theodorakis, K, 2019, *The Malawi crisis*, pp. 4–5

peace and prosperity with the country covertly sponsoring the proxies.

A Phase 3 escalation will rely heavily on the Internet to spread fear and promote appeasement pathways aimed at Australians and a worldwide audience. The Internet and the Electromagnetic Spectrum [EMS] give totalitarian nations and sub-national groups the freedom to misrepresent their motives, disguise their intentions and vindicate even their most monstrous actions. Both Response Force and Strike Force must have information operations capabilities, including counter-cyber and jamming technologies to counter an adversary's political, information, cyber and hybrid warfare in Australia and abroad.

This attribute involves having efficient approval processes to disseminate targeted narratives to counter an adversary's propaganda. Key messages from liberal democracies should always trump the negative concocted and disguised propaganda from authoritarian political and extremist adversaries. There is no intention to emulate the propagation of authoritarianism by compromising liberal democratic principles. Arguably, these principles always afford a competitive edge for the allegiance of populations in information warfare.

Strike Force must de-escalate simultaneously in several places using various modalities in several domains. This targeting tempo could be a 'game-changer' that achieves strategic decision-making paralysis.[355] The 24/7 tempo of acquiring and de-escalating targets anywhere and anytime to create a flurry of publicised and covert 'hurts' can create sufficient pressure to cause second thoughts and develop incentives for returning to negotiations and ceasing coercion. This 24/7 targeting tempo sits comfortably in a detect, deter, warn and de-escalate strategy. Arguably, well-targeted early and decisive surgical strike operations against an adversary and their proxies optimise the possibility of lowering their morale and dissuading them from pursuing and escalating their coercive campaign. Allies in Australia's near region are likely to appreciate this Strike Force capability to set conditions for negotiations.

---

355 Fadok, D, 1994, *John Boyd and John Warden*, p. 12

Stingers

Strike Force must not compete with maritime, land and air power priorities for resources. It is a fourth fighting force requiring technology and weapon systems to 'sting'. ASIS should command a range of weapon systems, including drones and underwater craft, counter-cyber, sea mine and other explosive technologies to create 'stings' that hurt but do not constitute acts of war. Some of these capabilities traditionally belong to the RAN, Army and RAAF. The Director-Generals of ASIS must be formation commanders like their RAN, Army and RAAF counterparts commanding their own forces. Strike Force stingers may well be employed to support ADF maritime, land and air operations but must not be beholden to the Services.

This attribute does not presume that a kinetic strike is a first and only option. It begins with the capabilities to detect and monitor existing and emerging threats. It then transitions from calling them out politically, informationally, and diplomatically to deter adversaries from plotting. It culminates – as a last resort – in conducting carefully-calibrated strikes to de-escalate threats. These actions are not provocations or triggers for war; they are preventative measures that 'hurt' to gain attention and avoid conflict. Modalities include obfuscation, deception, denial of responsibility and creation of confusion.

Armed drones that provide imagery for intelligence, surveillance and reconnaissance [ISR] are 'game changers' for surgical strike operations. The knowledge that Strike Force has armed ISR drones strengthens deterrence in the grey zone. And if deterrence does not work, their use destroys threats anywhere and at any time with minimal collateral damage. Armed ISR drones allow a degree of 'dwell' or a persistent 'stare' at areas of operation and potential targets. They are vital for discovering hostile groups and individuals who rely on complex populated urban areas to mask their movements and make them difficult to engage.[356]

Armed ISR drones enable strike teams to surprise and pounce on hostile groups and individuals confident of their security in cities and towns. Strike Force joint terminal attack controllers strike rapidly

---

356 Langford, I, 2017, 'Australia's Offset and A2/AD Strategies'

as soon as targets appear. The anticipated delivery of tactical armed medium-altitude drones to the RAAF is not sufficiently flexible or reliable enough for an enduring, constant level of support for Strike Force that has to own and operate them.

The best place to find and hurt military and commercial shipping is in their harbours. Acquisition of underwater craft would significantly increase Australia's ability to conduct long-range covert maritime subsurface operations in high-risk environments, such as ports, harbours, and inland waterways. These capabilities would take the opportunities missed in the Pacific War to find and disable shipping. This capability, enabled by sea mines and other sophisticated anti-vessel weapons, explosives, and electronic disruptors, would create an option of mauling vessels in port or soon after sailing. Equally, Strike Force should have the ways and means to neutralise aircraft in airfields and missiles in their bases and strike at headquarters and other high-value infrastructure employed for hybrid warfare. An adversary's political and military leaders should not feel safe from the possible uncomfortable personal consequences of their decisions to use hybrid warfare tactics against Australia.

It is also provident to enable others to 'sting' in the grey zone. Strike Force must have an enabling capability to train and shape proxies such as dissident political groups and local guerrilla networks capable of accessing areas of strategic importance. This option to use proxies is essential, especially where there is no reasonable possibility of deploying Australian military forces or strike teams. The modality would be forming Strike Force networks throughout Australia's neighbourhood as part of an Australian-facilitated regional de-escalation campaign plan. It operationalises an unconventional warfare dimension of Ross Babbage's grand strategy of partnership and leverage with regional neighbours. It also accords with Peter Varghese's engage and constrain prescription. This aggregation of 'stinging, poisonous shrimps' would contribute to regional solidarity and partnership and guarantee local access to Australian Strike Force teams.

Strike Force Memes

Strike Force will be the national instrument to orchestrate sophisticated Information-Age Australian Response Power in the grey zone to de-escalate threats. It should have three distinct roles: low signature, enabling, and offensive electromagnetic operations, three memes: *Ghosts*, *Enablers* and *Goblins*.

The Ghosts – Covet and Clandestine operations

Covet and Clandestine operations [CCO] represent future Strike Force capabilities for defending against and operating in the grey zone when no war is declared, but hybrid warfare is in the offing. The focus is on secret forms of small-group penetration anywhere in the world for as long as required for the specific purpose of intelligence collection, gaining situational awareness, and targeting. CCO can occur both in the physical sphere and through cyber and space vectors. Covert penetration of an electronic system is one example. They need to be undetectable; strike teams need to move in and out of areas without notice – they need to be *ghosts* – never truly discoverable, always a mystery and fear creators.

The Ghosts operate in the fog of the grey zone to defend against the sponsors of unethical and duplicitous hybrid warfare and other operations.[357] Hybrid warfare is persistent and population-centric, emphasising espionage, sabotage, and intimidation, combined with covert action, information warfare, and, when required, the use of proxies, partners and influencers. Countering this mix of activities is the CCO realm.

CCO mitigate Australia's vulnerabilities, such as small military force by global and regional standards, dependence on allies and little/no sovereign industrial base for the production of military materiel. CCO form the core of Australia's capacity to offset an adversary's comparative advantages in force size, as well as freedom of political action associated with authoritarian regimes and industrial might.

CCO add a secret dimension to familiar forms of international

357 Langford, I, 2014, 'Australian Special Operations: Principles and Considerations', pp. 27–29

engagement, such as military exercises, training activities, foreign military sales, port visits, key leadership exchanges, professional development, historical studies, conferences, and joint media press conferences. These activities facilitate a permanent 'warm start' for operations in particular regions and areas of interest. Australia will have 'a foot on the ground' in traditional military parlance should a threat emerge or change suddenly. This presence means Australia will have what it does not have now, a 'first strike' option using space, cyber, surgical strike or even maritime or air firepower. Put simply, CCO are about deterrent statecraft across a spectrum that includes competing for influence on one end to applying lethal force for strategic effect at the other. It is fruitless to counter grey zone campaigns without lawful, graduated and potent CCO options.

Enablers – Neighbourhood Watch

Enabling operations empower proxy forces in conjunction with information warfare activities, sometimes known as 'propaganda' operations. Enabling can create pre-conditions for carefully calibrated surgical strikes against grey zone combatants. Enabling processes emphasise the importance of gaining and maintaining access to Australia's areas of interest through the persistent presence and strategic investment on a country-to-country basis.

In the context of an international environment acknowledged as being in a permanent state of strategic competition, a deliberate decision to maintain a persistent presence through Response Force and Strike Force engagement would allow Australia to build its form of Anti-Access/Area Denial system in the grey zone.[358] Enabling is an ability to collaborate with Australia's partners and consider their critical contributions to a regional de-escalation strategy. This approach depends on a long-term plan to shape, understand, and influence Australia's near region or other priority areas of strategic interest, very much in the spirit of the Australian 2020 Strategic Update.

Enabling operations involve clandestine Strike Force personnel

358 Langford, I, 2017, 'Australia's Offset and A2/AD Strategies'

operating in small teams in areas of strategic influence. It is a long-term engagement campaign to identify and invest in people and places to shape and influence civilian, foreign military forces, and law enforcement colleagues. Enabling 'trade-craft' includes mentoring, training assistance, enablement with niche technologies, targeted diplomatic influence and capacity building through specialised aid.

De-escalation is an essential attribute of enabling operations. Strike Force would contribute to joint, interagency and alliance teams to destabilise an adversary's hybrid campaign or preliminary covert operations in preparation for their conventional campaign. This destabilisation acts as a deterrent to escalating hybrid operations or deciding to go to war. Enabling tactics deter armed conflict through a series of mutually reinforcing actions.

'Persistent presence' teams counter and defeat an adversary's unconventional and information warfare capabilities, both directly and indirectly, through the conduct of influence programs, building partner capability and setting information conditions favourable to Australia's interests. The resulting 'escalation dominance' establishes a position of strength against an adversary's unconventional and information warfare efforts. They act as a deterrent, giving other elements of Australia's national power the initiative and latitude to expand their own competitive space.

The Goblins – Electro-Magnetic Spectrum Operations

'Ghosts' and 'Enablers' are not enough. For Australia to have the total capacity or use modern parlance, a full spectrum of response and strike capabilities, the nation must also conduct offensive and defensive electromagnetic strike operations [EMSO] anywhere and at any time worldwide. Modern conflict involves all domains: land, maritime, air, space, cyber and information.[359] Cyber strikes, electro-magnetic storms, and non-detectable manoeuvre of Strike teams all feature significantly in Strike Force operations of the future – the realm of Ghosts and Goblins.

The traditional environmental domains (maritime, land and air) will

359 Ibid and Langford, I, 2017, podcast, Covert Contact podcast

still be the main battle-spaces of future conventional war. Still, emerging space, cyber and human information domains will determine the success or failure of both grey zone and traditional campaigns. Strike Force teams must be able to move inside, outside, and across all of these domains if they have a strategic impact disproportionate to their size or the superior conventional and unconventional capabilities of a national adversary or the asymmetric capabilities of a sub-national adversary. They must create winning advantages by employing forces and abilities in the space, cyber and human information vectors as a core capability.

EMSO strengthens Australia's resilience to an adversary's 'information confrontation capabilities' by mapping cyberspace to conduct deniable cyber offensive operations when and where necessary to do so. CCO and enabling operations capabilities, incorporating EMSO, facilitates deployment of Australian 'sovereignty' into highly contested threat areas for destruction, disruption, hostage rescue, high-value time-sensitive targeting, and setting of conditions for the conduct of other military operations and whole-of-government effects.

EMSO adds a dimension to Australia's independent reconnaissance-strike capabilities. The technological constituent of the contest in the grey zone will evolve to include weapons based on new information-age physical principles. One dimension will be Australian-generated 'information confrontation capabilities' that develops 'deep fake' propaganda. Its narratives would influence the will, emotions, behaviour, psychology, and morale of the adversary government and its population or a hostile sub-national group and its supporters.

Artificial Intelligence is an attribute of EMSO. Strike teams with swarms of self-learning, autonomous machines can distribute sensing, movement, targeting, and communications away from vulnerable areas and out to the edges of vast, dispersed networks. Adversaries would no longer concentrate on a few significant targets and instead need to search and scan for many things over larger spaces. These swarms would generate tempo, deception and mass – Clausewitzian friction.[360] These swarms contribute to neutralising opposing IT systems in Australia's area of strategic interest.

---

360 Watts, BD, 2004, 'Clauswitzian Friction and Future War'

Conclusion

Taken together, these Strike Force attributes and ways and means become part of an Australian strategic end-to-end system. EMSO, supported by CCO and enabling operations, constitute the essence of Australia's Response Power. This combination integrates Joseph Nye's hard, soft, smart and sharp power taxonomy.[361] They complement the ways and means of diplomatic, informational and economic power and hard military power (maritime, land and air). This approach accords with Shemella's prescriptions that integrate diplomatic, informational, military, economic, financial, intelligence and legal effort to shift the focus from responding to future attacks to anticipating and preventing them.[362]

If all of these measures fail to deter escalation, 'persistently present' Strike Force teams can assist inbound ADF Joint Task Forces with detailed tactical and operational intelligence preparation. Forward positioned 'Strikers' would conduct intensive preparations for future unconventional warfare in support of conventional operations. Strike teams would find targets for and coordinate long-range hypersonic missiles and space-based high energy weapons, as well as precision-guided munitions released from air, land and maritime weapons platforms. Strike Force will generate electro-magnetic 'storms' to 'keyhole' an adversary's Anti-Access, Area-Denial Systems. They will penetrate layered physical defences through a combination of cyber strikes, human activities via proxies and agents, as well as a physical manoeuvre of strike teams as part of a destructive effect.[363]

These Strike Force attributes are politically and ethically challenging for a liberal democracy like Australia. There will be no appetite to build a Strike Force until the prospect of political warfare transitioning to hybrid warfare is confirmed and accepted by most Australian people and their political and civil society elites. The lessons of the Strategic Reconnaissance Department during the Pacific War are there to learn.

---

361 Nye, J, 2011, *The Future of Power*

362 Shemella, P, 2011, *Fighting Back: What Governments Can Do About Terrorism,* p. 135

363 Langford, I, 2014, 'Australian Special Operations', and Langford, I, 2017, 'Australia's Offset and A2/AD Strategies'

The United States did not declare war on terror until grievously struck on 9/11. I hope Australia will not 'sleepwalk' to its strategic surprise. I am trying to make the threat real by echoing current warnings and proposing a de-escalation strategy. Still, I acknowledge that proposals for change like establishing a potent Strike Force must comprehend liberal democratic values, bureaucracies' sluggishness, and political and economic realities.

Building a Strike Force depends on the political will to direct it to act early, persistently, and sometimes, as a last resort, lethally. On the one hand, Strike Force operations come with political and physical risks. These risks increase when operating with and through international partners and proxy forces. It is essential to know the risks before taking them. On the other hand, Australia's Strike Force will be a risk mitigator. It does not seek or invite a military contest. It mitigates the risk of conflict and slows the bullying momentum. At worst, there will be some political embarrassment if covert and clandestine activities are compromised. But that will be lessened because all actions taken will ease tensions and de-escalate. There would be no sinister bellicose motives to discover. The rationale is to deter bullying and seek negotiation.

In sum, a Strike Force gives Australia the capability to detect threats and generate sufficient well-calibrated coercive force that can achieve deterrence and strategic effects anywhere and at any time. It offers Australian governments other options than conventional forces to protect threatened sovereignty and national interests. Strike Force warns and pushes against coercion while DFAT and Australia's political leaders invite discussion and negotiations to achieve rapprochement.

Afterthought

The history of the lost opportunities for SRD operations during the Pacific War is instructive. Still, I acknowledge that hindsight from 1942–45 is not a strong argument for changing Australia's strategic posture and developing a Strike Force in the 21st Century. Hindsight is notably cleverer than foresight.[364] But I would like to ask some

364 Ascribed to US Admiral Chester Nimitiz, quoted in Taylor, T, 2006, *The Magnificent Mitscher*, p. 266

hypothetical questions in addition to the lessons for concluding and setting the scene for the next chapter.

What if Australia had acted as a sovereign nation when the strategic warning bells began ringing in 1940 about Japan joining the Axis Alliance at war and hedged the Singapore Strategy with Special Operations Australia (SOA) as a fourth fighting force? What if SOA had been a fourth fighting force in 1942? Would Japan have had second thoughts about bombing Darwin and invading the Melanesian archipelago if SOA had destroyed significant numbers of Japanese ships in harbours and aircraft on airfields in Southeast Asia after the fall of Singapore?

Australia started to develop the equivalent of Response Power and a Strike Force in 1942 only after strategic surprise in December 1941 and the fall of Singapore in 1942. Service Chiefs opposed the diversion of their resources for SOA strike operations in 1942 and the following years. By the time SOA operations and technology were ready to disrupt the Japanese war effort in Southeast Asia, the war was over. By then, Service chiefs and political leaders acknowledged the significant contribution of SOA to shortening the war.

The Service Chiefs will be a significant impediment to the development of Australian Response Power in the 21st Century. They are likely to resist a de-escalation strategy because their focus is on warfighting, not 'war preventing'. Raising a Strike Force with high-technology de-escalation surveillance and stingers threatens the billions of dollars allocated to spend on ships, submarines, tanks, artillery, fighter aircraft and long-range missiles. They will argue against a fourth fighting force that dissipates their power. None will support Strike Force having autonomous rapid movement capabilities and high technology stingers. Special Forces will proudly declare that they are the force of choice, as they have been since 9/11. Undaunted, I offer a plan of action in the final chapter.

Part 5 – The way ahead

CHAPTER 7

The way ahead

Introduction

The strategic alarm bells are sounding for the US-led Western alliance about Chinese and Russian strategic ambitions. Borrowing from David Kilcullen, the Cold War dragons are back and have learned to fight the West on their terms in the grey zone. The Australian people are more anxious about the future than at any time since the Lowy Opinion Poll began 16 years ago. For a people who can become unsettled over toilet paper supplies, an escalation of the CPC's political and economic coercion to a hybrid war might precipitate contagion behaviour that divides communities and brings down governments. A grey zone campaign is already changing Australia by forcing more and more punitive legislation as the light grey Phase of political warfare escalates secretly.

It is time to toughen up. Australia needs a de-escalation strategy and Response Power to counter the CPC grey zone campaign in Australia and its regional neighbourhood. There is also a case for stopping China in China because China is attempting to undermine Australia in Australia. It is better to disappoint than provoke and, borrowing from Peter Varghese, to engage and constrain rather than attempt to isolate and contain. It is also better to aggregate regional de-escalation strategies rather than only aggregating conventional military power. Arguably, a traditional containment approach signalled by dialogues such as the Quadrilateral Security Dialogue, called the QUAD, gives CPC hardliners grounds for escalating Chinese conventional military power expenditure.[365] Banking only on containing China militarily

365 The Quad (Quadrilateral Security Dialogue) is a dialogue platform of like-minded countries (India, USA, Australia and Japan) that share the common attributes of democracy, pluralism and market-based economy with growing convergences in strategic and security perceptions, especially in the Indo-Pacific region.

gives hardliners more leverage over moderates in Beijing. Containment strategies allow them to argue that the United States and its allies are denying China's destiny aggressively and preparing for war. Still, investments in ships, land forces, strike aircraft and missiles will not trouble CPC grey zone campaigns.

Implementation

My proposed de-escalation strategy, involving the projection of Response Power and changes to institutional machinery for national security, does not fit neatly into any particular government portfolio's core business or current priorities. Defence, Home Affairs, DFAT, Attorney General's and the NIC are likely to resist implementation because a de-escalation strategy will re-direct some of their funds and organisational effort. However, DFAT and ASIS may appreciate the need to harden Australia's diplomatic posture to gain the CPC's respectful, albeit resentful, attention and acceptance of Australia's political and alliance preferences.

Let's look at a case study to inform the way ahead. The last time an Australian government received and adopted an externally developed de-escalation strategy for protecting national interests in its regional neighbourhood was in 2003. Dr Elsina Wainwright, then Program Director at the Australian Strategic Policy Institute, wrote *Our Failing Neighbour – Australia and the future of Solomon Islands.*[366] She took a draft to Defence and presumably to DFAT and possibly Attorney General's in December 2002. The establishment of the Department of Home Affairs was still 14 years away.[367] Officials ignored her despite warning about the consequences of Australia not doing enough for 'failing South Pacific neighbours.' The existing policies of advice, cash and patrol boats were not working.[368] She argued that a whole-of-government sponsorship of a regional intervention into Solomon Islands was not a neo-colonial provocation but the actions of a capable neighbour helping a neighbour under pressure. Though not naming

366 Wainwright, E, 2003, *Our Failing Neighbour*

367 Department of Home Affairs, 2020, 'Our History'

368 Breen, B, 2016, *The Good Neighbour*, pp. 361–62

it in 2003, she was advocating a de-escalation strategy. No one in the departments responsible for protecting Australia's national interests agreed with her. In January 2003, Australia's Foreign Minister, Alexander Downer, was emphatic about the folly of intervening in Solomon Islands.[369]

Wainwright's paper found support in the Solomon Islands Government. Prompted by a draft sent to the consulate in Canberra for comment, Prime Minister Alan Kemakeza wrote to Prime Minister John Howard on 22 April 2003 seeking Australian intervention. In a rare consolidation of departmental opinion, Defence, DFAT and Prime Minister and Cabinet advised Howard not to intervene. For their part, Defence officials by-passed advice from the Chief of the Defence Force, General Peter Cosgrove, who supported a 'circuit breaking' intervention – a de-escalation mission – to persuade Defence Minister Senator Robert Hill to suggest a 'package of targeted measures.'[370]

In the end, John Howard brought Alexander Downer and Robert Hill together and directed them to have their departments prepare intervention options for his consideration. He had decided that it was Australia's responsibility to step up its statecraft to act decisively to de-escalate the Solomon Islands crisis. It was an armed deterrence operation that would provide security for disarming militia groups threatening civil war.

Pre-publication copies of Wainwright's paper were available for policymakers and planners by this time. It provided a rationale, several prescriptions and a plan. Arguably, no one in Defence, DFAT or Attorney General's could have designed a whole-of-government intervention. An Inter-Departmental Task Force [IDTF] decided to appoint a senior Australian diplomat in charge, an AFP commissioner in command, and assign 1,200 ADF personnel and ships and helicopters in support. The IDTF also designed the intervention to be 'whole-of-region' by including contingents from police and military units from New Zealand and other Pacific Islands neighbours, thus *enabling* [author's emphasis] the region to deal with a regional

---

369 Downer, A, 2003, 'Neighbours cannot be recolonised', p.11

370 Breen, B, 2016, *The Good Neighbour*, p. 364

problem. There are still debates about the duration and expense of the Regional Assistance Mission to Solomon Islands.[371] Still, no one doubts its success as a circuit breaker on lawlessness and the collapse of governance in 2003–04. The intervention was Prime Minister John Howard's masterstroke of de-escalation.

Steps

Prime Ministerial leadership. Step one for implementing a de-escalation strategy is for Prime Minister Scott Morrison or his successor to bring Cabinet colleagues in the National Security Committee of Cabinet together to discuss this book. Each department will most likely provide contested advice and warn against the book's prescriptions. Defence officials may argue that espionage and foreign interferences are Home Affairs and DFAT problems. The RAN and RAAF may argue that developing a Strike Force for Response Power is an Army problem. The Army may agree that foreign interference is a Home Affairs issue but argue that Special Forces should focus only on counterterrorism at home and counter-insurgency operations overseas, as well as responses to sensitive incidents. Home Affairs may argue that the nature of hybrid warfare is a military threat, a Defence problem. DFAT may support muscling up ASIS to counter foreign interference but shy away from managing and employing the range of capabilities proposed for Strike Force. Diplomats may also argue that Strike Force capabilities will send too strong a message to the CPC that will provoke further economic retribution and other types of bullying behaviour. Hopefully, like John Howard, any Australian Prime Minister will comprehend the motives of departmental opposition and understand the grey zone. A Prime Minister should look to the bigger strategic picture and the sovereign responsibilities of Australian statecraft and 'bang ministerial heads together' to enhance Australian capabilities in the grey zone.

Inter-Departmental Task Force. The second step after Cabinet consensus is to establish an Inter-Departmental Task Force [IDTF]

---

371 Hayward-Jones, J, 2014, 'Australia's costly investment in Solomon Islands: The Lessons of RAMSI'

involving Federal, State and Territory representatives to produce unclassified and classified versions of Australia's de-escalation strategy and its Response Power requirements. This plan should be articulated publicly in an innovative National Security White Paper and secretly in a capability development plan. Each instrument of Australia's national power would contribute capability bricks. The Departments and agencies securing Australia will come together to provide the ways and means for projecting Response Power and building a Response Force and Strike Force.

Legislation. The third implementation step is to communicate this new strategy with laws and the media to shape both friends and foes' thinking about Australia's intentions to defend its sovereignty and national interests. The Australian public should know that its government is strategically astute and pro-actively developing capabilities to protect them against intrusive nations and sub-national groups employing political and hybrid warfare, including terrorism, in the grey zone. The strategic message is that Australia has a Response Force and a Strike Force that works with departmental and agency partners to identify threats to Australia's national interests and de-escalate those threats before they harm – precautionary and ethical, but potent. This strategy enables Australia's security machinery and force projection to be pre-emptive rather than reactive and reflexive.

Response Power. The fourth step is to develop Response Power, the instrument and practical modality of a de-escalation strategy. Response Power enhances force projection capabilities to integrate with and sharpen Australian national power's diplomatic, informational, military, and economic tools. Response Power depends on expertly selected, trained and rehearsed intelligent and capable people. It marshals Australia's ingenuity and optimises its human capital. Sophisticated technology must support the Response Power workforce. Notably, both Response Force and Strike Force must have the autonomous capabilities to deploy anywhere and at any time covertly and clandestinely. They should not be dependent on departments and agencies whose speed and agility will not meet their requirements. The preparatory functions of Response Power projection must be ready and capable, not the first urgent idea when surprised, and the threat is obvious as was the case on 6 December 1941 (Pearl Harbour) and 11 September 2001 (New York and Washington). The operational functions and organisational muscle groups must be 'stress-tested' with the robust rehearsal of contingencies under pressure to enable effective employment where and when necessary.

Smart and capable people

It is time to marshal Australia's human capital for national defence in increasingly uncertain times that Scott Morrison compared to the pre-Second World War 1930s.[372] There is no reason why Australia cannot develop the most sophisticated, technologically-enabled detection and deterrence arrangements supported by the most potent Strike Force in the world. There are plenty of educated and impressive Australian men and women with the right attributes. Hopefully, civilian and military leaders have the imagination, commitment, foresight, and ingenuity to step up to the challenge.

De-escalating grey zone threats will require Australia to select, train and manage intelligent and capable people. Multi-agency task forces will need specialists in intelligence analysis, cross-cultural analysis, sociology, psychology, surveillance, and cyber, political and information operations. DFAT, Defence and Home Affairs cannot generate the range of intelligent people necessary to meet Response Power requirements as single departmental efforts.

There should be civilian and military members of the Strike Force. This integration captures the spirit of a whole-of-government de-escalation approach and optimises talent. It will be essential to access skills, knowledge and attributes from civilian specialists, many ADF reservists from the corporate sector subject to the Defence Act and Official Secrets Act. Expert recruitment and training specialists should recruit and train military and civilian specialists to implement a de-escalation strategy.

Let's look at another case study. Some may argue that Australia does not have the human capital, ingenuity or organisational imagination to implement a multi-agency de-escalation strategy. An analogy would be

---

372 Morrison, S, 2020, 'Address – Launch of the 2020 Defence Strategic Update'

a New Zealander arguing that there is not enough human capital in New Zealand to field a world-class Rugby Union team. Other countries have larger populations, resources, imagination, experience, sophistication, technology, and ingenuity. The performance of New Zealand's national teams, the All Blacks and Black Ferns defy this pessimistic argument. Envious Australians argue that New Zealand's advantage is a national focus on Rugby Union to exclude other team sports. They opine that Australia has competing team sports that deny Australia's national Rugby Union teams, the Wallabies and the Wallaroos, the elite athletes they need to excel internationally.

These arguments are nonsense. New Zealand Rugby Union selects, trains and manages its human capital with organisational machinery, ingenuity and commitment that begins at the community level. New Zealand Rugby Union, with the enthusiastic support of the nation, employs specially-selected, trained and managed men and women with a strong ethos and skills for collective success against opposing nations with larger populations and more generic resources.

Professor John Blaxland calls for an Australian Universal Scheme for National and Community Service.[373] This compulsory marshalling and development of Australian human capital make sense for a specialised de-escalation strategy. There are two attractive features; the inclusion of generations of young Australians in common purpose to contribute their time and talent to Australia's common good and well-being; the freedom of choice for how that contribution can be made. Hopefully, the call to defend Australia by participating in a de-escalation strategy as a 'Striker' with Strike Force will resonate with educated and exceptional young Australians from all ethnic backgrounds who prefer to prevent war now rather than urgently and hurriedly train for one later.

Response Power needs a whole-of-government education and training system. This step is about integration rather than separate institutional development. Defence, Home Affairs and DFAT all have education and training systems for their workforces. These systems are for the core functions of those departments. Accordingly, the IDTF has to identify the expertise required for the Response Power workforce

---

373 Blaxland, J, 2020, *Developing a new Plan B for the ADF*, p. 22

and outsource the needs analysis that will lay the foundation for the design, development, delivery and evaluation functions of a Response Power education and training system. The intention is to enhance well-established department and agency education and training systems for the skilling of the Response Power workforce that will work within well-established arrangements for counter-terrorism and emerging arrangements for countering espionage and foreign interference anywhere and anytime.

Affordability

A de-escalation strategy with its Response Power instruments is affordable for middle and smaller powers. The ways and means are about human performance with technical augmentation rather than ships, submarines, tanks, artillery and strike aircraft using human operators. It is about ingenuity rather than firepower versus firepower. In short, investments in innovative and capable people, agile organisational machinery and technology cost less than just acquiring more ships, submarines, tanks, aircraft and missiles. Arguably, Australia's expenditure on conventional military power will never meet the threshold for deterring hard-line CPC ambitions for creating tribute states or landing a decisive blow on an invasion fleet as well as the airpower that will have to precede and protect it. Acknowledging that 'arming up' is still prudent, Response Power comes with a bonus. It optimises Australia's conventional military power and diplomatic, informational, and economic power when precision targeting, sharper negotiations, and immediate 'Fair Dinkum' consequences for rude and nasty behaviour are required.

Finally, I agree with Clive Hamilton when he concludes *Silent Invasion*, 'Our naivety and our complacency are Beijing's strongest assets. Boy Scouts up against Don Corleone. But once Australians of all ethnic backgrounds understand the danger, we can begin to protect our freedoms from the new totalitarianism.'[374] More optimistically, he concludes *Hidden Hand* with, 'People on the left and right who have opened their eyes to the threat posed by the CCP (sic), including those

---

374 Hamilton, C, 2018, *Silent Invasion*, p. 281

who have left China to escape it, are banding together. The pushback is growing by the day, and the party bosses in Beijing are worried.'[375] I am proud to be part of Australia's pushback. Hopefully, those in the CPC and China who seek a peaceful and prosperous world will respect Australia's efforts to de-escalate rather than defy; to disappoint rather than provoke; to always engage positively for rapprochement rather than exclude resentfully, or just rattle a $274 bn sabre over the next ten years.

Australia's de-escalation strategy and Response Power projection should be hard and hurtful enough to prompt Xi Jinping and CPC hardliners to have second thoughts about relations with Australia. A fair and equal relationship is a better option. Hopefully, Response Power creates both the disappointment and respect that leads to better relations. If not, it de-escalates in the grey zone as soon as possible and buys time before Australia's enhanced conventional military deterrence comes online. Alan Dupont made an insightful observation on 25 July 2020:

> Ultimately, however, we need to craft our own strategy for dealing with a more aggressive China and not rely on the goodwill of others. ... The objective of our policy is not to turn China into an enemy but to make Xi understand that while we value the relationship, we will not be coerced or threatened into compromising our sovereignty or values. ... Understanding that Xi is a devoted practitioner of hard power should inform our policy approach ...[376]

375 Hamilton, C & Onlbereg, M, 2020, *Hidden Hand*, p. 270

376 Dupont, A, 2020, 'Who's afraid of the big bad wolf warriors'

Bibliography

Australian Government

Australian National Audit Office 2020, *Future Submarine Program – Transition to Design,* Department of Defence, retrieved 23 January 2020, https://www.anao.gov.au/work/performance-audit/future-submarine-program-transition-to-design

Australian National Audit Office 2020, *Joint Strike Fighter – Introduction into Service and Sustainment Planning, Report No 14*, Department of Defence, Summary, retrieved 24 January 2020, https://www.anao.gov.au/work/performance-audit/joint-strike-fighter-introduction-service-and-sustainment

ASIO, Burgess, M, 2020, 'Director-General's Annual Threat Assessment 2020', Australian Security Intelligence Organisation website, 24 February, retrieved 23 May 2020, https://www.asio.gov.au/publications/speeches-and-statements/director-general-annual-threat-assessment-0.html

ASIO, 2020, Counter Espionage and Foreign Interference, ASIO website, retrieved 12 August 2020, https://www.asio.gov.au/counter-espionage.html

Attorney-General's Department 2020, 'Australia's counter-terrorism laws', Attorney General's website, retrieved 9 August 2020, https://www.ag.gov.au/national-security/australias-counter-terrorism-laws

Australian Government, 2015, *National Cyber Security Strategy,* Department of Prime Minister and Cabinet, Canberra

Australian Government, 2016, *Defence White Paper*, Department of Defence, Canberra

Australian Government, 2017, *2017 Independent Intelligence Review*, Department of Prime Minister and Cabinet, Canberra, retrieved 12 May 2020, https://www.pmc.gov.au/national security/2017-independent-intelligence-review

Australian Government, 2017, 2017 Foreign Policy White Paper, Canberra, retrieved 19 February 2021, https://www.dfat.gov.au/publications/minisite/2017-foreign-policy-white-paper/fpwhitepaper/pdf/2017-foreign-policy-white-paper.pdf

Australian Government, 2018, 'National Security Legislation Amendment (Espionage and Foreign Interference) Act 2018', C2018A00067, 29 June, Federal Register of Legislation, retrieved 9 August 2020, https://www.legislation.gov.au/Details/C2018A00067

Australian Government, 2018, Introduction of the Defence Amendment (Call Out of the Australian Defence Force) Bill 2018, 28 June, Parliament House, Canberra

Australian Government, 2020, *Australia's Pacific engagement, Stepping Up Australia's engagement with our Pacific family*, Department of Foreign Affairs and Trade website, retrieved 20 June 2020

Australian Government, 2018, National Security Legislation Amendment (Espionage And Foreign Interference) Bill 2017, Explanatory Memorandum, Circulated by authority of the Attorney-General, Senator the Honourable George Brandis QC, 29 June, retrieved 20 August 2020, https://www.aph.gov.au/Parliamentary_Business/Bills_Legislation/Bills_Search_Results/Result?bId=r6022

Australian Government, Counter-Terrorism Legislation Amendment Bill (No. 1) 2018, Explanatory Memorandum, Schedule 1 Amendments Current Threat Environment, Federal Register of Legislation

Parliament of Australia, 1901, The Constitution, Australian Government, Melbourne, retrieved 26 May 2018, retrieved 26 May 2018, https://www.legislation.gov.au/Details/C2005Q00193

Parliament of Australia, 1995, Criminal Code Act 1995, Australian Government, Canberra, retrieved 26 May 2018, retrieved 26 May 2018 https://www.legislation.gov.au/Search/C2018C00386%20accessed%20May%2026%202018

Australian Parliament 2018, National Security Legislation Amendment (Espionage and Foreign Interference) Act 2018, No. 67, Canberra, retrieved 14 July 2020, https://www.legislation.gov.au/Details/C2018A00067

Australian Parliament, Australia's Foreign Relations (State and Territory Arrangements) Bill 2020 and Australia's Foreign Relations (State and Territory Arrangements) (Consequential Amendments) Bill 2020, retrieved 20 October 2020, https://www.aph.gov.au/Parliamentary_Business/Committees/Senate/Foreign_Affairs_Defence_and_Trade/AustForeignRelations2020

Australian Government, 2018, Introduction of the Defence Amendment (Call Out of the Australian Defence Force) Bill 2018, 28 June, Parliament House, Canberra

Australian Parliament 2011, Human Rights (Parliamentary Scrutiny) Act 2011, retrieved 16 July 2020, https://www.legislation.gov.au/Details/C2011A00186

Parliament of Australia, 2018, *Call Out of the Australian Defence Force Bill 2018*, Australian Government, Canberra, retrieved 20 May 2020, https://www.legislation.gov.au/Details/C2018A00158

Department of Defence, 2003, *Future Warfighting Concept*, Canberra, retrieved 1 September 2019, https://www.defence.gov.au/publications/fwc.pdf

Department of Defence, *2020 Defence Strategic Update*, Canberra, 1 July 2020, retrieved 2 July 2020, https://www.defence.gov.au/about/publications/2020-defence-strategic-update

Department of Defence, 2020, *2020 Defence Force Structure Plan*, Canberra, 1 July 2020, retrieved 2 July 2020, https://www.defence.gov.au/about/publications/2020-defence-strategic-update

Department of Defence, 'Global Operations', Defence Department website, retrieved 7 June 2020, https://www.defence.gov.au/operations

Department of External Affairs, *Security Treaty between Australia, New Zealand and the United States of America [ANZUS]*, Australian Treaty series 1952 No 2, San Francisco, 1 September 1952, Article IV, retrieved 14 February 2021, http://www.austlii.edu.au/au/other/dfat/treaties/1952/2.html

Department of Home Affairs website Counter Foreign Interference, retrieved 12 August 2020, https://www.homeaffairs.gov.au/about-us/our-portfolios/national-security/countering-foreign-interference/cfi-strategy

Department of Home Affairs, 2020, 'Our History', Home Affairs website, retrieved 20 July 2020, https://www.homeaffairs.gov.au/about-us/who-we-are/our-history

Department of the Prime Minister and Cabinet, *Strong and Secure: A Strategy for Australia's National Security*, Commonwealth of Australia, Canberra

Department of Administrative Services, Mark, R, 1978, *Report to the Minister for Administrative Services on the Organisation of Police Resources in the Commonwealth Area and Other Related Matters*, Australian Government Publishing Service, Canberra

Australian Federal Police, Australian Federal Police Organisation Structure, AFP website, afp.gov.au, retrieved 15 February 2021, https://www.afp.gov.au/sites/default/files/PDF/AFPOrgStructure-08022021.pdf

Australian Federal Police, Specialist Response Group, AFP website, afp.gov.au, retrieved 15 February 2021, https://www.afp.gov.au/what-we-do/operational-support/specialist-response-group

Australian Federal Police 2014, Annual Report, 2014–15, Department of Home Affairs, Canberra, retrieved 11 August 2019, https://www.afp.gov.au/afp-annual-report-2014–15#chapter_4–2

Australian New Zealand Counter-Terrorism Committee 2017, *National Counter Terrorism Plan*, 4th ed, retrieved 23 March 2021, https://www.nationalsecurity.gov.au/Media-and-publications/Publications/Documents/ANZCTC-National-Counter-Terrorism-Plan.PDF

Australian Human Rights Commission, 2020, International Covenant on Civil and Political Rights – Human Rights at your Fingertips, AHRC website, retrieved 16 July 2020 https://humanrights.gov.au/our-work/commission-general/international-covenant-civil-and political-rights-human-rights-your

Australian Human Rights Commission 2020, Convention against Torture and Other Cruel, Inhuman and Degrading Treatment or Punishment – Human Rights at your Fingertips, AHRC website, retrieved 16 July 2020, https://humanrights.gov.au/our-work/commission-general/convention-against-torture-and-other-cruel-inhuman-or-degrading

Government of New South Wales

New South Wales Government, 2002, *Terrorism (Police Powers) Act 2002 No 115*, New South Wales Government, Sydney, retrieved 16 June 2018, https://www.legislation.nsw.gov.au/inforce/6f5a8912-c4e1-e5ba-aa92-93c10aa399a9/2002-115.pdf

Government of Victoria

State of Victoria 2010, R v Vinayagamoorthy & Ors. VSC 148, 31 March, Melbourne

State of Victoria 2017, Victorian Coroner's Inquest into the death of Yacqub Khayre, Melbourne

State of Victoria 2017, Justice Assurance and Review Office's review of Corrections Victoria's management of Khayre (JARO Review), Justice Assurance and Review Office, Melbourne

State of Victoria 2017, Expert Panel on Terrorism Report 2: The second report on how Victoria's legislation, powers and procedures are working to prevent, monitor, investigate and respond to terrorism, Department of Premier and Cabinet, Melbourne

Government of Western Australia

Western Australian Government, 2008, Billing v The State of Western Australia, WASCA, 21 January, Perth

Australian Defence Force

Australian Defence Force, 2020, Information Warfare–ADF Manoeuvre in the Information Environment, Commonwealth of Australia Publishing, Canberra

Australian National Archives

Official History of the Operations and Administration of Special Operations – Australia [(SOA), circa 1948, also known as the Inter-Allied Services Department (ISD) and Services Reconnaissance Department (SRD)] Volume 2 – Operations – copy no 4 [for Director, Military Intelligence (DMI), Headquarters (HQ), Australian Military Forces (AMF), Melbourne – abridged version of copy no 1]. Series no. A3269, O8/B, National Australian Archives Canberra, retrieved 31 August 2020, https://recordsearch.naa.gov.au/SearchNRetrieve/Interface/ViewImage.aspx?B=235326

Government of Estonia

Estonian Government, 2017, 'How Estonia Became a Global Heavyweight in Cyber Security', E-Estonia, Estonian Government, retrieved 21 October 2020 at https://e-estonia.com

Estonian Government, 2020, 'Estonian Demographics: 2020 Population', *Statistics Estonia*, Estonian Government, retrieved 20 October 2020 at http://www.stat.ee

NZ Government

New Zealand Ministry of Foreign Affairs and Trade, 'Building on a Success Story', MFAT website, retrieved 17 February 2021, https://www.mfat.govt.nz/en/trade/free-trade-agreements/free-trade-agreements-concluded-but-not-in-force/nz-china-free-trade-agreement-upgrade/overview/#:~:text=The%20New%20Zealand%2DChina%20Free,success%20story%20for%20both%20countries.&text=China%20is%20now%20New%20Zealand's,free%20trade%20agreement%20was%20signed

Australian New Zealand Counter-Terrorism Committee 2017, *National Counter Terrorism Plan*, 4th ed, p. 19, pp. 23–24, retrieved 23 March 2021, https://www.nationalsecurity.gov.au/Media-and-publications/Publications/Documents/ANZCTC-National-Counter-Terrorism-Plan.PDF

Government of Japan

Ministry of Foreign Affairs of Japan, 1960, Treaty of Mutual Cooperation and Security between Japan and the United States of America, 19 January, retrieved on 14 February 2021, https://www.mofa.go.jp/region/n-america/us/q&a/ref/1.html

US Government

US Department of Defense 2017, *Russia Military Power: Building a Military to Support Great Power Aspirations*, Defense Intelligence Agency, Government Printing Office, Washington DC, retrieved on 4 May 2020 https://www.dia.mil/Military-Power-Publications

US Department of Defense 2019, *China Military Power: Modernizing a Force to Fight and Win*, Defense Intelligence Agency, Government Printing Office, Washington DC, retrieved on 4 May 2020, https://www.dia.mil/Military-Power-Publications

United States Department of Defense 2014, *Strategy for countering weapons of mass destruction*, United States Special Operations Command, Tampa

United States Government, 2018, *National Strategy for Counter-terrorism- October 2018*, The White House National Security Committee, Washington DC, retrieved 11 March 2019, https://www.whitehouse.gov/wp-content/uploads/2018/10/NSCT.pdf

Central Intelligence Agency, Federal Bureau of Investigation, and National Security Agency 2017, Assessing Russian Activities and Intentions in Recent US Elections, *Intelligence Community Assessment*, 6 January, retrieved 4 February, https://www.dni.gov/files/documents/ICA_2017_01.pdf

US Embassies and Consulates in China, 2019, '2018 Report on International Religious Freedom: China (Includes Tibet, Xinjiang, Hong Kong, and Macau)', 21 June 2019, retrieved 14 July 2020, https://china.usembassy-china.org.cn/2018-report-on-international-religious-freedom-china

US Government, Kean, TH, Hamilton, LH, Ben-Veniste, R, Kerrey, B, Fielding, FF, Lehman, JF, Gorelick, JS, Roemer, TJ, Gorton, S, & Thompson, JR, 2004. *The 9–11 Commission' Report, National Commission on Terrorist Attacks Upon the United States,* United States Government, Washington DC, p. 346, retrieved 18 May 2020, https://www.9–11commission.gov/report/911Report.pdf

US Army 2017, *Multi-Domain Battle: Evolution of Combined Arms for the 21st Century 2025–2040*, Training United States Army 2011, Army Doctoral Publication 3–05 Special Operations, Government Printing Office, Washington, DC, Doctrine Command, Fort Eustis, VA, retrieved 12 September 2020 https://www.tradoc.army.mil/Portals/14/Documents/MDB_Evolutionfor21st%20(1).pdf

US Special Operations Command, JP 3–05, 2013, *Special Operations,* United States Special Operations Command, Tampa

UK Government

UK Government, 2017 Understanding Hybrid Warfare, Countering Hybrid Warfare (CHW), Multinational Capability Development Campaign (MCDC) Project, UK Government, London, retrieved 12 February 2020, https://www.gov.uk/government/publications/countering-hybrid-warfare-project-understanding-hybrid-warfare

UK Government, 2019, Countering Hybrid Warfare, Countering Hybrid Warfare, (CHW) Multinational Capability Development Campaign (MCDC) Project, UK Government, London, retrieved 12 February 2020, https://www.gov.uk/government/publications/countering-hybrid-warfare-project-understanding-hybrid-warfare

UK Government, 2014, 'The situation in Iraq and Syria and the response to al-Dawla al-Islamiya fi al-Iraq al-Sham (DAESH)', House of Commons Defence Committee, 7th Report of Session, 15, London

UK Government, 2018, *CONTEST – the United Kingdom's Strategy for Countering Terrorism, June 2018,* Home Department, London, retrieved 1 February 2019, https://www.safecampuscommunities.ac.uk/uploads/files/2019/03/contest_uks_counter_terrorism_strategy.pdf

North Atlantic Treaty Organisation

North Atlantic Treaty Organisation 1949, NATO Treaty, NATO website, retrieved 13 January 2021, https://www.nato.int/cps/en/natolive/official_texts_17120.htm

Books

Allison, G, 2017, *Destined for war: Can America and China escape Thucydides' trap?*, Houghton Mifflin Harcourt, Boston, MA

Bekjr Ilhan, *China's Evolving Military Doctrine after the Cold War,* Siyaset, Ekonomi Ve Toplum Araştirmalari Vakfi Foundation for Political, Economic and Social Research, Ankora, Turkey

Brady, AM, 2003, *Making the foreign serve China: managing foreigners in the People's Republic*, Rowman & Littlefield

Brady AM ed. 2012, *China's Thought Management*, Routledge, New York, retrieved 10 June 2020, https://trove.nla.gov.au/work/38962534?q&versionId=51751347

Breen, B, 2008, *Struggling for Self-Reliance: Four case studies of Australian Regional Force Projection in the late 1980s and the 1990s.* Australian National University Press, Canberra, retrieved 3 March 2022, https://press.anu.edu.au/publications/series/sdsc/struggling-self-reliance

Breen, B, 2016, *The Good Neighbour: Australian Peace Support Operations in the Pacific Islands 1980–2006*, Cambridge University Press, Melbourne

Clausewitz, C, 1984, Howard, M & Paret, P eds., *On War*, Princeton University Press, United States

Cronin, PM ed. 2008, *The Impenetrable Fog of War: Reflections on Modern Warfare and Strategic Surprise*, Greenwood Press Group, Praeger Security International, Westport, CT

Davies, W, 2021, *Special and Secret, The untold story of Z Special Unit in the Second World War*, Vintage Books, Australia

Dewar, M, 1985, *British Army in Northern Ireland*, Guild Publishing, Wilts, UK

Fitzgerald, J, (ed), 2022, 'Taking the low road: Chinese influence in Australian states and territories', 15 February, Australian Strategic Policy Institute, Canberra, retrieved 8 March 2022, https://www.aspi.org.au/report/taking-low-road-chinas-influence-australian-states-and-territories

Friedburg, AL, 2011, *A Contest for Supremacy: China, America, and the Struggle for Mastery in Asia*, W.W. Norton and Company, New York

Jacques, M, 2014, *When China Rules the World, When China Rules The World: The End of the Western World and the Birth of a New Global Order*, Penguin Books, London

Jian Hua To, J, 2014, *Qiaowu: Extra-Territorial Policies for the Overseas Chinese*, Brill, Leiden, Netherlands, retrieved 10 June 2020, https://books.google.com.au/books?id=KGe7AwAAQBAJ&pg=PR5&dq=qiaowu%E2%80%99+strategy&source=gbs_selected_pages&cad=3#v=onepage&q=qiaowu%E2%80%99%20strategy&f=false

Jonsson, O, 2019, *The Russian Understanding of War: blurring the lines between war and peace*, Georgetown University Press, Georgetown, Washington DC

Ganor, B, 2015, *Global Alert: The Rationality of Modern Islamist Terrorism and the Challenge to the Liberal Democratic World*, Columbia University Press, New York

Hai-Chi Loo, J, Shiu Hing Lo, S and Chung-Fun Hung, S, 2019, *China's New United Front Work in Hong Kong: Penetrative Politics and Its Implications*, Palgrave MacMillan, Singapore

Hamill, I, 1981, *The Strategic Illusion: The Singapore Strategy for the defence of Australia and New Zealand, 1919–1942*, Singapore University Press, Singapore

Hamilton, C, 2018, *Silent Invasion: China's influence in Australia*, Hardie Grant Books, Melbourne

Hamilton, C & Onlbereg, M, 2020, *Hidden Hand: Exposing how the Chinese Communist party is reshaping the world*, Hardie Grant Books, Sydney

Hoffman, F, 2007, *Conflict in the 21st Century: The Rise of Hybrid War*, Potomac Institute for Policy Studies, Arlington, VA, retrieved 23 January 2020, https://www.potomacinstitute.org/images/stories/publications/potomac_hybridwar_0108.pdf

Hoffman, F, 2007, *Thoughts on 21st century warfare*, Potomac Press, Washington

Horner, D, 1982, *High Command: Australia and Allied Strategy, 1939–1945*, Australian War Memorial and Allen and Unwin, Sydney

Horner, D, 1996, *Inside the War Cabinet: Directing Australia's War Effort 1939–1945*, Allen and Unwin, Sydney

Horner, D, 1998, *Blamey: Commander in Chief*, Allen and Unwin, Sydney

Ikenberry GJ, 2015, *America, China, and the Struggle for World Order: Ideas, Traditions, Historical Legacies and Global Visions*, Palgrave, New York

Kilcullen, D, 2020, *The Dragons and the Snakes: How the Rest Learned to Fight the West*, Scribe, Melbourne

Liang, Q & Xiangsui, W, 1999, *Unrestricted Warfare: China's Master Plan to Destroy America*, 2017 Kindle Edition, Shadow Lawn Press, New York

Mazarr, MJ, 2015, *Mastering the gray zone: understanding a changing era of conflict*, US Army War College Carlisle

McDonald, H, Ball, D, Dunn, J, van Kinken, G, Bourchier, D, Kammen, D & Tanter R, 2002, *Masters of Terror, Indonesia's military and violence in East Timor in 1999*, Policy Paper no 145, Strategic and Defence Studies Centre, ANU, Canberra

Neville, L, 2015, *Special Forces and the War on Terror*, Osprey Publishing, Oxford, UK

Petit, B, 2013, *Going Big by Getting Small: The Application of Operational Art by Special Operations in Phase Zero*, Outskirts Press, Parker, CO

Pillsbury, M, 2015, *The Hundred-Year Marathon: China's Secret Strategy to Replace America as the Global Superpower*, Henry Holt &Company, New York

Raby, G, 2020, 'China's Grand Strategy and Australia's Future in the New Global Order', Melbourne University Press, Melbourne

Rid, T, 2013, *Cyber war will not take place*, Oxford University Press, UK

Sanger, DE, 2018, *The Perfect Weapon*, Broadway Books, New York

Schelling, TC, 1966, *Arms and Influence*, Yale University Press, New Haven

Schelling, TC, 1980, *The Strategy of Conflict*, Harvard University Press, CT

Seidman, D, 2011, 'How: Why HOW We Do Anything Means Everything', John Wiley and Sons Publishing

Singer, PW and Brooking, ET, 2018, *LikeWar: The Weaponization of Social Media*, Houghton Mifflin Harcourt Publishing Company, New York

Silver, L, 2001, *Krait, the Fishing Boat that went to War*, Cultured Lotus, Sydney

Strachan, H, 2018, *The Direction of War: Contemporary Strategy in Historical Perspective*, Cambridge University Press, Cambridge, UK

Urban, M, 2012, *Big Boys' Rules: The SAS and the Secret Struggle Against the IRA*, Faber and Faber, London, UK

Valeriano, B and Maness, RC, 2015, *Cyber War Versus Cyber Realities*, Oxford University Press, New York

White, H, 2013, *The China Choice: why America should share power*, Black Inc, Melbourne

White, H, 2020, *How to Defend Australia*, Latrobe University Press/Black Inc, Melbourne

Yu-shek Cheng, J, 2020, *Political Development in Hong Kong*, World Scientific Publishing, Singapore

Book Chapters/Theses

Breen, B, 2006. Australian Military Force Projection in the late 1980s and the 1990s: What happened and Why, PhD Thesis, Australian National University, Canberra, retrieved 3 March 2022, https://openresearch-repository.anu.edu.au/bitstream/1885/7158/10/Breen-whole.pdf

Bury, RG, 1967, Plato, Plato in Twelve Volumes, vols 10 & 11, Harvard University Press, Cambridge, MA, retrieved 14 August 2020, http://www.perseus.tufts.edu/hopper/text?doc=Perseus%3Atext%3A1999.01.0166%3Abook%3D1%3Apage%3D626

Costello, J and McReynolds, J, 2020, 'China's Strategic Support Force: A Force for a New Era', Chapter 12 in Saunders, PC, Ding, AS, Scobell, A, Yang, AND and Wuthnow, J (eds) 2020, *Chairman Xi Remakes the PLA: Assessing Chinese Military Reforms,* National Defense University Press, Washington DC, retrieved 31 January 2020, https://ndupress.ndu.edu/Portals/68/Documents/Books/Chairman-Xi/Chairman-Xi.pdf

Dew, A, 2008, 'The Erosion of Constraints in Armed-Group Warfare: Bloody Tactics and Vulnerable Targets' in Norwitz, J ed. 2008, *Armed Groups: Studies in National Security, Counterterrorism and Counterinsurgency*, US Naval War College, Newport, RI

Kouretsos, P, 2019, 'A Literature Review' in Annex A: Contextualising Chinese Hybrid Warfare in Babbage, R, 2019 *Stealing a March: Chinese Hybrid Warfare in the Indo-Pacific: Issues and Options for Allied Defense Planners, vol. II Case Studies*, Center for Strategic and Budgetary Assessments, Washington DC, retrieved 12 February 2020, https://csbaonline.org/research/publications/stealing-a-march-chinese-hybrid-warfare-in-the-indo-pacific-issues-and-options-for-allied-defense-planners

Norberg, J, Westerlund, F & Franke, U 2014, 'The Crimea operation. Implications for future Russian military interventions' in Granholm, N, Malminen, J & Persson, G eds. 2014, *A rude awakening: ramifications of Russian aggression towards Ukraine,* FOI, Stockholm

Shemella, P, 2011, *Fighting Back: What Governments Can Do About Terrorism*, 1st edn., Stanford University Press, Redwood City, CA

Sparrow, R, 2011, 'Robotic Weapons and the Future of War', pp. 117–33, in Tripodi, P & Wolfendale J eds., *New Wars and New Soldiers: Military Ethics in the Contemporary World*, Ashgate Publishing Ltd, Surrey, UK

Taft, E, 2017, 'Outer Space: The Final Frontier or the Final Battlefield?', vol. 15, no. 1, *Duke Law & Technology Review*, Duke University, Durham, NC.

Whitmore, P, 2016 'Current Cyber Wars', in Janczewski, LJ and Caelli, W, 2016, *Cyber Conflicts and Small States*, Ashgate Publishing, Dorchester

Monographs

Babbage, R, 2015, *Game Plan: The Case for a New Australian Grand Strategy*, RG Menzies Essay, Menzies Research Centre, Connor Court Publishers, Ballarat

Babbage, R, 2016, *Countering Chinese Adventurism in the South-China Sea*, Centre for Budgetary and Strategic Assessments, Washington, DC

Babbage, R, Mahnken, T and Toshihara, T, 2018, *Countering Comprehensive Coercion-Competitive strategies against authoritarian political warfare*, Centre for Budgetary and Strategic Assessments, Washington, DC

Babbage, R, 2019, *Stealing a March: Chinese Hybrid Warfare in the Indo-Pacific; Issues and Options for Allied Defense Planners*, Centre for Budgetary and Strategic Assessments, Washington, DC

Babbage, R, 2019, *Winning Without Fighting: Chinese and Russian Political Warfare Campaigns and how the West can prevail*, Centre for Budgetary and Strategic Assessments, Washington, DC

Babbage, R, 2020, *Which Way the Dragon: sharpening allied perceptions of China's strategic trajectory*, Center for Strategic and Budgetary Assessments, Washington DC

Blaxland, J, 2019, 'A Geostrategic SWOT Analysis for Australia', Centre of Gravity series, no. 49, Strategic and Defence Studies Centre, ANU, Canberra June, retrieved 3 July 2020. https://sdsc.bellschool.anu.edu.au/sites/default/files/publications/attachments/2019-06/cog_49_swot_analysis_web.pdf

Burke, EJ, Gunness, K, Cooper C III, Mark Cozad MI, 2020, *People's Liberation Army Operational Concepts*, Rand Report, Rand Corporation, retrieved 31 January 2020, https://www.rand.org/pubs/research_reports/RRA394-1.html

Fox, AC, 2017, *Hybrid Warfare: The 21st Century Russian Way of War*, School of Advanced Military Studies, Defense Technical Information Center Leavenworth, KS, retrieved 4 July 2020, https://apps.dtic.mil/sti/citations/AD1038987

Hartcher, P, 2019, 'Red Flag: Waking up to China's challenge', *Quarterly Essay*, Black Inc Publishing, Sydney

Knight, C & Theodorakis, K, 2019, *The Malawi crisis – urban conflict and information operations*, Special Report, Australian Strategic Policy Institute, Canberra

Langford, I, 2014, *Australian special operations: Principles and considerations*, Australian Army, Department of Defence, Canberra

Kofman, M, Migacheva, K, Nichiporuk, B, Radin, A, Tkacheva, O & Oberholtzer J, 2017, *Lessons from Russia's Operations in Crimea and Eastern Ukraine*, The Rand Corporation, retrieved 15 June 2020, https://www.rand.org/pubs/research_reports/RR1498.html

Morris, LJ, Mazarr, MJ, Hornung, JW, Pezard, S, Binnendijk, A and Keep, M, 2019, 'Gaining Competitive Advantage in the Gray Zone. Response Options for Coercive Aggression Below the Threshold of Major War', Rand Corporation, CA, retrieved 19 February 2021, https://www.rand.org/pubs/research_reports/RR2942.html

Norberg, J, 2016, 'The use of Russia's military in the Crimea crisis.' Carnegie Endowment for International Peace Russia Programme', retrieved 15 February 2018, http://carnegieendowment.org/2014/03/13/use-of-russia-s-military-in-crimean-crisis

Parker, S & Chetfitz, G, 2018, *Debtbook Diplomacy: China's Strategic Leveraging of its Newfound Economic Influence and the Consequences for U.S. Foreign Policy*, Belfer Center for Science and International Affairs, Harvard Kennedy School, Cambridge, MA, retrieved 20 June 2020, https://www.belfercenter.org/sites/default/files/files/publication/Debtbook%20Diplomacy%20PDF.pdf

Paul, C and Matthews, M, 2016, *The Russian 'Firehose of Falsehood' Propaganda Model,* RAND Corporation Santa Monica, California

White, H, 2017, 'Without America: Australia in the New Asia', *The Quarterly Essay*, Black Inc, Melbourne

Papers

Lowy Institute 2020, '2020 Lowy Institute Opinion Poll,' June, Lowy Institute, retrieved 2 July 2020, https://poll.lowyinstitute.org/themes/security-and-defence

Bachmann, S, Oliver, V, Dowse, A & Gunneriusson, H, 2019, 'Competition Short of War – How Russia's Hybrid and Grey-Zone Warfare are a Blueprint for China's Global Power Ambitions', *Australian Journal of Defence and Strategic Studies*, vol. 1, no.1, retrieved 13 March 2020, https://papers.ssrn.com/sol3/papers.cfm?abstract_id=3483981

Bendett, S and Kania, E, 2019, A New Sino–Russian High Tech Partnership: Authoritarian innovation in an era of great-power rivalry, Policy Brief, Report No. 22 2019, Australian Strategic Policy Institute – International Cyber Policy Centre, 29 October, Canberra, retrieved 24 December 2020, https://s3-ap-southeast-2.amazonaws.com/ad-aspi/2019–10/A%20new%20Sino–Russian%20high-tech%20partnership_0.pdf?xAs9Tv5F.GwoKPiV9QpQ4H8uCOet6Lvh

Blaxland, J, 2020, *Developing a new Plan B for the ADF: Implications from a Geostrategic SWOT Analysis for Australia*, Australian Army Research Centre, retrieved 3 July 2020, https://researchcentre.army.gov.au/library/seminar-series/developing-plan-b-adf-some-implications-arising-geostrategic-swot-analysis-australia

Bongiorno, F, 2017, 'Up to a point, Professor Hamilton', *Inside Story*, Inside Story Publishing, Melbourne, retrieved 13 June 2020, http://insidestory.org.au/up-to-a-point-professor-hamilton

Brady AM, 2017, 'Magic Weapons: China's political influence activities under Xi Jinping', *Wilson Center*, 18 November, retrieved 2 June 2020, https://www.wilsoncenter.org/article/magic-weapons-chinas-political-influence-activities-under-xi-jinping

Brady, AM ed. 2010, 'Looking North, Looking South: China, Taiwan, and the South Pacific', *World Scientific*, vol. 26, series on contemporary China, https://www.bookdepository.com/Looking-North-Looking-South-China-Taiwan-South-Pacific-Anne-Marie-Brady/9789814304382

Brangwin, N, 2020, *Australia's military involvement in Afghanistan since 2001: a chronology*, Parliament of Australia, Parliament Library, Canberra

Carment, D & Belo D, 2018, 'War's Future: The Risks and Rewards of Grey Zone Conflict and Hybrid Warfare', *Policy Paper*, Canadian Global Affairs Institute

Czosseck, C, Ottis, R & Taliham, AM, 2011, Estonia after the 2007 Cyberattacks: legal, strategic and organisational changes in cyber security, case studies in information warfare and security, Cooperative Cyber Defence Centre of Excellence, Estonia, International Journal of Cyber Warfare and Terrorism, retrieved 13 January 2021, https://www.igi-global.com/article/estonia-after-2007-cyber-attacks/61328

Davies, A, Jennings, P & Schreer, B, 2014, A versatile force- the future of Australia's Special Forces, Australian Strategic Policy Institute, Canberra

Dibb, P, 2019, 'How the geopolitical partnership between China and Russia threatens the West', Special Report, SR148, 29 November, Australian Strategic Policy Institute, Canberra, retrieved 2 May 2020, https://www.aspi.org.au/report/how-geopolitical-partnership-between-china-and-russia-threatens-west

Dibb, P, Brabin-Smith R & Sargeant B, 2018, 'Why Australia Needs a Radically New Defence Policy', The Centre of Gravity series, Strategic and Defence Studies Centre, ANU, Canberra

Gerasimov, V, 2013, 'The Value of Science is in the Foresight: New Challenges Demand Rethinking the Forms and Methods of Carrying out Combat Operations,' *Voyenno-Promyshlennyy Kurier*, 26 February

Hamilton, C, 2018 Why do we keep turning a blind eye to Chinese political interference? 4 April, *The Conversation*, retrieved 19 April 2020, https://theconversation.com/why-do-we-keep-turning-a-blind-eye-to-chinese-political-interference-94299.

Hayward-Jones, J, 2013, 'Big Enough for All of Us: Geo-strategic Competition in the Pacific Islands', *Commentary*, Lowy Institute, May 2013

Hayward-Jones, J, 2014, 'Australia's costly investment in Solomon Islands: The Lessons of RAMSI', The Lowy Institute, 8 May, retrieved 3 May 2021, https://www.lowyinstitute.org/publications/australias-costly-investment-solomon-islands-lessons-ramsi

Hellyer, M, 2020, The Cost of Defence 2020–2021 Part 1: ASPI 2020–2021 Defence Budget Brief, 12 August, The Cost of Defence 2020–2021 Part 2: ASPI 2020–2021 Defence Budget Brief, 22 October, Australian Strategic Policy Institute, retrieved 28 April 2021, https://www.aspi.org.au/report/cost-defence-2020–2021-part-1-aspi-2020-strategic-update-brief

Jakobson, L, 2021, Why should Australia be concerned about rising tensions in the Taiwan Straits?, *China Matters Explores*, 9 February, retrieved 9 February 2021, https://chinamatters.org.au/policy-brief/policy-brief-february-2021

Joske, A, 2020, 'The Party Speaks for You: Foreign interference and the Chinese Communist Party's United Front System', *Policy Brief*, Report no. 32/2020, 9 June, Australian Strategic Policy Institute, Canberra, retrieved 10 June 2020, https://www.aspi.org.au/report/party-speaks-you

Kania, E, 2020, Innovation in the New Era of Chinese Military Power: What to make of the new Chinese defense white paper, the first since 2015, *The Diplomat*, retrieved 31 January 2020 https://thediplomat.com/2019/07/innovation-in-the-new-era-of-chinese-military-power

Kennan, GF, 1948, 'The Inauguration of Organized Political Warfare [redacted version]', Wilson Center, Digital Archive, International History Declassified, retrieved 6 August 2020 at http://www.digitalarchive.wilsoncenter.org

Kofman, M & Rojansky, M, 2015, 'A closer look at Russia's 'Hybrid War', *Kennan Cable*, no. 7, Wilson Center/Kennan Center, Washington DC, retrieved 23 May 2020 https://www.files.ethz.ch/isn/190090/5-KENNAN%20CABLE-ROJANSKY%20KOFMAN.pdf

Maclellan, S and O'Leary, N, 2017, 'Doing Battle in Cyberspace: How an Attack on Estonia Changed the Rules of the Game', Centre for International Governance Innovation, Cybersecurity, Surveillance and Privacy, retrieved 20 October 2020, https://www.cigionline.org

Norberg, J, 2016, 'The use of Russia's military in the Crimea crisis.' Carnegie Endowment for International Peace Russia Programme, retrieved 15 February 2018, https://carnegieendowment.org/2014/03/13/use-of-russia-s-military-in-crimean-crisis

Nye, JS, 2010, 'Cyber Power', Essay from the Belfer Centre for Science and International Affairs, Harvard Kennedy School, May

O'Neill, M, 2020, 'Punching at Air: The military and the Grey Zone', 26 June, *Land Power Forum*, Australian Army Research Centre, Canberra, retrieved 13 July 2020, https://researchcentre.army.gov.au/library/land-power-forum/punching-air-military-and-grey-zone

Smith, P, 2020, *Russian Electronic Warfare: A Growing Threat to U.S. Battlefield Supremacy,* American Security project, retrieved 20 October 2020 at http://www.americansecurityproject.org

Varghese, P, 2019, 'A new China narrative for Australia Submission by Peter Varghese,' *China Matters*, 23 April 2019, retrieved 6 July 2020, http://chinamatters.org.au/wp-content/uploads/2019/04/China-Matters_A-new-China-Narrative-Submission_Peter-Varghese-23042019.pdf

Varghese, P, 2019, What should Australia do to manage risk in its relationship with the PRC? *China Matters*, retrieved 6 July 2020, http://chinamatters.org.au/policy-brief/policy-brief-june-2020

Wallis, J, 2015, 'The South Pacific: arch of instability of arch of opportunity?', vol. 27, Iss. 1: The Sixth Oceanic Conference on International Studies: Transitions in the Asia Pacific, *Global Change, Peace & Security*, 3 February, pp. 39–53, retrieved 20 June 2020, https://www.tandfonline.com/doi/abs/10.1080/14781158.2015.992010?journalCode=cpar20

White, J, 2016, 'Dismiss, Distort, Distract, and Dismay: Continuity and Change in Russian Disinformation,' Policy Brief 13, *Institute for European Studies*, May, retrieved 6 August 2020, http://www.ies.be/policy-brief/dismiss-distort-distract-and-dismay-continuity-and-change-russian-disinformation

Journal Articles

Ackerman, RK, 2017, 'Russian Electronic Warfare Targets NATO Assets', *Signal magazine,* 01 November, retrieved on 20 October 2020 at http://www.afcea.org

Ayson, R, 2007, The 'arch of instability' and Australia's strategic policy, vol. 61, iss. 2, 22 May, *Australian Journal of International Affairs*, pp. 215–231, retrieved 20 June 2020, https://www.tandfonline.com/doi/full/10.1080/10357710701358360?src=recsys

Barber, N, 2017, 'A warning from the Crimea: hybrid warfare and the challenge for the ADF', no. 201, *Australian Defence Force Journal*, Canberra, pp. 46–58, retrieved 4 July 2020, https://www.defence.gov.au/adc/adfj/Documents/issue_201/Barber_April_2017.pdf

Bendett, S and Kania, E, 2020, The Resilience of Sino–Russian High-Tech Cooperation, *War on the Rocks*, 5 August, retrieved 24 December 2020, https://warontherocks.com/2020/08/the-resilience-of-sino-russian-high-tech-cooperation

Blasko, D, 2015, 'Chinese Special Forces: Not like 'Back at Bragg', *War on the Rocks,* retrieved 28 Jan 2019, https://warontherocks.com/2015/01/chinese-special-operations-forces-not-like-back-at-bragg

Byman, D & Merritt, I, 2018, 'The New American Way of War: Special Operations Forces in the War on Terrorism', *The Washington Quarterly*, vol. 341, iss 2, Georgetown University, Elliott School of International Affairs, Washington DC

Carrico, K, 2019, 'In defence of Silent Invasion', *Policy Forum*, Asia, the Pacific Policy Society, 1 March, retrieved 13 June 2020, https://www.policyforum.net/in-defence-of-silent-invasion

Chansoria, M, 2012, 'Defying Borders in Future Conflict in East Asia: Chinese Capabilities in the Realm of Information Warfare and Cyber Space', *Journal of East Asia Affairs*, Vol. 26, No. 1, pp. 105–06, retrieved 12 May 2020 at https://www.jstor.org/stable/23257910?seq=1

Fitzgerald, J, 2016, 'Beijing's *quoqing* versus Australia's way of life', 27 September, Inside Story, Inside Story Publishing, Melbourne, retrieved 8 June 2020, https://insidestory.org.au/beijings-guoqing-versus-australias-way-of-life

Florcruz, M, 2014, 'Chinese Military Professor: Maritime Disputes will lead to WWIII', *Business Insider*, 18 September, retrieved 1 February 2017, https://www.businessinsider.com/michelle-florcruz-maritime-disputes-will-lead-to-world-war-iii-2014-9?IR=T

Glenn, RW, 2009, 'Thoughts on 'Hybrid Conflict', *Small Wars Journal*, Bethesda, MD, retrieved 20 February 2020, https://smallwarsjournal.com/blog/journal/docs-temp/188-glenn.pdf.

Gray, CS, 2010, 'Gaining Compliance: The Theory of Deterrence and its Modern Application', vol. 29, iss 3, *Comparative Strategy*, 22 July, pp. 278–283, retrieved 14 February 2021, https://www.tandfonline.com/doi/full/10.1080/01495933.2010.492198?scroll=top&needAccess=true

Hollis, D, 2011, 'Cyberwar Case Study: Georgia 2008', *smallwarsjournal.com*, retrieved 12 January 2022, https://smallwarsjournal.com/blog/journal/docs-temp/639-hollis.pdf

Huth, P and Russett, B, 1984, 'What Makes Deterrence Work? Cases from 1900 to 1980', vol 36, no 4, *World Politics*, Cambridge University Press

Jakobson, L et al, 2021, A New China Narrative for Australia, *China Matters*, retrieved 9 February 2021, http://chinamatters.org.au/a-new-china-narrative-for-australia/text-of-a-new-china-narrative-for-australia

Johnston, R, 2018, 'Hybrid War and Its Countermeasures: A Critique of the Literature', Small Wars and Insurgencies, vol. 29, iss. 1, Routledge, Taylor & Francis Online, New York, pp. 141–163, retrieved 1 February 2020, https://www.tandfonline.com/doi/full/10.1080/09592318.2018.1404770?src=recsys

Karber, P and Thibeault, J, 2016, 'Russia's New-Generation Warfare', *Association of the United States Army*, retrieved 14 August 2020 at http://www.ausa.org

Kofman, M, 2020, The Emperor's League: Understanding Sino–Russian Defense Cooperation, War on the Rocks, 6 August, retrieved 24 December 2020, https://warontherocks.com/2020/08/the-emperors-league-understanding-sino-russian-defense-cooperation

Langford, I, 2017, 'Australia's Offset and A2/AD Strategies', no. 47, iss. 1, *Parameters*, Spring 2017, retrieved 10 November 2019, http://ssi.armywarcollege.edu/pubs/parameters/issues/Spring_2017/11_Langford_AustraliasOffsetAndA2AD.pdf

Nye JS, 2017, 'Deterrence and Dissuasion in Cyberspace', *International Security*, Vol. 41, No. 3

Pearlman, J, Parfitt S & Parfitt, T, 2014, 'Russia has sent a convoy of warships to Australia northern maritime border', *Business Insider,* 14 November, retrieved 2 June 2020, https://www.businessinsider.com/russian-warships-at-australias-border-2014–11?IR=T

Reilly, J, 2018, 'The Multi-Domain Operations Strategist', *Over the Horizon Journal,* 8 November 2018, retrieved 20 May 2020 at https://othjournal.com/2018/11/08/oth-mdos-reilly

Renz, B, 2016, 'Russia and 'hybrid war', *Contemporary Politics,* vol. 22, Iss. 3 in Russia the West and the Ukraine Crisis, pp. 283–300, retrieved 01 February 2020, https://www.tandfonline.com/doi/full/10.1080/13569775.2016.1201316?src=recsys

Schake, K, 2019 'Social Media as War?', *War on the Rocks*, 5 September 2019, retrieved 5 May 2020 at https://warontherocks.com/2018/09/social-mdeia-as-war

Segal, A, 2020, Peering into the Future of Sino–Russian Cyber Security Cooperation, *War on the Rocks*, 10 August, retrieved 24 December 2020, https://warontherocks.com/2020/08/peering-into-the-future-of-sino-russian-cyber-security-cooperation

Sechser, TS, 2011, 'Militarized Compellent Threats, 1918–2001', *Conflict Management and Peace Science*, Peace Science Society (International), Sage Publications, Newbury Park, CA, retrieved on 16 January 2020, https://journals.sagepub.com/doi/abs/10.1177/0738894211413066

Stoker, D & Whiteside, C, 2020, 'Blurred Lines: Gray-Zone Conflict and Hybrid War – Two Failures of American Strategic Thinking', vol 73, no 1, *Naval War College Review*, Newport RI, retrieved 3 February 2021 https://digital-commons.usnwc.edu/nwc-review/vol73/iss1/1

Strawser, BJ, 2010, 'Moral Predators: The Duty to Employ Uninhabited Aerial Vehicles', vol. 9, iss. 4, *Journal of Military Ethics*, pp. 342–68, retrieved 28 May 2020, https://www.tandfonline.com/doi/abs/10.1080/15027570.2010.536403

Talesco, C, 2020, 'Foreign Aid to Timor-Leste and the Rise of China', *Journal of International Studies*, pp. 131–150, retrieved 4 May 2020, https://www.jois.eu

Thornton, R, 2015, 'The Changing Nature of Modern Warfare, Responding to Russian Information Warfare', *The RUSI Journal*, Vol 160, 2015 – Issue 4

Trevithick, J, 2019, 'Ukrainian Officer Details Russian Electronic Warfare Tactics', *The War Zone*, retrieved 11 October 2020 at http://www.thedrive.com

Walker, C & Ludwig, J, 2017, 'The Meaning of Sharp Power', in *Foreign Affairs*, retrieved 10 November 2018, https://www.foreignaffairs.com/articles/china/2017–11-16/meaning-sharp-power.

Watts, BD, 2004, 'Clauswitzian Friction and Future War', *McNair Papers*, Institute for National Strategic Studies-National Defence University, Washington, DC

Williams, G, 2011, 'A Decade of Australian Anti-Terror Laws', *Melbourne University Law Review*, vol. 35, iss. 3, retrieved 9 April 2020, http://classic.austlii.edu.au/au/journals/MelbULawRw/2011/38.html#Heading82

Zhang D & Lawson, S, 2017, 'China in Pacific Region Politics', The Round Table, *The Commonwealth Journal of International Affairs*, vol. 106, Iss 2: Pacific Region Politics, 18 April, pp. 197–206, retrieved 20 June 2020, https://www.tandfonline.com/doi/full/10.1080/00358533.2017.1296705?src=recsys

Transcripts

Chivvis, C, 2017, 'Understanding Russian 'Hybrid Warfare' and What Can Be Done about it', Testimony presented before the House Armed Services Committee on March 22', Rand Corporation, retrieved 07 February 2020, https://www.rand.org/pubs/testimonies/CT468.html

Grattan M, 2014, 'In conversation with ASIO chief David Irvine', *The Conversation*, August 15, retrieved 25 July 2019, https://theconversation.com/grattan-on-friday-in-conversation-with-asio-chief-david-irvine-30536

Irvine, D, 2013, 'Director-General Speech: Address to the Security in Government Conference, 2013- Australia's current security and intelligence operating environment', Attorney-General's Department, 13 August, Canberra

Lewis, D, 2019, 'Address to the Lowy Institute', 5 September, retrieved 26 April 2020, https://www.lowyinstitute.org/news-and-media/multimedia/audio/address-asio-director-general-duncan-lewis

Keating, P, 2019, 'Paul Keating's speech on Australia's China policy – full text,' *The Guardian*, 18 November, retrieved 13 June 2020, https://www.theguardian.com/australia-news/2019/nov/18/paul-keatings-speech-on-australias-china-policy-full-text

Mattis, P, 2018, 'Testimony before the U.S.–China Economic and Security Review Commission: Hearing on China's Relations with U.S. Allies and Partners in Europe and the Asia-Pacific', 5 April, U.S.–China Economic and Security Review Commission website, retrieved 17 February 2021, https://www.uscc.gov/sites/default/files/USCC%20Hearing%20_Peter%20Mattis_Written%20Statement_April%205%202018.pdf

Morrison, S, 2020, 'Address – Launch of the 2020 Defence Strategic Update', 1 July, retrieved 13 July 20202, https://www.pm.gov.au/media/address-launch-2020-defence-strategic-update

Morrison, S, 2019, 'Stepping Up Australia's Response Against Foreign Interference', *media release*, Prime Minister of Australia website, 2 December, retrieved 19 July 2020, https://www.pm.gov.au/media/stepping-australias-response-against-foreign-interference

Morrison, S, Reynolds, L & Dutton, P, 2020, 'Statement on malicious cyber activity against Australian networks', *media release*, 19 June, Prime Minister of Australia website, retrieved 23 June 2020, https://www.pm.gov.au/media/statement-malicious-cyber-activity-against-australian-networks

Morrison, S, 2020, 'Australia's largest ever investment in cyber security', *media release*, 30 June, Prime Minister of Australia website, retrieved 1 July 2020, https://www.pm.gov.au/media/nations-largest-ever-investment-cyber-security

Nye, J, 2011, *The Future of Power*, Transcript, Chatham House, London

Ottis, R, 2008, 'Analysis of the 2007 Cyber Attacks against Estonia from the Information Warfare Perspective' in Proceedings of the 7th European Conference on Information Warfare and Security, 30 June – 1 July 2008, Plymouth University, Academic Publishing Limited, Reading, pp 163–168, retrieved 17 December 2020, https://ccdcoe.org/library/publications/analysis-of-the-2007-cyber-attacks-against-estonia-from-the-information-warfare-perspective

Payne, M, 2021, 'Joint statement on arrests in Hong Kong', DFAT website, 10 January, retrieved 17 February 2021, https://www.foreignminister.gov.au/minister/marise-payne/media-release/joint-statement-arrests-hong-kong

Singapore Government, 'Transcript of a talk given by the Prime Minister, Mr. Lee Kuan Yew, on the subject "Big and Small Fishes in Asian Waters" at a meeting of the University of Singapore Democratic Socialist Club at the University campus on 15th June, 1966', *media release*, MC.JUN.22/66(PM), retrieved 20 June 2020, https://www.nas.gov.sg/archivesonline/data/pdfdoc/lky19660615.pdf

Turnbull, M, 2017, National Security Statement, Transcript, 13 June 2017, retrieved 12 August 2020, https://www.malcolmturnbull.com.au/media/national-security-statement-tuesday-13-june-2017

Turnbull, M, 2017, A Strong and Secure Australia, transcript, 18 July 2017, retrieved 12 August 2020, https://www.malcolmturnbull.com.au/media/a-strong-and-secure-australia

Newspaper articles/Blogs/Online commentary

Ainge Roy, E, 2019, 'I'm being watched': Anne-Marie Brady, the China critic living in fear of Beijing', *The Guardian*, 23 January, retrieved 2 June 2020, https://www.theguardian.com/world/2019/jan/23/im-being-watched-anne-marie-brady-the-china-critic-living-in-fear-of-beijing

Armin, J, 2008, 'Russian Cyberwar on Georgia', 9 October, retrieved 18 May 2020, http://hostexploit.com/downloads/view.download/4/9.html

Australian Associated Press 2019, 'ASIO investigating Chinese plot to plant spy in Australia's parliament after Liberal party member found dead', 25 November, retrieved 3 June 2020, https://www.theguardian.com/australia-news/2019/nov/25/asio-investigating-chinese-plot-to-plant-spy-in-australias-parliament-after-liberal-member-found-dead

Barrett, J, 2019, 'Solomon Islands government says Chinese lease of island unlawful', *The Sydney Morning Herald,* 26 October, retrieved 3 July 2020, https://www.smh.com.au/world/oceania/solomon-islands-government-says-chinese-lease-of-island-unlawful-20191026-p534gv.html

Bashen, 2020, 'ASIO chases agents in the House', *The Weekend Australian*, 27–28 June

Baxendale, R, 2020, 'China-linked staffer's corona conspiracy', *The Australian,* The Nation, 2 June

Baxendale, R, 2020, 'Andrews staffer did Chinese propaganda course', *The Australian*, 29 June

Callick, R, 2021, 'Farewell to China's Most Sparkling Gem', Inquirer, *The Weekend Australian*, 20–21 January

Benson, S, 2020, 'Scott Morrison shoulders arms to China in 10 year $270bn plan', 30 June, *The Australian*, retrieved 1 July 2020, https://www.theaustralian.com.au/nation/politics/pm-shoulders-arms-to-china-in-10year-270bn-plan/news-story/1d130db628bde59abd6a02726bb94327

Birnes, WJ, 2017, Foreword, in Liang, Q & Xiangsui, W, 1999, *Unrestricted Warfare: China's Master Plan to Destroy America*. 2017 Kindle Edition, Shadow Lawn Press

Blainey, G, 2020, 'As the Pacific theatre opened, the nation was ill-prepared', *The Weekend Australian*, Inquirer, 15–16 August,

Buchanan, E, 2019, 'Hybrid warfare: Australia's (not so) new normal', *The Strategist*, Australian Strategic Policy Institute, Canberra

Buckley, C, 2013, 'China takes aim at Western ideas', 19 August, *The New York Times*, retrieved 4 June 2020, https://www.nytimes.com/2013/08/20/world/asia/chinas-new-leadership-takes-hard-line-in-secret-memo.html?mcubz=1

Campbell, A, 2019, 'Political Warfare', ASPI Keynote Address, 18 June 2019 retrieved 20 July 2020 at https://www.youtube.com/watch?v=P7O40S9W7ks

Carr, B, 2018, 'Bob Carr replies to China critics', *The Australian Financial Review*, 11 November, retrieved 11 June 2020, https://www.afr.com/opinion/despite-the-cold-warriors-australia-reverts-to-pragmatism-on-china-20181111-h17r92

Condon, M, 2020, 'The boy who kicked the hornet's nest', *The Weekend Australian Magazine*, 30–31 May, retrieved 4 June 2020, https://www.theaustralian.com.au/weekend-australian-magazine/how-drew-pavlous-university-of-queensland-protest-enraged-china-and-started-a-free-speech-battle/news-story/82f5fd86413844c724e64322b11abb69

Croucher, G & Powell D, 2019, 'Our ties to China must be subtle and nuanced', *The Australian*, 30 October, retrieved 13 June 2020, https://www.theaustralian.com.au/higher-education/our-ties-to-china-must-be-subtle-and-nuanced/news-story/f1f75abe01896bc61d48633c12a24b82

Downer, A, 2003, 'Neighbours cannot be recolonised', *The Australian*, 8 January 2003

Dupont, A, 2019, 'A New Type of War at Our Door', *The Australian*, Inquirer, 10 August, retrieved 5 February 2019, https://www.theaustralian.com.au/inquirer/a-new-type-of-war-at-our-door/news-story/243b8fcaee5e0fa8bcb817f7ce971073

Dupont, A, 2020, 'Australia must stand strong against Beijing's political warfare', *The Australian*, Inquirer, 4 January, retrieved 7 June 2020, https://www.theaustralian.com.au/inquirer/australia-must-stand-strong-against-beijings-political-warfare/news-story/1d88706d02cc0a8f65c24ff8d23540a2.

Dupont, A, 2019, 'A New Type of War at Our Door', *The Australian,* 10 August, retrieved 05 February 2019 https://www.theaustralian.com.au/inquirer/a-new-type-of-war-at-our-door/news-story/243b8fcaee5e0fa8bcb817f7ce971073

Dupont, A, 2020, 'Who's afraid of the big bad wolf warriors', 25 July, *The Australian*, Inquirer, retrieved on 25 July 20202, https://www.theaustralian.com.au/inquirer/whos-afraid-of-chinas-big-badwolf-warriors/news-story/78ecb0971212799b83ea18ce6b10a12d

Dupont, A, 2021, 'China strategy: Get a bigger stick with which to protect ourselves', 30 April, *The Australian*, retrieved 30 April 2021 https://www.theaustralian.com.au/commentary/china-strategy-get-a-bigger-stick-with-which-to-protect-ourselves/news-story/9bf2fe8f2024ef6d61e0cc9e2df4eaf6

Dziedzic, S, 2021, 'New Zealand Trade Minister advises Australia to show China more 'respect', *ABC News*, 28 January, retrieved 17 February 2021, https://www.abc.net.au/news/2021–01-28/nz-trade-minister-advises-australia-to-show-china-more-respect/13098674

Fitzgerald, J, 2018, 'Australia on its own when managing foreign influence on Australian soil', *The Australian Financial Review*, 15 March, retrieved on 8 June 2020, https://www.afr.com/world/asia/australia-is-on-its-own-as-beijing-demonstrates-its-power-in-the-region-20180312-h0xbze

Freedberg Jnr, SJ, 2018, 'Electronic Warfare Trumps Cyber for Deterring Russia', Breaking Defense, 01 February, retrieved 20 October 2020, https://breakingdefense.com

Galbally, F, 2021, 'We must bolster our cyber war defences', *The Australian*, 12 January, retrieved 12 January 2021

Grenfell, O, 2019, Australian media's 'Chinese spy defection story' unravels', International Committee of the Fourth International, World Socialist Website, 5 December, retrieved 3 June 2020, https://www.wsws.org/en/articles/2019/12/05/wang-d05.html

Hamilton, C, 2019, 'Why Gladys Liu must answer to parliament about alleged links to the Chinese government', *The Conversation,* 11 September, retrieved 7 June 2020, https://theconversation.com/why-gladys-liu-must-answer-to-parliament-about-alleged-links-to-the-chinese-government-123339

Hamilton, C, 2020, 'Sheets pulled back in search for reds in bed with ALP', *The Weekend Australian*, 27–28 June

Harris, R, 2019, 'Gladys Liu's Beijing confession deepens dispute over loyalty', *The Sydney Morning Herald*, 11 September, retrieved 7 June 2020, https://www.smh.com.au/politics/federal/gladys-liu-s-beijing-confession-deepens-dispute-over-loyalty-20190911-p52qec.html

Jennings, P, 2019, 'The many ways China is pushing us around ... without resistance', 8 June, *The Australian*, retrieved 8 June 2020, https://www.theaustralian.com.au/inquirer/the-many-ways-in-which-china-is-pushing-us-around-without-resistance/news-story/2de4e239607062fd8859f486fd82403c

Jennings, P, 2020, 'China will be surprised how long it took us to act', *The Australian*, 8 June, p. 10, retrieved 8 June 2020, https://www.aspi.org.au/opinion/china-will-be-surprised-how-long-it-took-us-act-foreign-investment-laws

Keating, P, 2019, Video: 'China is a great state' – Ex-Aussie PM Paul Keating tears into spooks over Beijing suspicions', Hong Kong Free Press, retrieved 13 June 2020, https://hongkongfp.com/2019/05/06/video-china-great-state-ex-aussie-pm-paul-keating-tears-spooks-beijing-suspicions

Kearsley, J, Bagshaw, E & Galloway, A, 2020, 'If you make China the enemy, China will be the enemy': Beijing's fresh threat to Australia, 18 November, *The Sydney Morning Herald*, retrieved 4 February 2021, https://www.smh.com.au/world/asia/if-you-make-china-the-enemy-china-will-be-the-enemy-beijing-s-fresh-threat-to-australia-20201118-p56fqs.html

Kelly, J & Benson, S, 2020, 'Raided Labor MP in fundraising boast', *The Weekend Australian*, 27–28 June

Kelly, J & Packham, B, 2020, 'Sweeps first test of laws on foreign interference', *The Weekend Australian*, 27–28 June

Kelly, P, 2020, 'Shift on Beijing was Turnbull's gift to Morrison', *The Australian*, 29 April

Kennedy CM & Erickson, A, 2016, 'China's Uniformed, Navy-trained Fishing 'Militia', CIMSEC series, part 2, 17 May, retrieved 15 June 2020, https://www.maritime-executive.com/editorials/chinas-uniformed-navy-trained-maritime-militia and http://cimsec.org/new-cimsec-series-on-irregular-forces-at-sea-not-merely-fishermen-shedding-light-on-chinas-maritime-militia/19624

Lindley-French, J, 2019, 'Briefing: Complex Strategic Coercion and Russian Military Modernisation', *Policy Perspective*, Canadian Global Affairs Institute, Calgary, January, retrieved 21 October 2020, https://d3n8a8pro7vhmx.cloudfront.net/cdfai/pages/4117/attachments/original/1548354852/Complex_Strategic_Coercion_and_Russian_Military_Modernization.pdf?1548354852= also The Lindley-French Analysis: Speaking Truth Unto Power, blog, 9 January, retrieved 21 October 2020, http://lindleyfrench.blogspot.com/2019/01/briefing-complex-strategic-coercion-and.html

McKenzie, N, Sakkal, P & Tobin, G, 2019, 'China tried to plant its candidate in Federal Parliament, authorities believe', *The Age*, 24 November, retrieved 8 June 2020, https://www.theage.com.au/national/china-tried-to-plant-its-candidate-in-federal-parliament-authorities-believe-20191122-p53d9x.html

Korporaal, G, 2021, 'Hong Kong activists arrested in China show of force', *The Australian*, 7 January 2021, retrieved on 7 January 2021, https://www.theaustralian.com.au/world/hong-kong-activists-arrested-in-china-show-of-force/news-story/62299971397a5543b05fb1f6b8a504a9?utm_source=&utm_medium=&utm_campaign=&utm_content=

McGuinness, D, 2017, 'How a cyber-attack transformed Estonia', *BBC News,* 27 April 2017, retrieved 16 December 2020, https://www.bbc.com/news/39655415

Medcalf, R, 2018, 'Silent Invasion: the question of race', *The Interpreter*, The Lowy Institute, 21 March, retrieved 13 June 2020, https://www.lowyinstitute.org/the-interpreter/silent-invasion-question-race

Milhiet, P, 2017, 'China's Ambition in the Pacific: Worldwide Geopolitical Issues', Institute de Relations Internationale et Strategiques, Asia Focus #49 – Asia Program, retrieved 20 June 2020, https://www.iris-france.org/wp-content/uploads/2017/10/Asia-Focus-49.pdf

Moses, A, 2008 'Georgian websites forced offline in 'cyber war'', 12 August, *The Sydney Morning Herald*, retrieved 4 February 2021, https://www.smh.com.au/technology/georgian-websites-forced-offline-in-cyber-war-20080812-gdsqac.html

Munro, K, 2019, 'Australian attitudes to China shift: 2019 Lowy Poll', 27 June, Lowy Institute, retrieved 21 June 2020, https://www.lowyinstitute.org/the-interpreter/australian-attitudes-china-shift-2019-lowy-poll

Needham, K, 2019, 'Beijing supports 'patriotic' protests against Hong Kong students in Australia', *The Sydney Morning Herald*, Fairfax Media, Sydney, retrieved 10 October 2019, https://www.smh.com.au/world/asia/beijing-supports-patriotic-protests-against-hong-kong-students-in-australia-20190820-p52iu7.html

Norington, B, 2020, 'MP China-link raids underline ASIO's anxiety', *The Australian*, 29 June

Packham, B, 2020, 'Influencer cosied up to Chinese leaders', *The Australian*, The Nation, 1 June

Oliver, A & Kassam, N, 2020, 'Happy to hop away from these bounders: The 2020 Lowy Institute Poll finds us squaring up to an uncertain future', *The Australian*, Commentary, 24 June 2020

Packham, B, 2020, 'Cyber spy agency on high alert over hack', *The Australian*, 24 December, retrieved 24 December 2020, https://www.theaustralian.com.au/nation/cyber-spy-agency-on-high-alert-over-hack/news-story/a4879aac7be8536b662af8b29f2d3d20?utm_source=&utm_medium=&utm_campaign=&utm_content=

Packham, B, 2021, 'China dangles $39bn carrot to build city on our doorstep', *The Australian*, 5 February, retrieved 5 February 2021 https://www.theaustralian.com.au/nation/china-dangles-39bn-carrot-to-build-city-on-our-doorstep/news-story/0c8b1219fb3db6d51a5a8d95e224f50b?utm_source=&utm_medium=&utm_campaign=&utm_content=

Paterson, T, 2019, 'The Grey Zone: Political Warfare is Back', *The Interpreter*, The Lowy Institute, retrieved 19 May 2020 https://www.lowyinstitute.org/the-interpreter/grey-zone-political-warfare-back

Riordan, P, 2018, 'China to host Pacific Islands meeting ahead of APEC', *The Weekend Australian*, 10 July, retrieved 20 June 2020, https://www.theaustralian.com.au/national-affairs/foreign-affairs/china-to-host-pacific-islands-meeting-ahead-of-apec/news-story/961c0cb7fe2ab07e5fdf7166eb7fa005

Sheridan, G, 2020, 'Scott Morrison right to say times as dangerous as 1930s', *The Australian*, 2 July, retrieved 26 July 2020, https://www.theaustralian.com.au/commentary/scott-morrison-backs-tough-words-with-robust-actions/news-story/ce0f4f5ffecc97e90ab415661c23cbbc and https://www.theaustralian.com.au/author/Greg+Sheridan

Slattery, L, 2020, 'Hitting Home', 25–26 April, *The Weekend Australian*, retrieved 4 June 20202, https://www.theaustralian.com.au/weekend-australian-magazine/swimmer-mack-hortons-family-reveals-fallout-from-drug-protest/news-story/a3f11ec2851c90b4171b8021c168a200

Sun, W, 2019, 'What do we learn about the experience of Mandarin-speaking migrants from Chinese-language media in Australia?', *ABC Religion and Ethics*, 25 November 2019, retrieved 14 June, https://www.abc.net.au/religion/what-we-learn-from-chinese-language-media-in-australia/11735478

Sweeny, L et al. 2017, 'Sam Dastyari resignation: How we got there', 12 December, *ABC News*, retrieved 3 June 2020, https://www.abc.net.au/news/2017–12-12/sam-dastyari-resigns-from-parliament/9247390 and https://www.abc.net.au/news/2017–12-12/sam-dastyari-resignation-how-did-we-get-here/9249380

Sakkal, P & Mackenzie, N, 2019, 'How Nick Zhao made enemies, faced charges, and was allegedly asked to spy for China', *The Age*, 29 November, retrieved 8 June 2020, https://www.theage.com.au/national/how-nick-zhao-made-enemies-faced-charges-and-was-allegedly-asked-to-spy-for-china-20191128-p53ezs.html

Tillett, A, 2021, 'Chinese city plan on PNG island highlights concerns about Beijing', *Australian Financial Review*, 5 February, retrieved 9 February 2021, https://www.afr.com/politics/federal/chinese-city-plan-on-png-island-highlights-concerns-about-beijing-20210205-p56zwm

Varga, R, 2020, 'Key BRI advisor linked to Communist Party', *The Australian*, The Nation, 1 June

Varghese, P, 2020, 'How to best manage our relationship with Beijing: Adopting a policy of engaging and constraining China suits Australia's interest far better', *The Weekend Australian*, 27–28 June 2020

Walden, M, 2021, 'China again blames Australia for diplomatic spat, issues warning to Five Eyes intelligence partners', *ABC News*, 20 November, retrieved 17 February 2021, https://www.abc.net.au/news/2020–11-20/china-blames-confrontational-australian-government-for-spat/12902774

Wall, J, 2020, 'China to build $200 million fishery project on Australia's doorstep', *The Strategist*, Australian Security Policy Institute, 8 December, retrieved 9 February 2021, https://www.aspistrategist.org.au/china-to-build-200-million-fishery-project-on-australias-doorstep

White, H, 2017, 'China's Power and the Future of Australia', *ANU TV*, YouTube, retrieved 13 June 2020, https://www.youtube.com/watch?v=8JWLnaVvuJg&feature=youtu.be

White, H, 2017, 'We need to talk about China', Asia and Pacific Policy Society, 4 May, retrieved 13 June 2020, https://www.youtube.com/watch?v=8JWLnaVvuJg &feature=youtu.be

White, N, 2020, 'Why two of Australia's richest men are backing China in diplomatic row sparked by push for a coronavirus inquiry as Beijing threatens to destroy our economy as revenge,' *The Daily Mail – Australia*, 4 May, retrieved 3 July 2020, https://www.dailymail.co.uk/news/article-8272347/Andrew-Twiggy-Forrest-Kerry-Stokes-China-diplomatic-row.html

Zhou, N & Smee B, 2020, 'We cannot be seen: the fallout from the University of Queensland's Hong Kong protests', *The Guardian*, 4 August, retrieved 8 June 2020, https://www.theguardian.com/australia-news/2019/aug/04/we-cannot-be-seen-the-fallout-from-the-university-of-queenslands-hong-kong-protests

Podcasts/Documentaries

Jennings, P, 2016, 'Peter Jennings on China, Australia and soft power', podcast, 20 September, ASPI, retrieved 3 June 2020 https://www.aspi.org.au/video/peter-jennings-china-australia-and-soft-power

McKenzie, N, 2019, 'China's Spy Secrets', *60 Minutes*, 9 Entertainment Co, retrieved 3 June 2020, https://9now.nine.com.au/60-minutes/chinas-spy-secrets/9f3b7622–28a1–4823-888f-878aa2146698

Langford, I, 2017, podcast, Covert Contact podcast, 25 September 2017, *Australian Special Forces*, retrieved 10 November 2017, http://covertcontact.com/tag/col-ian-langford

Matisek, J & Bertram, I, 2017, 'The Death of American Conventional Warfare: It's the Political Willpower, Stupid', Strategy Bridge podcast, 5 November, p. 4, retrieved 11 November 2017, https://thestrategybridge.org/the-bridge/2017/11/5/the-death-of-american-conventional-warfare-its-the-political-willpower-stupid

McKenzie, N, 2019, 'World Exclusive: Chinese spy spills secrets to expose Communist espionage', *60 Minutes* 24 November 2019 https://www.youtube.com/watch?v=zdR-I35Ladk

Mulyanto, R & Tobin, M, 2019, 'East Timor's China friendship won't compromise its national interests: foreign minister', *This Week in Asia*, 23 August, retrieved 20 June 2020, https://www.scmp.com/week-asia/politics/article/3023934/east-timors-china-friendship-wont-compromise-its-national

www.ingramcontent.com/pod-product-compliance
Lightning Source LLC
Chambersburg PA
CBHW062051270326
41931CB00013B/3027

9781922603104